# CONFRONTING
# ANTISEMITISM
## ON THE
# LEFT

# CONFRONTING ANTISEMITISM

## ON THE

# LEFT

## ARGUMENTS FOR SOCIALISTS

## DANIEL RANDALL

**Daniel Randall** is a railway worker, trade union representative, and socialist activist based in London. He is a member of the Labour Party and a supporter of the revolutionary socialist group Alliance for Workers' Liberty (AWL). He has written extensively about antisemitism on the left and edited the AWL pamphlet *Left Antisemitism: What it is and How to Fight it.*

The AWL and its predecessor organisations have engaged in a critical analysis of left antisemitism for over thirty years. Members of Socialist Organiser, the AWL's immediate antecedent, helped promote Steve Cohen's *That's Funny, You Don't Look Antisemitic* on the British left when it was first published in 1984.

While Randall's own Jewish identity inevitably informs his work and analysis, he endeavours to avoid an identitarian frame, and attempts to approach the question of left antisemitism historically and theoretically.

He tweets at @therubykid

# CONTENTS

# ACKNOWLEDGEMENTS

My first thanks go to No Pasaran Media, for helping the arguments in this book reach a wider audience than they otherwise might have, and for their consistent support throughout the publishing process. I am particularly grateful for their hard work and assistance in editing the book in a way that greatly improved issues of structure and style without altering the political message. NPM gave me full control over the political content of the book, and at no point attempted to intervene in or influence it, something for which I am extremely grateful.

I am also especially grateful to Camila Bassi and Tom Cohen for their forewords. Camila is a comrade whose work on left antisemitism I have always found immensely valuable, and who also gave helpful feedback on early drafts of the book. Given how much I am influenced by the work of Steve Cohen, and how directly this book draws on his writing, for his son Tom to write a foreword was a particular honour.

Numerous people gave up their time to read drafts of some or all of the book at various stages of completion and provide feedback. My sincere thanks go to Edd Mustill, Holly Smith, Ralph Levinson, Charlotte Fischer of L'Taken, Joey Ayoub, Hannah Polin-Galay, Barry Finger, Paul Hampton, Spencer Sunshine, David Renton and Michael Richmond. Several people on that list are writers and activists whose work around this subject I have learned from, sometimes referring to it directly in the book, so I was honoured by the fact they took time to read drafts and share their thoughts and criticism. Special thanks go to Stan Crooke, on whose research and writing I have drawn in much of this book, especially the fourth chapter, for his feedback. Thanks also to Rabbil Sikdar for giving his permission for our dialogue on the 2019 general election to be reproduced here as an appendix.

I have also learned from and drawn on the work of many other scholars, activists and writers about antisemitism – some of whom, whilst they were not able to provide direct feedback on the book, I have benefited from correspondence with, including Keith Kahn-Harris, whose work I have quoted extensively, and Brendan McGeever. I also acknowledge the work of April Rosenblum, whose pamphlet *The Past Didn't Go Anywhere* is, like Steve Cohen's *That's Funny, You Don't Look Antisemitic*, a vital contribution to the critique of antisemitism on the activist left, from *within* the activist left.

Special thanks are also due to Mudar Kassis and Maher Al Hashweh, Palestinian socialists and academics at Birzeit University in Palestine, with whom I was connected by Ralph Levinson. They provided valuable critiques and feedback on my fifth chapter. Although we don't agree on everything, they approached the exchange in a spirit of intellectual openness, genuine critical enquiry and solidarity, and I am hugely grateful for their time and efforts.

I owe an enormous debt of gratitude to Matt Cooper, who gave up far more of his own time than I had any right to expect in order to provide assistance and research, and acted variously as a sounding board and constructive critic.

It goes without saying that any errors in the book are wholly my own.

Thanks to all the comrades – and I use that term here in its broadest sense – who have taught me, and with whom I have discussed and debated these issues, throughout nineteen years of involvement, so far, in socialist politics. Those exchanges helped me develop and hone the arguments set down here. I hope we will continue the discussion.

Finally, thanks to my parents, Norman and Ronne, who also read drafts of this book and gave feedback, and to whom I owe much.

# FOREWORD
## BY CAMILA BASSI

The indignation expressed by many on the left at the idea that an antisemitic common sense exists anywhere in our circles is an indication of how pervasive, and how little understood, left antisemitism is. Such indignation reflects an intolerance, closed-mindedness and absence of thought from activists and academics who otherwise advance anti-racism.

Indeed, left antisemitism is the exception of the anti-racist imagination. This exception is rationalised by designating antisemitism as coming solely from the right: from the populist and far right, or from a right-wing Israel, as a reaction against Israel's military onslaughts and ongoing occupation of Palestine, and as a manufactured accusation by Israel and its global Zionist lobby to shut down criticism of its actions. Those on the left who raise concerns about antisemitism in our ranks are reasoned away as fake leftists and Zionists. Zionism in this imagination is the racist pariah: nothing more than the ideological roots and tentacles of a settler-colonial state in an era of decolonisation, the domination of a white people over a Black people. Left antisemitism is not just the exception of the anti-racist imagination, it is often outcast as a racist allegation in itself.

How did the left – as a movement for liberty, democracy and radical equality – end up here, and how do we navigate ourselves out of this dead end? There is, after all, no liberation, democracy and equality if we exclude a part of our class; there is no path to liberation via a politics that advocates inequality and oppression for some.

With a deep activist knowledge and a scholarly rigour, Daniel Randall provides us with a crucially important interlocution and map. This book should be seen as an invitation – *from the left, to the left* – to open-mindedness, critical thinking and debate. Randall's comprehensive critique of the ideological trends and manifestations of left antisemitism does not steer us away from the ideas of socialism and Marxism, as numerous critiques do, but rather is a call to reconnect with such ideas in an effort to transform and reinvigorate the movement for progressive societal change.

Throughout *Confronting Antisemitism on the Left*, one finds both a detailed assessment of the problem of left antisemitism and the provision of a politics that gives answers to overcoming this problem. Randall develops a consistently democratic and internationalist politics of workers' solidarity and equal rights as a map for our movement to progress. This is not a book damning the left while pontificating in despair; this is a book sharp and hopeful in thought and action. Academics and activists on the left must engage with *Confronting Antisemitism on the Left* if we genuinely want to deliver a humane universalism that includes everyone.

*Dr Camila Bassi is Senior Lecturer in Human Geography at Sheffield Hallam University, and a socialist and trade union activist who has written extensively about antisemitism on the left, and racism and anti-racism more widely. She blogs at anaemiconabike.com and tweets at @dr_camila_bassi.*

# FOREWORD
## BY TOM COHEN

Antisemitism matters.

Antisemitism is important.

Antisemitism is not 'a touchy subject'.

As proud members of the left, we need to own and understand our own perspectives, and, yes, prejudices, so we can overcome them. If not, they will overcome us and drown out everything else.

Irrespective of whether Jeremy Corbyn is or was an antisemite – and, frankly, that is immaterial right now – not addressing and challenging this issue has damaged the Labour movement and the broader left in general. We have allowed ourselves to be accused of 'ignoring antisemitism' or 'being soft on our own', and 'applying different tests' than we would to others.

We have only ourselves to blame for not grasping this thorny problem – and our enemies instead have beaten us with the rest of the bush and left us bloodied. I am ashamed that a narrative now exists where people feel they have to define themselves for or against not merely Israeli policy but 'Israel'; I am ashamed that people no longer want to discuss Israeli politics – simply 'Israel'.

Failure to challenge the bigotries that exist within our own movement undermines our ability to challenge bigotries in wider society. And there are many that need challenging. I am ashamed to be living in a country which is becoming increasingly insular, which is pandering to Little England prejudices and using racist tropes and Trumpian political strategies to perpetuate a divisive race to the bottom, under the auspices of St Boris of the Vaccine. I am consistently amazed at how 'free trade' in our new 'independent' Britain means free transport of goods and services, but not the free movement of people; the left is at fault on this as well, as parts of it have peddled the myth that free movement is a threat to wages. This is wrong: no one is illegal.

Labour has been out of power for over a decade. We need to rethink and relearn what our values are, and what our values should be. To do this, we need to learn from our past as we consider our future. This book is part of this learning and growth.

My father, Steve Cohen, in his book *That's Funny, You Don't Look Antisemitic*, challenged the left over its views on antisemitism in the 1980s, using history and polemic in equal measure. In this book, Daniel continues both this narrative and this challenge. I may not agree with everything he says, or all his conclusions; that is a good thing. We need to live in a world where we are challenged, and where arguments are not always meant to make us feel safe. I encourage everyone not just to read this book but also to actively engage with it. Discuss these issues with your colleagues and comrades, read more, argue more, and keep challenging antisemitism wherever it occurs.

*A luta continua!*

*Tom Cohen is the son of Steve Cohen, author of* That's Funny, You Don't Look Antisemitic, *and a member of the Labour Party.*

# CHAPTER ONE
# INTRODUCTION

Antisemitism on the left is not a new phenomenon. It has roots stretching back 150 years or more. However, many readers may have been alerted to the issue only relatively recently. Between 2015 and 2019 the issue was thrust into the national spotlight in Britain by the unexpected ascendancy of a section of the left to the leadership of the Labour Party.

I saw that ascendancy as an immense opportunity to renew left-wing politics in Britain, push back the Thatcherite orthodoxy that dominated political life and revitalise working-class struggle. I also saw it as a vital opportunity for the socialist left to reckon with its own imperfections and flaws – a reckoning made both more difficult and more necessary by the pressure of circumstance. One of those flaws was the presence of antisemitic ideas within sections of the left.

## WHY LEFT ANTISEMITISM MATTERS

Antisemitism is not merely 'Jew hatred'. It is connected to, and ultimately stems from, an ideological narrative based on claims of a world-shaping power, which is identified, implicitly or explicitly, as Jewish. Antisemitism can manifest as direct bigotry, prejudice or chauvinism towards Jewish people, expressed in writing, speech or actions. It can also manifest as expressions of that ideological narrative, or versions of it.

For proponents of that narrative, such expressions may not imply hostility to individual Jews, but are claimed to be only a political opposition to a perceived power. Antisemitism is, therefore, a toxic force even when those expressing antisemitic ideas have no personal animus towards Jews as such.

The primary focus od this book is revolutionary socialist parties and groups, radical social movements, and the Labour Party, particularly its left wing. Most attention will be on the left in Britain, but examples from other countries will sometimes be referred to.

Left antisemitism hugely distorts left-wing politics. As a fuel for bigotry, it undermines the left's ability to fight for equality. As a form of conspiracy theory, which attempts to identify the individual 'bankers' or 'elite financiers' pulling the strings of world affairs, it undermines the left's ability to explain capitalism as a system of openly functioning class relations that can be overthrown by mass collective action. Left antisemitism thereby miseducates and misleads, serving to protect, rather than challenge, existing systems of power. It peddles conspiracy theories about Zionism and promotes a perspective that sees the world as divided into discrete 'imperialist' and 'anti-imperialist' blocs, with the entire 'anti-imperialist' bloc ordained as necessarily progressive, regardless of the actual political programme of the states and movements claimed to comprise it. Thus, left antisemitism distorts necessary solidarity with the Palestinian struggle for self-determination by cheerleading for reactionary forces that cynically claim to represent it, and by insisting that such solidarity can be built only on a political foundation that opposes Israeli-Jewish national rights and therefore rejects equality.

I am not writing this book because I think left antisemitism is worse, or more of an immediate threat to Jews, than other forms of antisemitism, particularly far-right, white-supremacist antisemitism. Forms of far-right nationalism are in power, or close to power, in many countries across the world. This demands a distinct analysis of antisemitism's place at what the anti-racist activist Eric Ward called the 'theoretical core of white nationalism'.[1] The labour movement also needs to take anti-fascist and anti-racist direct action and self-defence seriously, and particular work must be done to foster anti-racist solidarity between Jews and other victims, historic and contemporary, of racialised oppression.

But the fact that there may be other forms of antisemitism that are more dangerous, in an immediate physical sense, does not absolve the left of the responsibility to confront the forms of antisemitism that exist within our own movement. On the contrary, doing so becomes even more urgent. If we are unable to do that, our efforts to combat antisemitism in general will be significantly hindered. And, beyond that, if we are unable to confront reactionary ideas in our own movement, we will always be inhibited in pursuing our ultimate aim: the socialist transformation of society.

## LABOUR'S ANTISEMITISM DEBATE: AN ALTERNATIVE POSITION

Much has been made by defenders of Labour's 2015–19 leadership of the way in which the issue of antisemitism was 'exploited' or 'weaponised' by centrist or right-wing critics, inside the party and beyond, in order to attack the left. Even some leftists who accepted that left antisemitism was a real phenomenon expended more energy lamenting its exploitation by our opponents than in actually confronting it within our own ranks.

Others have insisted the entire notion is a 'fabrication' or a 'smear'. In the more lurid versions of this position, it was claimed that the issue was fabricated directly by the Israeli state. Some local Labour parties passed motions accusing pro-Israel MPs of being agents of 'interference by a foreign power'.[2] The irony of denying the existence of left antisemitism while advancing a conspiracy theory about the hidden hand of Israel and Zionism manipulating political affairs in Britain was apparently lost on the partisans of this particular viewpoint.

Conversely, some critics of left antisemitism insisted that the problem was not the ideas of a section of the left, even a large and influential section, but radical left-wing politics *as such*. This argument reached its risible logical conclusion in March 2019 when Labour MP Siobhain McDonagh drew an equivalence, and causal link, between antisemitism and *any* opposition to capitalism. McDonagh said in a radio interview that 'it's very much part of […] hard left politics to be against capitalists and to see Jewish people as the financiers of capital. Ergo you are anti-Jewish people.' When asked by the interviewer, 'To be anti-capitalist, [do] you have to be antisemitic?' McDonagh replied, 'Yes.'[3] In other words, because some antisemites code capitalism as 'Jewish', to be against capitalism is to be against Jews. Ironically, in her efforts to oppose antisemitism, McDonagh allowed antisemites to set the terms of debate.

Between this anti-left tendency on one side and the denialists and downplayers on the other, there was and is what might be called a third camp – not a point of neutral equidistance between the two, but an entirely alternative, independent position. This position acknowledges the existence of left antisemitism, but rather than seeing it as a logical or even inevitable outgrowth of foundational left-wing ideas – such as radical democracy, equality and social ownership – understands it as a distortion that threatens those ideas.

Although the issue has sometimes been raised cynically, or was less widespread than sometimes claimed, that did and does not mean it was unworthy of attention. It is right to criticise the exploitation of antisemitism by those whose wider agenda is to block the advance of any form of left-wing politics at all, and, like critics of antisemitism from, for example, the Tory right, are often at best inconsistent opponents of other forms of bigotry or even of antisemitism itself. Nor did many figures from the 'New Labour', Blairite wing of the Labour Party – who, in government, also pursued anti-migrant policies and appealed to nationalist and chauvinist prejudices – have an entirely consistent record of opposition to all forms of bigotry. But the highlighting, or even exploitation, of antisemitism by such people does not mean left antisemitism does not exist. Antisemitism has indeed been 'weaponised', but as the socialist writer and lawyer David Renton succinctly put it: 'You can't weaponise something that isn't there.'[4]

The way to deal with such a problem is *to deal with it*, rather than continually bemoaning that our opponents have called attention to it. Against both those who deny the existence of the problem and those who claim the problem is left-wing politics as such, the third, independent position understands that the most articulate analyses of left antisemitism come from within the far left itself, and that, far from requiring a break from the classical ideas of leftism, the task of confronting left antisemitism requires a reconnection with them.

It is that position that this book seeks to advance.

### CHALLENGING ANTISEMITISM ON THE LEFT, FROM THE LEFT

This book stands in the tradition of an earlier one, Steve Cohen's *That's Funny, You Don't Look Antisemitic* (which will be referred to hereafter as *That's Funny*), first published in 1984 and reprinted twice since, once in 2005 and, most recently, in 2019 by No Pasaran Media, by whom this book is also published.

*That's Funny*, while pioneering in the context of the British far left of the 1980s, was by no means the first attempt to grapple with the problem of antisemitism on the left. A century earlier, activists in Germany's Social Democratic Party, then a mass revolutionary workers' party, used the label 'socialism of fools', originating with the Austrian liberal Ferdinand Kronawetter, to critique invective against 'Jewish capitalists'. Their critique was often flawed and limited, but it represented an acknowledgement of a specific challenge posed to left-wing politics by antisemitism.[5]

In the British labour movement and left of the late-nineteenth and early-twentieth centuries, Jewish radicals and their allies, including Eleanor Marx, the daughter of Karl Marx, confronted the nationalist antisemitism that impelled many labour move-ment bodies, including the Trades Union Congress, to lobby the state to impose the restrictions on Jewish immigration that would become the 1905 Aliens Act – an episode surveyed in some detail in *That's Funny*. Marx spoke on the platform of rallies opposing immigration controls, and Jewish workers' unions sponsored the publication of a pamphlet entitled *A Voice from the Aliens*, which argued against nationalist antisemitism and for solidarity between British-born and Jewish migrant workers.

Jewish activists in the international socialist movement attempted to win the movement to a more combative stance against antisemitism, often unsuccessfully. The 1891 Brussels congress of the Second International, the main international network of socialist and labour parties, voted down a resolution proposed by American-Jewish socialist Abraham Cahan, found-ing editor of the Yiddish socialist newspaper *Forverts* (*Forward*), advocating a determined fight against antisemitism. Instead, the congress supported a resolution that opposed 'antisemitic and philosemitic incitement' equally.[6]

In the late 1920s Trotskyist dissidents in the USA such as Max Shachtman criticised the Communist Party of the USA, and other communist parties internationally, by then past the point of no return on their journey to Stalinisation, for supporting antisemitic attacks against Jewish settlers in Palestine.[7] In the late 1930s Leon Trotsky called out antisemitic attacks on himself and other dissident Bolsheviks by the Stalinist regime. In the 1960s dissident Polish socialists denounced the antisemitism of the Stalinist regime in that country. Jacek Kuroń, one of the authors of the 'Open Letter to the Party' that would provide some of the ideological foundations of Solidarność, the mass Polish workers' movement of the 1980s, declared: 'There are certain situations in which any honest person should consider himself Jewish.'[8]

On the British left, several Jewish supporters of the Communist Party of Great Britain (CPGB) left, or were expelled, as dissident critics of antisemitism in the Eastern Bloc and the CPGB leadership's suppression of discussion of it.[9] In the late 1970s and early 1980s, when some far-left groups led a campaign to ban 'Zionists', and later to ban campus Jewish societies, others on the left opposed that campaign for what it was: an expression of antisemitism on the left, even though the advocates of the bans were usually careful to talk about 'Zionists' rather than 'Jews'.[10]

What Cohen's book did was to set down in one place a comprehensive analysis of left antisemitism, tracing its historical origins and suggesting a political framework via which it could be confronted. Cohen did not assess left antisemitism as an outsider to the left, but as a far-left activist, aiming to help transform the left. While reams of commentary on left antisemitism has been written since 2015, very little has come close to Cohen's book in terms of being comprehensive yet succinct and highly accessible. Other compact left-wing, activist critiques of left antisemitism written more recently, such as April Rosenblum's *The Past Didn't Go Anywhere* (2007) and the anti-fascist activist Spencer Sunshine's essay 'Looking Left at Antisemitism' (2019), have recommended Cohen's book as key further reading.

Such is the enduring value of its analysis that, in 2019, the Jewish Labour Movement – a group whose politics Cohen did not share, and the majority of whose contemporary leaders certainly do not share many, probably most, of Cohen's political conclusions – chose to distribute a copy of the reprinted edition to every single one of their members.[11] The Labour left group Momentum, in what has been one of a well-intentioned, if sporadic and inconsistent, series of attempts to confront the issue of antisemitism, also urged supporters to read Cohen's book.[12] In both instances,

I felt at the time that if the leadership of the Labour Party itself had chosen to do the same, it would probably have had more of a positive impact via that one act than via the aggregated effect of almost everything else it said or did on the issue.

I write, as Cohen did, as a grassroots activist of the far left, and intend this book as a work of polemic rather than scholarship. This book, like his, sees the task of uprooting left antisemitism as a fundamental imperative for the left itself, a prerequisite for making our movement fit to achieve its aims, which must be situated within a general effort of transformation, aiming to forge a left more consistently committed to equality and liberation. Cohen wrote of his book that 'what is written here is not in any way presented as a last word, rather it is an attempt to open up a genuine debate on the left'.[13] The same is true of this work.

While I hope anyone interested in antisemitism, political thought in general and historic engagements between Jews and the left specifically will find this book valuable, or at least thought-provoking, its primary intended audience is socialist activists concerned to improve the political health of our movement, hence its subtitle 'arguments for socialists'.

Like Steve Cohen, I believe in a socialism based on the values of liberty, equality and solidarity. Like him, I see working-class struggle as the means for achieving such a society, and anti-Stalinist and pre-Stalinist revolutionary socialism as the best available intellectual and activist tradition for politically orienting the means and ends of that struggle. And, like him, I believe that this involves an unflinching confrontation with ideological trends that threaten to distort our politics, as part of a wider effort to transform, renew and reinvigorate our movement in order that we can hope to accomplish the goals we set for ourselves.

This book aims to be a contribution to that effort.

# CHAPTER TWO

# WHAT IS LEFT ANTISEMITISM?

Anti-Jewish bigotry and persecution has a long and complex history, far predating the common use of the word antisemitism as the main term for it. It has taken distinct forms in different historical periods: the religious persecution of Jews by the Seleucid and Roman Empires was distinct from subsequent persecution by Christian and Islamic states, which differed in type from each other and which differed in turn from the exterminationist anti-Jewish racism of the Nazis.

Despite these distinctions, however, the very antiquity and longevity of varied forms of anti-Jewish bigotry have led to the creation of what some writers have called a 'reservoir' of anti-Jewish tropes and ideas that have 'accumulated over centuries and [which] are embedded deeply within our culture', with 'some images and narratives persisting over time and others emerging anew'.[1]

Moishe Postone, a Marxist academic who taught at the University of Chicago, and who was one of the most sophisticated critics of left antisemitism, summarised modern antisemitism as:

an ideology, a form of thought, that emerged in Europe in the late nineteenth century. Its emergence presupposed earlier forms of antisemitism, which had for centuries been an integral part of Christian Western civilisation. What is common to all forms of antisemitism is the degree of power attributed to the Jews: the power to kill God, to unleash the bubonic plague, and, more recently, to introduce capitalism and socialism [...]

It is not only the degree, but also the quality of power attributed to the Jews that distinguishes antisemitism from other forms of racism. Probably all forms of racism attribute potential power to the Other. This power, however, is usually concrete, material, or sexual. It is the potential power of the oppressed (as repressed), of the 'Untermenschen'. The power attributed to the Jews is much greater and is perceived as actual rather than as potential. Moreover, it is a different sort of power, one not necessarily concrete.[2]

Despite antisemitic ideas being 'deeply embedded within our culture', the notion of a 'left' antisemitism can seem counter-intuitive and contradictory. Isn't the left against bigotry and prejudice, and for equality between peoples? Surely antisemitism is the sole ideological property of the right? Why would the left collude in the attribution of world-shaping power to Jews?

The apparent paradox has led some to deny that left antisemitism *can* exist at all: antisemitism is incompatible with the values of the left, therefore if someone advances antisemitic ideas, they're not really on the left. They must be expressing ideas they picked up elsewhere and importing them into the left. The possibility of forms of antisemitism that might exist within left-wing discourse, and present themselves as consistent with an otherwise left-wing worldview, is denied. Often, the denial functions in reverse: an idea cannot possibly be antisemitic if it is expressed by someone whose wider political beliefs and activist record show them clearly to be left-wing, or that if an idea presents itself as only a critique of a form of politics – for example, Zionism – rather than of 'Jews as Jews', it cannot be antisemitic.

Alas, if only things were that simple. The history of the left is sadly full of expressions of various forms of bigotry – national, inter-communal, gender or sexuality-based and others – and attempts to make bigoted ideas serve a would-be left-wing worldview.

Take, for instance, the example of Jim Larkin, the great Irish workers' leader, who, in 1906, led a demonstration of Liverpool dockers opposing Chinese immigrant labour, which they claimed was undercutting British workers' conditions. Larkin and others dressed as 'Chinamen', donning fake pigtails and using dye to make their skin appear yellow. They paraded a coffin draped with a Union Jack through Liverpool, proclaiming the 'burial of freedom'.[3]

This disgraceful episode does not represent the totality of Larkin's legacy. I regard Larkin as a heroic figure in many ways. But he was also clearly someone who believed anti-migrant bigotry was compatible with his socialism. Does this episode prove that Larkin was not really of the left, that all his prior efforts in the cause of socialism were an act, and he was showing his true, racist colours in 1906? Or that Larkin wasn't *yet* a leftist, but became one later? But he was already a member of the Independent Labour Party in 1906, and is nowhere on record as having later regretted or recanted the episode. So it must be conceded that there is, in fact, historical precedent for the incorporation of bigoted ideas into a worldview that sees itself as – and may, in general terms, sincerely *be* – left-wing. There is clearly such a precedent with antisemitism, too.

Antisemitism on the left can broadly be seen as having three primary historical phases, each generating a strand of ongoing thinking. These, to varying degrees, still persist on the contemporary left, sometimes functioning separately but often overlapping and intertwining. The first, which could be called the primitive strand, took shape in the nineteenth century, based on a conflation of Jews with capital and finance. A second strand developed in the early 1950s, in the USSR and its satellite states, emerging from a phase of intensive state propaganda accusing Jewish dissidents, real and alleged, of being part of 'cosmopolitan' and anti-national conspiracies to undermine the state. That phase is best understood as transitional between the first phase, whose conspiracy-theorist frame it recycled, and the third, which began when Stalinism's 'anti-cosmopolitan' campaigns segued into a discourse that focused primarily on 'anti-Zionism'.

The strand of left antisemitism that emerged from that third phase has an attendant political programme asserting that any expression of self-determination by the Israeli-Jewish national group embodies the racist-colonial essence of Zionism, and must therefore be opposed. It sits within a wider political framework, originating with Stalinism but taken up in parts of the non- and even anti-Stalinist left, of a dualistic anti-imperialism. This framework sees any opposition to hegemonic imperialism as necessarily progressive, regardless of the positive social content a given form of anti-imperialism represents. Crucially, imperialism is understood not as a system of policies that states pursue on international terrain to advance their financial or territorial interests, but as an almost innate condition or essence that certain states or even peoples embody and which other states and peoples do not. According to this line of argument, within which Zionism is seen as a subset of imperialism, or even its vanguard or driver, any form of anti-Zionism should be supported by the left.

## THE FIRST STRAND: PRIMITIVE ANTISEMITISM ON THE LEFT

The first strand of historic left antisemitism predates the popularisation of the word antisemitism to describe hostility to Jews. According to the academic Nancy Green, the utopian socialist Charles Fourier, active in France in the early nineteenth century, 'saw the Jews as the incarnation of commerce: parasitical, deceitful, traitorous and unproductive'.[4] There are antisemitic ideas, of varying degrees of intensity, in the work of several other nineteenth-century leftists and radicals, including the theoretical forefather of anarchist communism, Mikhail Bakunin, who wrote that 'the whole Jewish world' comprised 'a single exploiting sect, a kind of blood-sucking people, a kind of organic destructive collective parasite, going beyond not only the frontiers of states, but of political opinion'.[5]

Pierre-Joseph Proudhon, another theoretical pioneer of anarchism, described Jews, in a note for a future article to be entitled 'On the Jews', as 'this race that poisons everything by sticking its nose into everything without ever mixing with any other people'.[6] Wilhelm Marr, who popularised the term antisemitism to describe hostility to Jews, was not some clerical or aristocratic reactionary, but a sometime revolutionary of the 1848 generation and proto-anarchist who became a convinced racist and nationalist.

The French revolutionary syndicalist and anarchist leader Emile Pouget – who, like Larkin, I regard as a highly respectworthy figure in the history of class struggle in Europe – wrote that, while 'masked antisemitism' was not present in the revolutionary workers' movement, neither was 'blind philosemitism', making his declaration in order that 'the sensitive epidermis of our Jewish comrades does not tremble anew'.[7] Pouget's claim of a movement free from antisemitism is somewhat complicated by the record of his comrade Emile Pataud, the electricians' union leader and fellow anarcho-syndicalist, with whom Pouget co-authored *How We Shall Bring About the Revolution: Syndicalism and the Cooperative Commonwealth*; Pataud spoke at an anti-Jewish rally in 1911, where the crowd chanted '*A bas les Juifs!*' (Down with the Jews).[8]

At the rally, Pataud said it was 'not his fault if ninety-five per cent of the capitalists he was attacking in connection with labour conflicts were Jewish'.[9] In so doing, he was expressing one of the most frequent bases for the incorporation of antisemitic ideas into would-be radical worldviews – the old association, even the conflation, of Jews with commerce and finance, a plank of antisemitism since well before 'left-wing' existed as a concept, with roots in the forced exclusion of Jews from trades other than mercantile and commercial. By the nineteenth century such rhetoric was being incorporated into some developing critiques of capitalism. As Nancy Green put it, with specific reference to the French context: 'An amalgam occurs whereby all Jews are supposed to be capitalists and all capitalists are supposed to be "Jews", regardless of their origin. […] In the linguistic equation between capitalist and Jew, the socialists thus inherited a language in which the negative characteristics ascribed to all capitalists were also attributed to all Jews.'[10] Jewish capitalists were not seen merely as capitalists who happened to be Jewish, but as *the* capitalists, embodying capitalism's essence, with capitalism seen as an intrinsically Jewish endeavour.

The association of Jews with capital and finance was sometimes present as a trope even in nineteenth-century leftist writing supportive of Jewish emancipation. Writers including Hal Draper, one the great theorists and organisers of the heterodox Trotskyist tradition on the US left, and Robert Fine, a socialist activist and academic who wrote extensively on left antisemitism, have argued clearly and convincingly that the substance of Karl Marx's argument in his infamous work 'On the Jewish Question' is opposed to antisemitic oppression.[11] Notwithstanding this, Marx undeniably deployed the language of antisemitism. His acceptance of the 'economic-Jew stereotype' as a fixed fact of political culture, which he referred to even when advancing an argument for Jewish rights and freedom, shows how entrenched this association was in political consciousness.

The conception of the Jew as not simply a racial or national inferior, but the embodiment of some powerful, socially manipulative force, expresses the specificity of antisemitism. Modern antisemitism has not functioned as a simplistic dualism – Jews bad, non-Jews good – but as an explanatory narrative for how the world is organised. We often speak of 'antisemitic conspiracy theories', but this is, in a sense, tautologous. Antisemitism itself *is* a conspiracy theory, seeking to explain social structure and events by claiming that the world is secretly controlled by a shadowy cabal of Jews. As Steve Cohen put it: 'The peculiar and defining feature of antisemitism is that it exists as an ideology. It provides its adherents with a universal and generalised interpretation of the world.'[12] This specificity also highlights the inadequacy of attempting to define antisemitism solely as 'Jew hatred'. While many antisemites undoubtedly do hate Jews, it is not necessary for antisemitism as an ideology to proceed from individualised animus towards individual Jews, but from opposition to an alleged form of intangible power and control, which is identified as Jewish or 'Zionist'.

Postone called antisemitism 'a primitive critique of the world, of capitalist modernity'. He therefore viewed antisemitism as 'particularly dangerous for the left [...] precisely because [it] has a pseudo-emancipatory dimension that other forms of racism rarely have'.[13] Postone wrote elsewhere that antisemitism presents itself as 'antihegemonic, the expression of a movement of the little people against an intangible, global form of domination'.[14]

Antisemitism therefore has a distinct potential to undermine radical, transformative politics, in part by appearing to embody them. As the writer and activist April Rosenblum put it:

Antisemitism's job is to make ruling classes invisible. It protects ruling class power structures, diverting anger at injustice toward Jews instead. But it doesn't have to be planned out at the top. It serves the same ends, whether enshrined in law or institutionalised only in our minds; whether it's state policy, popular 'common sense', or acts of grassroots movements.[15]

Unlike more contemporary forms of left antisemitism, which take assumed political, rather than supposed biological or racial, characteristics as the basis for their hostility to Jews, primitive antisemitism on the left frequently had an explicitly racialised element, fusing the idea of Jews as a 'blood-sucking people', in Bakunin's phrase, with a critique of finance and financiers as playing a vampiric role within a nation.

As we will explore in Chapter Three, a notable, and alarming, feature of the antisemitism encountered particularly in Labour Party spaces since 2015, and often expressed by individuals in online forums and on their personal social media platforms rather than in physical meetings, is how much of it seems to belong to this primitive strand, the themes of which appeared to have been superseded by a contemporary strand consisting of narratives focusing on Israel and Zionism.[16]

## THE SECOND STRAND: CONSPIRACY THEORIES IN THE 'COMMUNIST' BLOC

A second historical strand of left antisemitism, examined in more detail in Chapter Four, consisted of conspiracy theory propaganda produced in so-called 'Communist' – in fact Stalinist – states from the 1950s onwards. Stalinist antisemitism predates the 1950s, with Stalin and his supporters exploiting antisemitic arguments against his factional opponents inside the Bolshevik party, most prominently Leon Trotsky, in the mid-late 1920s.[17] In the 1920s and 30s, Stalinist Communist parties supported antisemitic attacks against Jewish settlers in Palestine, claiming the attacks were 'anti-imperialist'.[18] But it is from the 1950s that an especially virulent strain of conspiracy-theorist antisemitism becomes a central feature of Stalinist ideology.

Antisemitism was rife, and state-sponsored, in pre-revolutionary Russia, and it did not dissolve overnight upon the overthrow of the Tsar, or following the Bolshevik-led workers' revolution of October 1917. The Bolsheviks made various attempts to confront the question, in society and within their own ranks, with varying degrees of success.[19] But the overthrow of the ideals of October 1917 by the Stalinist counter-revolution ultimately saw those attempts frustrated.

Beginning in earnest with the Doctors' Plot of 1951 and the Slánský Trial of 1952, claims that Jews were involved in various conspiracies to overthrow the Stalinist states began to be produced on an industrial scale. In the former case, a group of mainly Jewish doctors were accused of involvement in a plot to assassinate Stalin. In the latter, Rudolf Slánský, a Jewish leader of the Czech Communist Party, was put through a show-trial, along with thirteen other alleged dissidents, ten of whom were Jewish. Again, they were accused of conspiring to bring down Stalin, and later executed. Appeals to antisemitism became an almost default mechanism used by Stalinist ruling classes to deflect domestic dissent. In Poland in 1967–8, against a backdrop of radical student protests, the Stalinist bureaucracy whipped up antisemitic, 'anti-Zionist' fervour.

This strand of antisemitism on the left shared a basic framework with the first, primitive-anti-capitalist, strand: a conspiracy-theorist narrative that claimed to expose secret cabals of rootless, transnational Jews organising behind the scenes to subvert or take over the state. A largely new element in the second strand, which became the central basis of the third, was the ubiquity of the label 'Zionist', slapped on any Jewish dissident, real or imagined. The Jewish doctors accused in the Doctors' Plot were 'Zionists'. Rudolf Slánský was a 'Zionist' – and a 'Trotskyite': the two words often went together.

### THE THIRD STRAND: STALINIST ANTI-ZIONISM

The 'Zionism' that existed in Stalinist antisemitism bore little relation to what Zionism was in the real world: a nationalist response to Jewish marginalisation and oppression, that became the founding ideology of a small nation state. Rather, it was an immensely powerful, world-shaping force. As the *New York Times* report on the Slánský Trial noted:

> The charge [is] that Slánský and the majority of his fellow-defendants, who are of Jewish origin, were members of a vast Jewish conspiracy, betraying their country to 'American imperialism' in order to serve the state of Israel. Here we have the infamous *Protocols of the Elders of Zion*, but in the Stalinist version. So the Prague trial is not merely a comedy; rather it may well mark the beginning of a major tragedy as the Kremlin swings further and further towards antisemitism masked as anti-Zionism.[20]

This particular form of anti-Zionism, which linked Zionism to a conspiracy of 'millionaires of Jewish origin' to engage in a project of imperialist expansion in the Middle East, comprises the third strand of left antisemitism. In this strand, Zionism is inflated into an almost mystical force, the quintessential expression of colonialism and imperialism, and directly and wholly synonymous with racism, and sometimes even with fascism.[21]

Steve Cohen's term for this form of anti-Zionism was 'transcendental', arguing that it transcended any relationship with Zionism as it actually existed.[22] Much of what has passed for anti-Zionism on the far left since the 1960s has more closely resembled this transcendental anti-Zionism than the anti-nationalist critiques of Zionism developed on the pre-Stalinist revolutionary left. Those critiques counselled the Jewish working classes to look to class unity with non-Jewish workers in a struggle for socialism as the best means to win emancipation, rather than to separatism and 'national' unity with the bourgeoisie in their own communities.

Zionism is, at root, Jewish nationalism – the belief that the Jews constitute a national people who should collectively self-determine. It is also, at root, a response to antisemitism. As summed up by the

Lebanese-French socialist academic and writer Gilbert Achcar, it is 'indisputable that eastern European Zionism emerged in reaction to an unbearable form of racist oppression that, ultimately, defined the Jews as a race and culminated in the Nazi genocide'.[23] Historic Zionism has been a diverse movement, differing within itself on what form a Jewish national home should take. Zionism has encompassed everything from a Marxist far left, whose adherents organised detachments to fight in the Bolshevik Red Army in the Russian civil war, and who, in 1934, advocated in Palestine for 'Jewish and Arab workers' solidarity',[24] to a racist far right, some of whose partisans sympathised with Mussolini.[25]

The achievement of Zionism's central policy aim, the realisation of Jewish nationhood in the form of an independent state in historic Palestine, has meant displacement, subjugation and oppression for the pre-existing Arab communities of the territory. The contemporary Israeli state, heavily militarised, stands in an essentially colonial relationship to the Palestinian people of the West Bank and Gaza, and as a deeply discriminatory power towards the Palestinian minority in Israel itself.

Does that justify collapsing all of historic Zionism, and the more diffuse affinity most Jews feel with Israel – seen as, in Isaac Deutscher's useful phrase, a 'lifeboat, a raft, [...] a float'[26] for post-Holocaust Jewish refugees – into nothing more than a racist, colonial-imperialist impulse? That idea is supportable only by the erasure of Jewish history and experience. The Orientalist scholar Maxime Rodinson, himself a strident critic of Zionism, who pioneered the analysis of Israel as a 'settler-colonial' state, wrote: 'The Jews of Israel too are people like other people. [...] Many went there because it was the life preserver thrown to them. They most assuredly did not first engage in scholarly research to find out if they had a right to it according to Kantian morality or existentialist ethics.'[27] Forms of anti-Zionism that ignore these complexities and tensions, which some commentators on left antisemitism have called 'absolute anti-Zionism', necessarily bring those who advance them into implied hostility with the majority of Jews alive.[28]

To maintain its claim that it is not antisemitic, absolute anti-Zionism implies a separation between 'Jews' and 'Zionists', as if these are two mutually exclusive categories. This is expressed by the oft-repeated claim that anti-Zionism cannot, definitionally, be antisemitic, because 'not all Zionists are Jews, and not all Jews are Zionists', implying that an idea is antisemitic only if based on hostility to traits or characteristics that it alleges *all* Jews possess.[29] As the sociologist Keith Kahn-Harris put it in his book *Strange Hate: Antisemitism, Racism, and the Limits of Diversity*:

> How is it that victims can become perpetrators? For [some on the left], these ['Jews' and 'Zionists'] are two entirely separate categories of persons; to willingly switch from one to another is incomprehensible, a sign of catastrophic moral failure. So it has to be explained away by treating Zionists as separate to Jews, as perpetrators only, and hence categorisable alongside Nazis. The Jews that were killed in the Holocaust were victims of two sets of perpetrators. The survivors and their descendants that embraced Zionism were either duped by the Zionists or were never really victims at all. Circle square. Job done. Simple.[30]

Transcendental and absolute forms of anti-Zionism offer an appealing emotional and moral simplicity. They suggest fixed historical classifications of easily identifiable good and bad people, whose status as good or bad is a matter of essence. Emotion has its place in the construction of a revolutionary politics, but it is not sufficient. And if not tempered with historical analysis, it can be counterproductive. Historical materialism, the method underpinning the Marxist approach to history, involves an analysis of the social and economic conditions in which events take place. Friedrich Engels summarised this as the belief that the 'determining element in history is the production and reproduction of real life'.[31] To confer an essential moral condition on any national or communal people is incompatible with that approach. It is also an affront to the humanism that must be the core of any socialist politics.

The experiences of persecution and genocide that turned Zionism from a minority current amongst Jews into something much closer to a reflex are harsh realities that continue to resonate in Jewish identity. And Jewish identity, like any ethnic, cultural, or national identity, is complex and sometimes contradictory. Some level of identification and affinity with Israel makes up an aspect of that identity for most Jews. This affinity is not limited to the Ashkenazi Jews of central and eastern European background, who can be made to fit superficially the mould of white Europeans supporting of a project of colonial-imperialist expansion in the Middle East, which subjugates indigenous peoples of colour in the process.* Jews from Arab and other Middle Eastern and North African backgrounds also experienced persecution and expulsion from their home states. Many found refuge – if not, as yet, equality – in Israel itself. Today, Mizrahi (North African and Middle Eastern-background) Jews make up around half of Israel's Jewish population.

Academic research from 2015, the most recently conducted research of its type, found that 93 per cent of British Jews felt

---

\* Whether Ashkenazi Jews could be said, in the period of Jewish settlement in Palestine and at the time of the foundation of the state of Israel, to have been meaningfully integrated into the constructed category of 'whiteness' is dubious, as is whether Palestinian Arabs are 'Black'. Several prominent Black nationalists and Pan-Africanists, such as W. E. B. Du Bois and Eldridge Cleaver, identified with Zionism, rather than with Palestinian or wider Arab nationalism. Some of these issues are discussed in further detail in Chapters Four and Seven.

that Israel forms some part of their identity, while 90 per cent supported its continued existence as a Jewish state. The establishment of an independent Palestinian state alongside Israel was supported by 71 per cent, and 75 per cent said the West Bank settlements were a 'major obstacle to peace'.[32] The Stalinist form of conspiracy-theorist anti-Zionism cannot begin to engage with the complexities of this identity and these political views. It necessarily implies hostility to 93 per cent of Jews in Britain, and probably a similar proportion of Jews around the world, and not merely to their political views, but to the very fabric of what, for them, comprises their Jewish identity.

All of this is why statements like 'it's not antisemitic to oppose Zionism' or 'it's not antisemitic to criticise Israel' are banal truisms with little explanatory value. Of course, it's *not* antisemitic to oppose Zionism or to criticise Israel, but *some* criticisms of Israel and Zionism *can be* antisemitic. Making a reflexive and mechanical insistence that 'anti-Zionism is not antisemitism' – the default response to any allegation of antisemitism on the left – engenders a collective political ignorance of forms of anti-Zionism that *are* antisemitic.

The antisemitic potential of certain forms of anti-Zionism were highlighted in the late 1970s and early 1980s, when sections of the far left, including the Socialist Workers Party (SWP), conducted a campaign on college and university campuses to impose 'no platform for Zionism', including a ban on campus Jewish societies on the basis that their Zionism made them 'racist', and it was a principle of the left that racists should be given no space to organise.[33] The campaign was partially successful, with several students' unions banning their Jewish societies.

The implied demand posed to the Jewish societies and their members by their left-wing critics was that they should disavow Zionism, not only as a formal ideology but also as a catch-all term for any degree of affinity with Israel. Disavow and reject your own relief that Jewish people, perhaps including your own relatives, were able to escape to Palestine, often despite significant obstruction. Do not allow the historical experience of your community, of your parents and grandparents, perhaps even of yourselves, to have any shaping effect on how you consider the world. That remains the demand left antisemitism poses to Jewish people today.

In 2021 a controversy sparked by comments made by David Miller, a professor of sociology at the University of Bristol, reprised debates surrounding the 1980s agitation against campus Jewish societies. Miller denounced Bristol's Jewish Society by claiming it was, 'like all [Jewish societies], an Israel lobby group'. Professor David Feldman, of Birkbeck College's Pears Institute for the Study of Antisemitism, wrote in response: 'The university's Jewish Society, [Miller] points out, through a series of affiliations, is "formally" a member of the Zionist movement. In saying this, Miller aims to discredit their complaints against him, as if Zionists complaining about antisemitism are necessarily acting in bad faith'.[34]

Miller's claims were consistent with his wider view that almost every major organisation and individual in Jewish communal life were effectively paid agents of the Israeli state. Miller sees 'Zionism', standing as a singular and reified force, behind almost all of politics, domestically and internationally. He had previously accused Labour leader Keir Starmer of being in receipt of 'money from the Zionist movement',[35] because of an individual donor's Zionist politics, and, at an online rally of the Labour Left Alliance in June 2020, argued that even an interfaith initiative held at the East London Mosque, which involved Jews and Muslims cooking together, was an 'Israel-backed project', part of a drive to 'normalise Zionism in the Muslim community'.[36] Zionism, according to Miller, is 'the enemy of world peace' which 'has no place in any society' and must be 'ended'.[37]

As Feldman rightly argued, 'In the context of [Miller's] other remarks, we can see that he identifies members of the university

[Jewish Society] as people whose political attachments have no place in any society and, by implication, as enemies of world peace.'[38]

Prior to the controversy, Miller was perhaps best known as a member of the 'Working Group on Syria, Propaganda, and Media', a collective of academics and independent researchers, which denied the atrocities of the Assad regime in Syria.[39] The group also includes Vanessa Beeley, who posted on Twitter that 'Zionists rule France'[40] and, in 2014, circulated an article on social media claiming that Kristallnacht, the anti-Jewish pogrom carried out by the Nazis on 9–10 November 1938, was a 'false flag' organised by Mossad, the Israeli secret service, an organisation that did not exist until 1949.[41] Whether or not Miller shares Beeley's views on this matter, their collaboration makes clear that there are sections of the would-be left in which conspiracy-theorist anti-Zionism, of a necessarily antisemitic type, is the common sense.

During the February 2021 controversy, Miller was defended by several prominent figures on the left. A letter supporting him attracted hundreds of signatories, including Noam Chomsky, John Pilger and current and former SWP leaders such as Alex Callinicos and Lindsey German. The letter did not merely defend Miller's right to speak and publish, against calls for censorship and dismissal, but explicitly lauded and celebrated his work, calling him 'an eminent scholar', who is 'known internationally for exposing the role that powerful actors and well-resourced, coordinated networks play in manipulating and stage-managing public debates, including on racism. [...] The impact of his research on the manipulation of narratives by lobby groups has been crucial to deepening public knowledge and discourse in this area.'[42] The writer Tom Mills insisted the campaign against Miller was 'McCarthyism, pure and simple'.[43] Kerry-Anne Mendoza, founding editor of The Canary, a prominent pro-Jeremy Corbyn website with whom Corbyn himself had, in December 2020, conducted an exclusive interview, denounced Miller's critics as 'pro-apartheid fanatics'.[44]

These defences dismissed the possibility that Jewish students on Bristol's and other campuses might sincerely object to the assertion that they were agents of a Zionist plot for political domination. For Miller and many of his supporters, any link with Israel, of any sort, no matter how diffuse or notional, is enough to justify an unqualified categorisation as a racist. This not only significantly over-inflates the power of Israel in the world but also reifies Zionism, a historically diverse ideology, into a concrete and singular agency that must be confronted and, to quote Miller, 'ended'.

This thinking necessarily designates the majority of Jews, who have some degree of affinity with Israel and who are likely to call themselves 'Zionists', mortal political enemies. Whatever the intent of its adherents, and however strongly they insist they are merely anti-Zionist rather than antisemitic, they have classified the majority of Jews not merely as people who might hold ideas with which the left disagrees, but as an enemy Other. Moreover, their wilful ignorance of, and insensitivity to, the historically accumulated reasons why Jews and Jewish organisations might feel a connection to Israel has an inevitably antisemitic logic.

As an opponent of the bans on Jewish societies in the 1980s put it at the time:

> Zionism is part of the identity that modern history – centrally, Hitler's massacres, and the callous attitude of the big powers to those massacres and their survivors – has stamped on Jews. To differentiate between banning Zionists and banning Jews is no more than a thin fiction when the vast majority of Jews today identify with Israel and are supporters – active or passive, callous or guilty, blinkered and happy, or deeply troubled supporters – of the existing Jewish state. This is part of their identity as Jews, and not easily detachable.[45]

Much of the left acts precisely as though this aspect of historically developed Jewish identity *is* 'easily detachable', and implies those who do not detach from it should be treated as straightforward reactionaries. Those sections of the left prefer to leap over the complexity and contradictions history has created in Jewish identity and consciousness in a way they tend not to with the consciousness and identity of other minority groups.

In *Strange Hate*, Kahn-Harris suggested:

> Group identities are neither fixed nor eternal. They do not contain an ahistorical 'essence'. Yet an anti-essentialist view of identity has also to recognise the fact that group identities often 'feel' like they carry the weight of essence. [...] All of which leaves us with an appalling dilemma as to how to conduct politics when it impinges on closely held group identities. [...] On the left, there is at least some awareness of the need to find a way to grapple with these issues. However, when it comes to Jewish Zionists, there is a limited recognition that the problem even exists.[46]

No one, Jewish or otherwise, is the mere imprint of what history has 'stamped' on them. The reflexes that our own experiences, and the inherited memory of the historical experiences of our forebears, produce in us can and should be engaged with critically. And internationalist revolutionary socialism does attempt to reshape identity. It appeals to all peoples to aspire to a universalist-humanist, rather than particularist, identity and consciousness. The realisation of our politics does require some amount of overcoming of reflexive responses to historical injustice, which can tend towards nationalism or separatism, with all that those perspectives imply in terms of the othering of other peoples.

But for Jews, sections of the left present the matter not as an appeal or an attempt at persuasion, but as an ultimatum, on pain of being considered racists who ought to be banned. Instead of understanding diaspora Zionism and affinity with Israel as residual products of the bludgeoning history meted out to Jews during twentieth century and earlier, much of the left treats them as something akin to a mortal sin.

Group identities cannot be reliably changed by sheer force of denunciation, or by ostracism. To repurpose an adage from Karl Marx, although we can shape our own identity and consciousness, we do so in circumstances not of our own choosing. Through an insensitivity to the circumstances in which Jewish identity and consciousness have been made and remade – in other words, through ignorance of 'the production and reproduction of real life' – sections of the left are brought into implied hostility towards most Jews alive. This can only entrench nationalism, making it less likely that Jewish identity could be remade again on the basis of universalist-humanist ideals.

These perspectives are not incidental, the products of an aberration that impels otherwise egalitarian-minded people towards hostility to Jews, but belong to a wider ideological frame – a dualistic anti-imperialism that sees Zionism as imperialism's quintessence.

'Imperialism' in this context is a concept stripped of its real meaning and descriptive value. As already stated, it describes not a system of policies pursued on international terrain by capitalist ruling classes to secure advantage for their states, but a behind-the-scenes conspiracy of some compact and singular group, the imperialists – or, sometimes, the Zionists – to dominate the world. Anything and anyone opposed to the imperialists, regardless of whether the alternative in the name of which they oppose imperialism is any better, is automatically ordained as an agent of historical progress. Thus, referring back to the 'socialism of fools' label, used by some in Austria and Germany in the late nineteenth century to describe antisemitism on the left,[47] Moishe Postone said that left antisemitism could, 'given its subsequent develop-ment, […] also have been called "the anti-imperialism of fools"'.[48]

This view, which some writers have called 'campist',[49] contends that the world is essentially divisible into relatively discrete blocs, or camps (hence 'campism'), comprising states and satellite parties and movements linked to or supported by those states. Campism is also a legacy of Stalinism. It is in part a hangover of Cold War logic, with a nebulous 'anti-imperialism' having taken the place of the 'actually existing socialism' that the Stalinist bloc was once held to represent. Dissident traditions within revolu-tionary socialism consistently challenged the campist worldview, most coherently the heterodox Trotskyist tendency emerging in the USA in the late 1930s and early 1940s led by Max Shachtman, Hal Draper and others, which advocated support for the 'Third Camp' of the working class, constituted as an independent polit-ical force, against both Western capitalism and Stalinism. This perspective was summarised by the slogan 'neither Washington nor Moscow, but international socialism'. This was the tradi-tion Steve Cohen consciously invoked when he wrote, in a 2007 article, 'For the Third Camp – Yes to Palestinian Liberation! No to Antisemitism!'[50]

Within the campist 'anti-imperialism of fools', Israel and Zionism are held to be synonymous with 'imperialism' (meaning Western imperialism), and sometimes even imperialism's driving force. The cartoon adorning the cover of *Israel: The Hijack State – America's Watchdog in the Middle East*, a 1986 pamphlet produced by the SWP, shows a ferocious dog, teeth bared in a slavering maw, with a weedy-looking Uncle Sam holding its leash.[51] The cartoon could serve either interpretation – that Israel is solely an instru-ment, a pet, of US imperialism, and therefore illegitimate; or that Israel in fact drags the USA behind it. It is a recurrent theme of left antisemitism that Zionism is not merely a form of nationalism that may, like any other form of nationalism, broker deals with big-power imperialism, but is in fact in the driving seat, determining the policy of the big powers, perhaps even against the wishes of the big powers themselves. As Steve Cohen wrote: 'Much of what the left poses as anti-Zionism [...] is concerned with ascribing world power to Zionism.'[52]

It is an indication of how hegemonic Stalinist-inspired ideas have been across the far left that the SWP, in its origins and according to its self-conception an anti-Stalinist, Trotskyist organisation, could become a primary carrier of them. How and why this happened, and how another would-be Trotskyist tendency, the Workers Revolutionary Party, could become another key well-spring for left antisemitism, is discussed further in Chapter Four.

The left should, of course, oppose imperialism. But our point of departure in that is not an abstract, negative anti-imperialism, or anti-Zionism, but a positive support for the principle of equality between all peoples and national groups, including an equal right to self-determination. Consistent support for democracy and equal rights comes first; opposition to policies and structures that suppress such rights flows from that. Placing the negative opposition ahead of the support for positive rights leads to what Susie Linfield, author of *The Lion's Den: Zionism and the Left from Hannah Arendt to Noam Chomsky*, has called 'a sort of Pavlovian anti-Zionism' on the left. 'Of course,' Linfield goes on, 'vehement criticism of Israel is absolutely justified, but by "Pavlovian" I mean that the hostility to Israel is a reflex, often without any historic knowledge.'[53]

Within the framework of the 'anti-imperialism of fools', the Israeli Jews are not a national community, which should be entitled to national democratic rights on an equal basis to all other national peoples; they are simply 'the Zionists', a settler caste, the carriers of the colonial conspiracy. The language habitually used by sections of the far left to describe Israel and its people, and its differences from the language used by them to describe other states and national groups, implies a clear double standard. There is no habit in leftist discourse of referring to Turkey as 'the Kemalist state' when describing its oppression of the Kurds, or to Sri Lanka as 'the Sinhalese nationalist entity' when describing its oppression of the Tamils; nothing equivalent, in other words, to the historic description of Israel as 'the Zionist entity' or 'the Zionist state', labels originating in Arab nationalist discourse, the use of which the Palestinian academic and writer Edward Said called a 'foolish and wasteful policy'.[54]

All nation states are on some level instruments for the nationalism of the national group on which the state is based. In this, Israel is a 'Zionist state' in the same sense that Britain is a 'British nationalist state' and France is a 'French nationalist state'. But leftists critiquing the actions of those states usually find it sufficient to refer to them simply as 'Britain' and 'France', rather than insisting that the nationalist character of the state voids the right of the people of the nation to self-determination. The increasingly virulent Hindu-nationalist character of the Indian state, based on the ideology of Hindutva, is not used by any group on the left to inform the conclusion that contemporary India must be destroyed. No one on the left claims 'anti-Hindutva' is an adequate political descriptor or point of departure, that can denote an entire worldview, in the way often implied for 'anti-Zionist'.

As the socialist writer and activist Martin Thomas points out:

Israeli Jews, as a collective, are frequently referred to as 'the Zionists', and thus, unlike any other nation on earth, equated with a political faction. (As if Poland, as a country, were routinely referred to as 'the Polish nationalists'.) Then the big majority of Jews worldwide, who for historically rooted reasons not changeable at will, mostly have some reflex (maybe critical or very critical) identification with Israel, are also 'Zionists'.[55]

According to these arguments, Israel's oppression of the Palestinians is resolvable not by the levelling-up of rights, so the oppressed nation gains its independence from the oppressor nation, but by the wholesale destruction and dismantling of the oppressor state. An article in the SWP's *Socialist Worker* expressed it succinctly: there can be no peace in the Middle East, it suggested, 'while the state of Israel continues to exist'.[56] But beyond general appeals to 'resistance' and 'revolution', neither the means for bringing about the extinction of Israel, nor what should happen to the Israeli Jews, the people on whose national community that state is based, if they oppose the destruction of the state, is spelled out explicitly.

The academics Sina Arnold and Blair Taylor argued in their survey of antisemitism on the left that,

> because it calls for an end not only to the occupation but the very existence of Israel, ['absolute' anti-Zionism] has come to represent the obvious 'radical' position on the left. Yet this radicalism rests on deeply liberal and ahistorical presumptions about the nature of nation-states. It assumes Israel is a uniquely violent exception rather than the more mundane rule [and] selectively ignores that every state in existence today is equally 'artificial', birthed and maintained by violence, dispossession, and exclusion.[57]

Given this, the desirability of *any* state existing in its present form can, in the abstract, be made a matter for debate. It is not necessarily antisemitic to imagine, and hope for, a future in which the present state of Israel has been superseded by a unitary constitutional settlement, freely entered into by the peoples of the region, encompassing the whole territory of historic Palestine. Various models have been advanced – a binational federation, a wider regional federation with autonomy for the distinct national groups, a post-national republic which leaves constitutional categories of 'Israeli Jew' and 'Palestinian Arab' behind altogether, and others.

Ultimately, that is a debate to be settled by democratic accommodation amongst Israelis and Palestinians. Leftists internationally can discuss, from a distance, the possible plausibility and desirability of various models without trafficking in antisemitism. My own view is that democratic confederation, not just in Israel/Palestine but in the wider region, is a desirable destination. Any consistent internationalist should aspire to a world with fewer borders, not more. If our aim is to lower borders and erode national boundaries, why stop at Israel/Palestine? Socialists should hardly consider the colonially-imposed pre-1948 borders as sacrosanct. Why not a federal socialist republic of the Middle East?

These are worthy aspirations. But a unitary state in Israel/Palestine seems to me unlikely to be achieved without an almost certainly quite prolonged transitional settlement based on two independent states. Any kind of post-national settlement emerging fully formed, an unprecedented occurrence in world history, from over fifty years of occupation and an even longer history of displacement and violence, seems especially utopian. Nevertheless, it is not antisemitic to discuss any of this; indeed, it is being discussed by Palestinian and Israeli leftists all the time, against the backdrop of worsening conditions, as successive Israeli governments have aimed to definitively block any possibility for the emergence of a viable Palestinian national entity and impose a chauvinist, one-state model in which Palestinians will be condemned to permanent subject status.

But what is almost unavoidably antisemitic is the claim that the Israeli Jews – undeniably today, and for many generations, a national group by any operable definition of the concept – should have no national rights at all. Some on the left scoff at the claim that 'Israel has a right to exist', countering that, while peoples may have a right to self-determination, no *state* has 'a right to exist'. That rebuttal might be more persuasive if the left routinely made the demand for the non-existence of states, rather than the cessation of particular policies, the main focus of its opposition to colonialism or national oppression.

Echoing Hal Draper, US socialist activist Daniel Fischer draws a distinction between

> anti-Zionism, which opposes a regime, and anti-Israelism, which opposes a country and its people. [...] Unfortunately, some in the Palestine solidarity movement conflate anti-Zionism and anti-Israelism. Anti-Israelism is [musician] Roger Waters conjuring up a false story about Israeli concert attendees failing to applaud his call for regional peace. Anti-Israelism is [...] *Socialist Worker*[58] declaring 'unconditional' support for Hamas, a far-right group that intentionally kills Israeli civilians. Anti-Israelism is [feminist academic] Judith Butler bizarrely remarking, 'Yes, understanding Hamas and Hezbollah as social movements that are progressive, that are on the left, that are part of a global left, is extremely important.' Maybe more Israeli Jews would join the global left if they felt as invited as their theocratic enemies are.[59]

I would go further, and be more explicit, than Fischer. It is precisely at the point of 'conflation' of anti-Zionism with 'anti-Israelism' that contemporary left antisemitism resides. At the point at which it opposes national self-determination for Israeli Jews; the point at which it denies any progressive potential for the Israeli-Jewish working class; the point at which it supports murderously reactionary forces, merely because they oppose Israel; and the point at which it insists Israel's very existence, not merely its policies, is illegitimate – that is when anti-Zionism becomes antisemitic.

If one's point of departure for assessing Israel/Palestine is that one of the two national communities living there should, uniquely amongst all the nations of the world throughout history, give up any claim to nationhood and self-determination, this necessarily applies a double standard to the world's only majority-Jewish national group. Taken on its own, this might only amount to a peculiarly singular form of chauvinism directed against a particular national people. But the origins of the Israeli Jews as a distinct nation are so bound up with flights from antisemitic oppression and attempted genocide that this position has an inbuilt tendency towards antisemitism.

## ANTISEMITISM ON AND OF THE LEFT

These three strands, then – primitive and reactionary critiques of capitalism that conflated Jews with capital, the Stalinist conspiracy theories beginning prominently with the Doctors' Plot and the Slánský Trial, and the subsequent 'anti-imperialism of fools', which 'ascribes world power to Zionism' and insists on the absolute inadmissibility of Israeli Jews' national rights – represent the primary forms in which antisemitism has manifested on the left. The third strand, as the most contemporary, is the most recently prevalent; while transcendental and absolute forms of anti-Zionism are relatively common on the far left, it has for some time been rarer to find anyone in left-wing spaces making explicit arguments about nefarious Jewish financiers – although, as explored in Chapter Three, it remains not entirely unheard of and is becoming less rare. The three strands, while distinct, share key parallels and points of overlap, including a common conspiracy-theorist frame.

The term 'left antisemitism' has limitations. The three strands of antisemitism on the left are sufficiently different in proportion and character that grouping them all under the label 'left antisemitism' might obscure more than it clarifies. While using the term 'left-wing antisemitism' as a shorthand, the sociologist Marcel Stoetzler draws a useful distinction between 'antisemitism *on* the left' – forms of antisemitism found elsewhere in society manifesting on the left – and 'antisemitism *of* the left' – forms of antisemitism relatively specific and organic to the left itself.[60] In the work of Pears Institute academics David Feldman, Ben Gidley and Brendan McGeever, the emphasis on the 'reservoir' metaphor suggests that, while antisemitism can manifest in particular forms, its varied narratives and images are drawn from a common source, and therefore that identifying a distinct left antisemitism is unhelpful.[61]

But, despite its limitations, I believe the concept of 'left antisemitism' has value. The 'reservoir' approach, although a helpful metaphor for thinking about the functioning of antisemitism across political culture and society in general, risks blurring what is distinct in how antisemitism has manifested in left-wing movements and discourse specifically, and how that is linked to wider ideological trends and social forces affecting and shaping the left – above all, Stalinism and campism more generally, a key source for left antisemitism, which is explored in Chapter Three.

Subsequent chapters aim to address in greater detail issues within each of the three strands, some of which have been flagged up in this summary, as well as other related questions, such as recent trends in the left's relationship to Jewish communities, and the question of whether left antisemitism can be meaningfully categorised as 'racism', or understood as a form of 'oppression', and what implications such categorisation might have for our responses to it. The final chapter suggests some practical ideas for undertaking a confrontation with left antisemitism.

The socialist left is not an antisemitic movement. Even in the sections of it where antisemitic ideas are entrenched, they invariably function implicitly rather than directly. I echo the clarifications Arnold and Taylor offered for their own work on this issue:

> Let us first avoid persistent confusions by reiterating what we are *not* saying: that antisemitism is the worst or most pressing form of oppression today; that the left is a hotbed of rabid antisemites; that any and all criticism of Israel is antisemitic. Instead, we are suggesting antisemitism remains an 'invisible prejudice' for much of the contemporary left. [...] When it does occasionally surface, its articulation is not generally explicit, but rather takes coded and fragmented forms.[62]

The presence of antisemitism, even in 'coded and fragmented forms', and the thinking from which those forms emerge, distorts left-wing politics, and will continue to do so if it is not overturned. To take just one small example, the praise and support from many prominent leftists for the work of David Miller shows, at the very least, a profound confusion over these issues. This cannot be dismissed as resulting from marginal quirks at the edges of the left, such that might be found in any movement inevitably reflecting some of the prejudices that exist in the society around it. To overcome left antisemitism, we must understand it as the product of a political common sense that prevails amongst sections of our movement, and then work to replace that common sense with a different one: a rational, historical-materialist, class-based analysis of capitalism and imperialism, and a consistently democratic, internationalist politics of working-class solidarity and equal rights.

# CHAPTER THREE

# THE RE-EMERGENCE OF PRIMITIVE ANTISEMITISM ON THE LEFT

In 2018 Jeremy Corbyn's 2012 defence of 'Freedom for Humanity', a mural painted in East London by the artist Mear One, hit the headlines. The mural drew on imagery suggesting a conspiracy of mainly Jewish financiers as the source of oppression and exploitation in the world. Journalist Michael Segalov described the mural in an article for the *Guardian*:

> Sitting around a table is a group of rotund men: one has a full beard, and is counting money. That, in and of itself, is an antisemitic symbol. It's not just the big, hooked noses and evil expressions that make this iconography offensive and troubling, these depictions mirror antisemitic propaganda used by Hitler and the Nazis to whip up hatred that led to the massacre of millions of Jews. This extends to the table these figures are sat at, resting on human bodies, as the Nazis also depicted.[1]

Lutfur Rahman, mayor of Tower Hamlets when the mural was painted, said at the time that 'the images of the bankers perpetuate antisemitic propaganda about conspiratorial Jewish domination of financial institutions'. And, to ensure no one was left in any doubt, the artist himself explained the painting was explicitly intended to demonise Jewish financiers: 'Some of the older white Jewish folk in the local community had an issue with me portraying their beloved #Rothschild or #Warburg etc., as the demons they are.'2

References to the Rothschilds and Warburgs, two Jewish families with extensive involvement in banking, who are frequent focuses of the antisemitic imagination, place this matter on the terrain of conspiracy theories about Jewish financiers, the primitive strand of left antisemitism.

Since the 1950s, left antisemitism has been expressed primarily through discourse about Israel/Palestine and Zionism. It has consisted of a particular political narrative about the formation of Israel, both as a state and as a national community, and a radical over-inflation of the power of Israel and Zionism in the world. The older antisemitic themes that found traction in the late-nineteenth and early-twentieth-century left, conflating Jews with finance, had by no means receded entirely, but the primitive-reactionary critique of capitalism, which some have called the 'socialism of fools', appeared to have faded, and an 'anti-imperialism of fools' that foregrounded anti-Zionism had been amplified.

But, as the Mear One mural episode reflected, a notable feature of the expressions of antisemitism in the Labour Party since 2015, and in broadly left-wing spaces more widely for the last decade or more, has been how much of it has borne only a tangential connection to any concrete political argument about Israel/Palestine. Instead, these expressions have much more closely resembled a more primitive form of antisemitism – conspiracy theories about Jewish financiers and their alleged power over world affairs. More widely, and alarmingly, as conspiracy-theorist thinking spread across the political spectrum, much of the left not only failed to adequately critique it, but sometimes reproduced it.

Other high-profile incidents also expressed conspiracy-theorist antisemitism. For instance, the claim made by Jackie Walker, the former co-chair of the Labour left group Momentum, that Jews were amongst 'the chief financiers of the sugar and slave trade',[3] recycled a canard about the role of specifically Jewish financial power that has been comprehensively debunked on a number of occasions.[4] It too has no direct relationship whatsoever to the politics of Israel/Palestine. Former council leader and MP Chris Williamson, a sometime standard-issue career politician who reinvented himself as a left-winger to ride the wave of the Corbyn surge, tweeted in support of Vanessa Beeley, whose promotion of antisemitic claims was discussed in Chapter Two. Williamson also spoke in support of Cyril Chilson, who has attacked 'Jew funding' of British political parties.[5]

The Labour Party report into its own Governance and Legal Unit's work on antisemitism, leaked in the factional spasms around the 2020 leadership election, noted that while instances of antisemitism were 'sometimes framed in terms of support for the Palestinian people', they incorporated 'traditional tropes about Jewish power/influence'.[6]

One Labour member, for instance, wrote about 'zioscum ... behind all the conflict on the planet in pursuit of debt slavery of all the countries', and shared posts about 'Zio-Jewish nonce arch-Buggerers of British Children at the British Brainwashing Corporation'.[7] Another 'shared a meme about Jacob Rothschild controlling people's lives',[8] and another posted about 'Jews' deceitful infiltration of UK's politics'.[9] Another Labour member expressed 'support for a wide range of antisemitic conspiracy theories, about "Zionist Western banksters", Soros and the Rothschilds'.[10]

The social media output of another was found to include 'repeated Rothschild conspiracies; posting about Jews receiving a "Jew call" on 9/11 [a common theme of 9/11 conspiracy theories which alleges Jewish workers in the Twin Towers were warned about the attacks in advance and therefore stayed at home]; the "Jewish House of Rothschild"; "Zionist neocon Jews"; and Zionist Hollywood "Media programming".'[11]

A Labour Party member and organiser of a local Momentum group wrote that Tony Blair was 'Jewish to the core', and that he was under the 'protection' of the Rothschilds, who 'control all the money in the world'.[12] Members of the Momentum group in Barnet defended an activist who had written about the 'over-representation of Jews in the capitalist ruling class'.[13]

Another Labour member wrote that: 'the Rothschild family (at the top of the NWO[14] pyramid) financed the Third Reich, and Hitler was an illegitimate son of one of the Rothschilds [...] [Hungarian-Jewish investment banker George] Soros was an SS member when a youth, and proud of it. Planet Zion.'[15] Many of these examples veer towards straightforward neo-Nazi-style anti-Jewish racism. One member tweeted: 'National Socialist Germany 1933–1945. Its flaws were few, its achievements many. Don't believe Jewish-Zionist lies.'[16]

Although some instances relate to the social media output of individuals who may have been only passive or paper members, elected officials, candidates for office and activists at the heart of the life of local parties also expressed such ideas. In addition to his support for Beeley and Chilson, Chris Williamson, then a Member of Parliament, also wrote in support of Pedro Baños, a right-wing former military officer from Spain,[17] whose book *How They Rule the World: The 22 Secret Strategies of Global Power* promoted conspiracy theories about Jewish financiers.[18] One Labour councillor posted links to an antisemitic article entitled 'World War 3: Trump Begins Paying His Homage to Rothschilds', commenting 'we must remember that the Rothschilds are a powerful financial family (like the Medicis) and represent capitalism and big business'.[19]

Another councillor shared an image of Jacob Rothschild with the caption 'these people control the world'.[20] A council candidate posted on Facebook that 'it's the super rich families of the Zionist lobby that control the world. Our world leaders sell their souls for greed and do the bidding of Israel.[21] Yet another councillor shared a meme of a hook-nosed Israeli soldier, covered in blood, with the caption 'Israel was created by the Rothschilds'.[22] A Labour activist who had been a parliamentary candidate in the 2015 general election shared a meme, originating with a neo-Nazi, which read:

Israel owns the Senate, the Congress, and the executive branch … but who owns Israel? The Rothschild family who has been creating almost all of the world's money at interest for a couple hundred years. They have used usury alongside modern Israel as an imperial instrument to take over the world and all of its resources, including you and I … and if you have a problem with that, you're an 'antisemite'.[23]

The former Labour candidate who shared the meme, who had also been an elected councillor and chair of his local council, said that, while it expressed 'an oversimplified view of the world economy', it also 'contained a great deal of truth'.

The terms 'Israel' and 'Zionism' appear in this discourse, but rarely in connection to any concrete argument about Israeli policy or advocacy of Palestinian national liberation. Claims that 'Israel was created by the Rothschilds', or that the Rothschilds 'have used usury alongside modern Israel as an imperial instrument to take over the world and all of its resources', for example, are not 'criticisms of Israel' in any rational sense. They are straightforward, conspiracy-theorist, antisemitic canards. The futility of making the truism that 'it's not antisemitic to criticise Israel' the reflexive response to allegations of antisemitism on the left is thus reaffirmed. The mere fact that something purports to be a 'criticism of Israel', rather than naming itself as a racist attack on all Jews, does not cast a magic spell that cleanses it of antisemitism. 'Criticisms of Israel' that are based on conspiracy-theorist lies *are* antisemitic.

These forms of antisemitism are the ones whose manifestations on the left have the most crossover with generic antisemitism – to use Marcel Stoetzler's distinction, these are instances of 'antisemitism *on* the left' more than 'antisemitism *of* the left'.[24] Anti-capitalist-sounding critiques of Jewish bankers and their alleged conspiracies are also found in far-right strains of antisemitism, including Nazism.

Moishe Postone's analysis of antisemitism representing a 'primitive critique of [...] capitalist modernity', which aspires to be 'the expression of a movement of the little people against an intangible, global form of domination' resonates particularly here.[25] The motif of intangibility – the untouchable, the unseen, the hidden – occurs repeatedly in antisemitic ideology: the Rothschilds and the Soroses pulling behind-the-scenes strings, the 'Zionist lobby' controlling US foreign policy, the incorporeal, rootless, international nature of Jewish financial power. Against this intangible enemy, the endeavour of would-be radical politics is thereby reduced not to any real struggle for power or greater equality, but simply to an attempt to pull back the curtain, touch the intangible, name the hidden threat.

As well as being deeply bigoted, this analysis is thoroughly miseducating and utterly disempowering. Capitalist global 'domination' is far from 'intangible'. It is perfectly perceivable, conducted primarily in the open and consisting – not exclusively, but essentially – in the exploitation of wage labour. Far from being a shadowy conspiracy shrouded in darkness that must be exposed, capitalism as a social relation is something the majority of people are directly and personally engaged in, as members of an exploited class. Under the deadening pressure of capitalist normality, that reality can be obscured – as the aphorism attributed to Rosa Luxemburg puts it, 'those who do not move do not notice their chains'. But, noticed or not, the chains of capitalist exploitation are there, the structuring reality of our society, not a mysterious manipulation taking place beyond our sight or perception. It is from realisation of, and mass collective action which leverages, our class position that we derive socially transformative power, not from the imagined discovery of an unseen conspiracy controlling the world.

This is why Postone argued antisemitism is 'particularly dangerous' for the left. Antisemitism's 'primitive critique of capitalist modernity' competes with the left on common terrain – an attempt to explain the nature of capitalism, and build an 'antihegemonic' movement. Its disempowering 'pseudo-emancipatory' claims directly draw people away from genuinely and sincerely emancipatory ones. As the activist and writer Michael Richmond put it in an article for the *New Socialist*'s website, conspiracy theory represents a 'process of profound disempowerment for participants, many of whom (often white men in my experience) adopt the masculinised figure of the "brave truth-teller". […] People become enmeshed in a tangled, self-reinforcing and ultimately dangerous set of logics and argumentation that can be incredibly difficult to break out of.'[26]

The question of how people could reconcile obviously antisemitic ideas with a would-be left-wing worldview does not have an easy answer; every individual's process of ideological formation is somewhat distinct. Some people are simply extremely confused. But whatever the precise political trajectory of these particular individuals, conspiracy theories have been able to fester on the left, broadly defined, in part because the organised left has been insufficiently alive to them as an ideological threat, and insufficiently combative in asserting a distinct alternative. In some instances the left has even encouraged conspiracy-theory-adjacent modes of thought.

Some caveats are necessary before we proceed. It is emphatically not my argument that the antisemitism expressed above is in any sense broadly representative of 'the left' as such. The people expressing it will not have learned their arguments about 'the Rothschild family at the top of the NWO pyramid' from the far-left press, or from meetings of far-left groups. It is also clear that the numbers involved here are relatively small, although we should remember that the cases referred to in the leaked report represent only people who expressed these ideas online or in meetings, and subsequently had complaints made against them. Many more may have gone unreported, or expressed in speech of which no lasting record remains.

But even tiny numbers of people in the Labour Party, or in left-wing spaces more broadly, making virulently bigoted conspiracy-theorist claims about Jews controlling British and international government policies is something that requires interrogation and explanation. As we have noted, these numbers include prominent representatives and elected officials, who were able to obtain and retain their positions despite holding antisemitic beliefs. Whether these people formed and shaped their views within left-wing spaces, or formed them elsewhere but came to see a left-led Labour Party as an appropriate political home, there is a problem that needs addressing.

The usual explanation given by those seeking to downplay the issue is an argument from scale. At its height under Corbyn, Labour had nearly 600,000 members, and any mass organisation will reflect, to some degree, the society around it. So if bigotry exists in society, the argument goes, it is inevitable that it will find expression in the Labour Party too. Antisemitism is thereby reduced to a kind of marginal detritus unfortunately and accidentally caught in the net of the Labour Party as it expands, and the possibility of antisemitic ideas already being present on the left, or emerging from erroneous would-be-left-wing analyses and critiques, is ruled out.

It is true that no organisation can entirely seal itself off from the prejudices that exist in the society around it. But unless one is to conclude that all the individuals in question here are simply ardent supporters of renationalised railways who just happen to believe that Jewish financiers run the world, in a way unconnected to any of their other beliefs, this explanation will not suffice. What shaped the conclusion of someone who believes in Rothschild conspiracy theories that a left-led Labour Party was the most appropriate arena for their politics? How could the left-wing *leader* of the Labour Party fail so spectacularly to identify antisemitism, and why was Chris Williamson able to pose as a prominent standard bearer for the left? Why were people who believed the Rothschilds 'visibly control the world' able to be selected to represent the Labour Party in elections?

Those inclined to downplay or deflect might assert that the problem, in the worst individual cases, *was* eventually addressed. Their views are cited in the report precisely because action was taken, in the form of suspension or expulsion from the Labour Party; Chris Williamson was also eventually suspended and later quit the party. But taking disciplinary action against individuals does not address the ideological question of why this kind of conspiracy-theorist antisemitism can coexist with a would-be left-wing worldview. Besides which, it was not true in all cases: the councillors who shared Rothschild conspiracies were reselected *after* having done so, without appearing to have acknowledged the antisemitic nature of these ideas or meaningfully changed their views.

## ANTI-GLOBALISATION, THE CRASH, OCCUPY, AND ANTISEMITISM

Finding our way through this requires looking back to the 'anti-globalisation' wave of the late 1990s and, more recently, the echoes of the 2007/8 financial crash. The anti-globalisation movements of the 1990s and early 2000s, such as the World Social Forum movement and mobilisations such as the 1999 'Battle of

Seattle' protests against the World Trade Organisation (WTO), often focused their critique on 'globalisation' and 'trade' rather than capitalism as such. By highlighting these apparently rootless – incorporeal and transnational – elements of capitalism as the primary sources of global injustice and exploitation, nationalist and antisemitic political narratives could assert themselves.

As the academic Werner Bonefeld put it:

> 'Anti-globalisation' gives in to reactionary forces if its critique of globalisation is a critique for the national state. […] The critique of, for example, the WTO is not enough. Trade, whether deemed fair or unfair, presupposes capitalist relations of exploitation. Further, without the critique of exploitation, the critique of speculation leads with necessity to xenophobia and antisemitic denunciations of money. It conceals the relations of exploitation and is complicit, whether intentionally or not, in the critique of finance as parasitic.[27]

The 2007/8 financial crash again thrust to prominence questions about the nature and stability of capitalism as a global system. The consequences of that crash caused significant material harm to working-class living standards across the world, leading to mass job losses, evictions, wage freezes and stagnations. On the ideological level, the crash shook the mystique of capitalism in a way it had not been shaken since the Great Depression, and possibly before. In the context of global communications and the rise of social media, competing explanations and narratives about what the crash meant, and what the appropriate political response was, could circulate in a new way. The left had an opportunity, and a responsibility. Our opportunity was to persuade people of an alternative to capitalism, the system wreaking such acute social misery. Our responsibility was to educate those people about what that system actually was – how it operated, and how it could be overthrown and replaced. The most high-profile left responses to the crisis failed to do that.

The dominant responses were the populist ones generated by broad, amorphous movements like Occupy, rather than political parties or revolutionary socialist groups. The Occupy movement's key idea was the '99%' versus 'the 1%', an almost classically populist motif, positioning 'the people' against an 'elite'.

The appeal of the populist response to the crisis was obvious. As an article in the socialist newspaper *Solidarity* put it:

> The work had already been done to popularise these ideas. It also seemed a way around forty years of calumnies against socialism, a route around the historical weakness of working-class consciousness and the low level of working-class struggle. Yet a problem with the left adopting populism is that its explanatory power fails when it comes to the more fundamental workings of capitalism, the nature of the state, and ruling-class ideology. It explains the world in moral rather than structural terms.[28]

The 'We are the 99%' slogan, by itself, is not a gateway to antisemitism. That notion would surely have horrified its originator, the late anthropologist and anarchist activist David Graeber. The slogan invites those who might otherwise feel alienated and atomised to express a sense of mass collectivity, and echoes the stirring conclusion of 'The Masque of Anarchy', Percy Shelley's 1819 poem about the Peterloo Massacre: 'Ye are many, they are few'.

But despite these virtues, it is nevertheless a step away from an explanation of capitalism in structural, class-based terms. The ruling class is certainly a small minority compared to the working class, but it is not merely 1 per cent of society. And the working class, while certainly the overwhelming majority class, does not comprise 99 per cent of the population. The exact nature of the social collectivities we talk about when we use concepts like 'the many' and 'the few' matter. The writers Frederick Harry Pitts and Matt Bolton expressed this succinctly in their book *Corbynism: A Critical Approach*, arguing that 'not everything that purports to be a critique of capitalism is actually a critique of capitalism'.[29]

As the left-wing Labour Party activist Edd Mustill argued in the *Clarion*, substantial sections of the left appeared to have

> given up the teaching and learning of a structural analysis of capitalism in favour of simpler and quicker explanations. Conspiracism is bolstered by, for example, the sort of shallow analysis of the last recession that blamed 'greedy bankers' or 'the 1%' – effective for short-term sloganeering but ultimately [...] reducing complex social relations to a few bad individuals pulling society's strings. Left-wing alt-media further encourages this, with sites like Skwawkbox and The Canary appearing to view everything as a Manichean struggle, a Hollywood script of goodies versus baddies both inside and outside the Labour Party.[30]

Identifying injustice as the product of the manipulative greed of an infinitesimal minority, perhaps consisting of only a tiny handful of individuals, is always dangerous terrain. Here, Feldman, Gidley and McGeever's concept of antisemitism as a 'reservoir' is especially useful.[31] The long-established presence of antisemitic-populist ideas in political culture, with roots going back centuries, means that antisemitic answers to questions about the nature of social and economic power are always close at hand, recently all the more so thanks to rapid transmission and circulation of ideas via the internet and social media.

The depth of this reservoir means that populist explanations about minority elites, often operating secretively, to manipulate society to the detriment of the majority are never very far from naming Jews, often specific, individual Jews, as the key figures in these elites, as the Mear One mural incident shows. The hoary conspiracy theories about the Rothschilds, which lie about the extent of their power and involvement in specific events, and focus on them out of all proportion to their actual wealth and influence even relative to other financial dynasties, are a clear example of this. More recently George Soros has been added to the line-up of Jewish financiers pulling the strings, as Soros is literally depicted as doing in numerous widely circulated memes, of economic and political life.[32]

Much of the post-2008 agitation focused not on capitalism itself, but on 'bankers'. The identification of a particular financial elite as the source of the problem is precisely a personalised, moral rather than structural, understanding of the enemy. Sometimes this enemy has been named as finance capital, rather than capital as such. Just as the 1990s anti-globalisation movement's underdeveloped and miseducating critique of 'trade' left room for antisemitic conclusions, an inchoate post-2008 analysis that blamed bankers and financiers, whose reckless gambling with incorporeal finance ended up costing people their jobs and homes, could develop in an antisemitic direction.

Antisemitism has long peddled imagery of the parasitic Jewish financier, conjuring his wealth via incorporeal, phantasmic commercial processes, to the disadvantage and ruin of the honest, nationally rooted capitalist who wants to make his money from bricks-and-mortar factories producing material commodities, and who would undoubtedly pay his workers well were it not for the vampiric figure of the Jewish financier bleeding him dry. Antisemitism imagines 'a capitalism not of productive labour and industry but of parasites: money and finance, speculators and bankers'.[33] Nationalist political narratives on both left and right that trace the source of social dislocation to the supplanting of the 'real' economy of 'British manufacturing' by an invisible, and implicitly foreign, financial economy can easily dovetail with these antisemitic themes.

Antisemitic imagery was found in literature distributed at Occupy movement demonstrations and camps, and in publications influential within the broad Occupy milieu. The anti-corporate magazine *Adbusters* is seen by many as having launched the Occupy movement, with a July 2011 article calling for a peaceful occupation of Wall Street. In 2004 the same magazine had published an article by its joint founding editor Kalle Lasn entitled 'Why won't anybody say they are Jewish?', alleging disproportionate 'Jewish' influence over the administration of George W. Bush. Lasn's article positioned him as the 'brave truthteller', to use Michael Richmond's phrase, exposing the conspiracy at work behind the scenes. *Adbusters* has also published articles by the musician Gilad Atzmon, who has written: 'The time is ripe for Jewish and Zionist organisations to draw the real and most important lesson from the Holocaust [...] to look in the mirror and try to identify what it is in Jews and their culture that evokes so much fury.'[34] *Adbusters* also published Ken O'Keefe, who proposed expanding Occupy Wall Street to include 'Occupy Rothschilds'.[35] As the anti-fascist activist Spencer Sunshine's article 'The Right Hand of Occupy Wall Street' shows, there were relatively extensive attempts by various far-right and explicitly antisemitic forces to orient to and intervene in the Occupy movement.[36]

At the Occupy London camp in the churchyard of St Paul's Cathedral, a group promoting the Zeitgeist film series, a set of wildly antisemitic conspiracy-theorist documentaries purporting to critique 'bankers' and 'banking', had a permanent base. Others within the camp promoted different views – organisers strung a giant banner reading 'Capitalism Is Crisis' above the main cluster of tents, an admirable attempt to express a structural analysis – but the very nature of the Occupy movement made it more difficult to directly challenge it politically. Occupy had what Australian socialist activist Daniel Taylor called a consciously 'anti-political' culture,[37] and, as Sunshine put it, 'loudly proclaimed that it was open to everyone and refused to define even its most basic concepts or demands'.[38] Not enough was done by class-struggle anti-capitalists active within these movements to fight for alternative models of organisation and an alternative culture.

Neither Occupy, nor any of the similar social movements that emerged in the post-2008 periods, were consciously left antisemitic movements. To suggest this would be calumnious, and a slander against the hundreds of thousands of participants drawn to such movements out of radically progressive instincts. A magazine like *Adbusters*, while influential, was in some ways an outlier. But the failure to move past populist explanations for the crisis, and the failure of the organised left to do more to catalyse such movement, left an ideological vacuum that primitive-reactionary anti-capitalism could fill.

The left has not been able to use the period since 2008 to rebuild and reawaken class consciousness. The lasting political beneficiaries of the 2008 crisis and its sequels have not been left-wing movements, but movements based on right-wing identity politics of various kinds – Orban, Modi, Bolsonaro, Trump, the Brexit movement in Britain and more. Despite all having an explicitly pro-capital economic policy – the late Marxist academic Leo Panitch called Trump's economic vision 'neoliberalism with a white nationalist face'[39] – several of these movements, especially Trump and Orban, have also instrumentalised antisemitic critiques of 'globalism', in terms that sound vaguely anti-capitalist.

The final advertisement of Trump's 2016 campaign featured footage of prominent Jewish figures from the financial world, including Soros, former Goldman Sachs chair Lloyd Blankfein and then Federal Reserve chair Janet Yellen, and included lines such as: 'It's a global power structure that is responsible for the economic decisions that have robbed our working class, stripped our country of its wealth and put that money into the pockets of a handful of large corporations and political entities.'[40] The idea of Donald Trump as an anti-capitalist is ludicrous, but he has been prepared to exploit quasi-anti-capitalist, antisemitic rhetoric in order to cohere a nationalist base.

When a section of the left in Britain found itself in the leadership of the Labour Party, and therefore able to promote a counter-narrative, the opportunity was largely squandered. Instead, Corbynism often recycled populist framing, particularly via the use of the concept of the 'rigged economy' and the 'rigged system'. Bolton and Pitts summed up the dangers of this rhetoric for anyone seeking to develop a working-class anti-capitalism, saying the concept of the 'rigged economy' was: 'Qualitatively distinct from both the analysis of class as a social relation, and that of capitalism as a system of socially mediated labour. [...] A critique of a "rigged system" implies that capitalist social relations are consciously and covertly designed by a minority of individuals or groups in order to exploit everyone else.'[41]

### 'THE SOCIALISM OF FOOLS': HOW TO COMBAT CONSPIRACY THEORIES

Why did much of the organised far left appear unprepared, unwilling or incapable of effectively combating populist and conspiracy-theorist thinking? Specifically Marxist, materialist ideas about class struggle were, by 2008, highly marginal. They had been bludgeoned by triumphant neoliberalism, and were still reeling from the collapse of Stalinism, a social system that claimed to represent them and which even many avowedly anti-Stalinist Marxists still desperately insisted was a 'degenerated' form of workers' rule. In radical academia, approaches that rejected universalist and historical materialist narratives had become dominant. As early as 1986 the Marxist academic Ellen Meiksins Wood had identified a widespread 'retreat from class' across the left, with large sections collapsing into forms of postmodernist identity politics and populism.[42]

When Occupy exploded, many left groups undoubtedly saw either a shortcut out of marginality, by presenting socialism as a version of the populist, bankers-versus-the-people narratives it and other similar social movements advanced, or a means of giving political expression to those narratives without having to develop or revise very much of their existing analysis. Some Marxists sought to piggyback on the catchcry success of the '99% vs 1%' framing, recycling the narrative rather than challenging it.

Despite these failings, neither the Marxist left nor the Corbyn leadership is in any direct sense to blame for the rise of conspiracy theories, and the resurgence in primitive left antisemitism they have impelled. There is a delusional tendency on the far left to see every political moment as evidence of a 'crisis of revolutionary leadership'. They imagine that if only 'the revolutionaries' – who exactly 'the revolutionaries' are usually depends on who is advancing the argument at the time – had been able to manoeuvre themselves into a position of leadership, all would have gone well.

There was no single strategic master stroke that class-struggle Marxists could have deployed to somehow give the post-2008 social movements 'revolutionary leadership'. Any attempt to extrapolate a direct sequence of counterfactuals that starts with Marxist groups, or the wider labour movement, taking a clearer and more critical line against populism and ends with the decisive defeat of those ideas, would be utterly futile.

We can, however, say for sure that populist narratives are inevitably fertile ground for an antisemitic, 'pseudo-emancipatory' anti-capitalism, which the left needed to do more to challenge, rather than attempting to surf the populist wave by instrumentalising ideas such as 'the rigged economy'. Even if the individuals cited in the leaked Labour Party report learned their ideas somewhere entirely other than the post-2008 social movements or their online echoes, had the left been more robustly critical of populist and conspiracy-theorist thinking within those movements, that would surely have been better preparation for combating and, in the first instance, *recognising* such ideas if and when they appeared within the Labour Party.

The reactionary anti-capitalist conflation of Jews with capital has often been described as 'the socialism of fools'. In 2018 Jeremy Corbyn wrote, in one of his most comprehensive acknowledgements of a specifically left-wing antisemitism: 'The phrase "Socialism of Fools" was deployed by the German Social Democrats in the late nineteenth century to describe fellow socialists who mixed opposition to capitalism with conspiracy theories about Jewish bankers.'[43]

The term has taken on a more general meaning since its usage in the 1890s, and Corbyn, Steve Cohen, Postone and others have all used it as a shorthand to designate as 'foolish' the idea that socialism and antisemitism are in any way compatible. It is a snappy and useful label. But its frequent attribution to German socialist leader August Bebel is inaccurate – a mistake I have made myself in the past. The common usage of the term in the nineteenth-century German socialist movement has more negative lessons to impart for the fight against antisemitism on the left than positive ones. Those negative lessons are particularly valuable for socialists considering how to combat primitive antisemitism in a contemporary context.

According to the writer Dale Street's article 'The "Idiot of Vienna"', the phrase's origins can be traced to a speech by Ferdinand Kronawetter, an Austrian liberal democrat, given in Vienna in 1889.[44] His specific target was a reactionary, antisemitic movement led by Karl Lueger, a right-wing politician who would go on to be the mayor of Vienna from 1897 to 1910. Kronawetter said that antisemitism was 'nothing but the socialism of the idiot of Vienna', referencing a well-known idiom roughly the equivalent of the English term 'village idiot'.[45] He said antisemitism would lead 'back into the darkness of the Middle Ages'. But when the term gained currency in the German socialist movement, it was given a different twist, and often used in the context of arguments implying antisemitic narratives about Jewish capitalists were half-way to socialist good sense, and that what was 'foolish' or 'idiotic' about them was that they limited their opposition to Jewish capitalists only.

An 1892 article in the SPD newspaper *Hamburger Echo* declared:

> Antisemitism is the socialism of the idiot [...] and the socialism of the petty bourgeoisie. Suffering more and more under the crushing force of big capital, the petty bourgeoisie rebels against its oppressor and enemy, but against a part rather than the whole, against individuals rather than the system, against the Jews rather than against capitalism, and precisely for this reason is antisemitism the socialism of the idiot.[46]

Implicit in this formulation is an acceptance of the idea that 'the Jews' are 'a part' of capitalism, and that the conflation of Jews with capital merely needs to be extended and developed into an opposition to *all* capitalists, rather than challenging that conflation directly.

The following year, when Bebel, one of the SPD's greatest leaders, gave a speech on the Jewish question to the SPD congress in Cologne, he argued that antisemites who railed against Jewish capitalists would eventually be logically compelled to confront 'capital in general'. Then, Bebel argued, 'the moment will have come when our ideas can and will fall on fertile ground'.

Antisemitism, said Bebel, had a 'contradictory reactionary-revolutionary nature', and if its adherents were able to extend their hatred of Jewish capitalists to all capitalists, then 'against its will, but of necessity, it must become revolutionary, and thereby plays into our hands, the hands of social democracy'.[47] The idea that antisemitism could somehow develop into socialism was also expressed in an article in the SPD paper *Die Neue Zeit* in 1897. In a review of Zionist leader Theodore Herzl's *The Jewish State*, it argued that, should incipient Zionism succeed in establishing a Jewish state on a capitalist basis, 'antisemitism would follow [Jewish capitalists] to the new Jewish state; it would certainly then dispense with the name and character of the "socialism of the idiot" and emerge unmasked and in its true form as the struggle of the exploited masses against the exploiters.'[48]

Thus, as Street points out, "'the socialism of the idiot (of Vienna)" ceased to be a statement of unqualified condemnation of antisemitism. It was transformed into a statement which attributed a "progressive" dimension to antisemitism.'[49]

The point here is not to cast August Bebel, one of the most important Marxists of his generation, down from the place of great esteem he rightly occupies in the memory of the revolutionary socialist movement. Nor is it to condemn the German SPD, one of the world-historic high points of revolutionary socialist organisation and the model that inspired the Bolsheviks, as a left antisemitic movement. Far from it. Bebel and the SPD had no doubt that antisemites were deserving of condemnation and opposition. And they were right to attempt to grapple with the ways in which antisemitic critiques of capitalism competed with, inhibited and stymied the advance of Marxist critiques, by misnaming and misidentifying the enemy faced by workers and the poor, who had reached antisemitic conclusions at least partially in an attempt to explain social grievances that were real and legitimate. But the ultimately limited and opportunistic nature of their analysis, and the flaws in their conclusions, can be instructive for contemporary efforts to confront a re-emergence of primitive antisemitism on the left.

A narrative that conflated Jews with capital had to be challenged *as such*. Its adherents may have opposed Jewish capitalists *as capitalists*, but they also opposed them *as Jews*. They understood capitalist exploitation not as a relation between classes, but as a conspiracy perpetrated by Jews specifically. The figure of the 'Jewish capitalist' did not merely describe a capitalist who happened to be Jewish, and might just as easily be of any other religious or ethnic background. Rather, it referred to a specific type, a figure engaged in an exploitative process because of something inherent in their Jewishness. Telling antisemites that their analysis was on its way to socialism, albeit by a 'contradictory' route, and could arrive there merely by extending the same hatred to all capitalists, without confronting the specifically anti-Jewish content of the analysis, was a significant misjudgement.

Similarly, in a contemporary context, we cannot respond to narratives which indict 'financial elites', and name George Soros and Lloyd Blankfein as the chief enemies, merely by suggesting that Soros and Blankfein shouldn't be mentioned, or that the names of non-Jewish financiers are added for balance. Direct ideological confrontation with the conspiracy-theorist mode of thought, whether its antisemitism is explicit or merely latent, is needed. Capitalism must continually be explained and re-explained as a class society, the essential mechanics of which take place in the open, rather than a conspiracy conducted by shadowy, unseen forces.

The 2013 pamphlet *How to Overthrow the Illuminati*, which critiques and debunks prominent conspiracy theories from an explicitly Marxist perspective, is a good example of the kind of direct educational campaigning that was, and remains, necessary. It stands out for being a rare example of its type. We need more tools like it. The pamphlet was presented as an explicit critique of populism, in both right- and left-wing variants, arguing:

Populist movements join poor people with the petty bourgeoisie, against imagined elite enemies. They speak in the
name of the 'common man', but they're guided by middle-
class elements, and screw over poor and working participants
in the end. Contemporary examples of populism include the
Tea Party, some parts of Occupy Wall Street, and the Nation
of Islam. Illuminati theories are often populist in character.
Many populist theories draw on antisemitism to identify an
evil elite that runs the world.[50]

The pamphlet concludes that the conspiracy theory 'leaves no
room for chance or error, and so views the enemy as unbeatable. It
relies on circular logic and innuendo, rather than logical scientific
argument. And it provides no clear strategy to end oppression and
liberate humankind.'[51]

An influential strand of contemporary anti-imperialism on
the left often takes a similarly disempowering conspiracy-theorist
form, and figures from this wing of the left have sought dialogue
and collaboration with figures from the far right, and other
antisemitic conspiracy theorists. Popular would-be leftist platforms such as The Grayzone have amplified Soros conspiracies,
and increasingly insist that every uprising in a so-called 'anti-
imperialist' country is directed by the CIA and the 'Soros-funded
regime change machine'.[52] The journalist Alex Rubinstein, whose
writing has frequently appeared on The Grayzone, has called for
rapprochement between the left and the far right, arguing that it's
'time to rethink the left–right paradigm'.[53] Jimmy Dore, a journalist and podcaster popular on sections of the US left, interviewed
Magnus Panvidya, an activist with the far-right group Boogaloo
Boys, on his show. Dore himself appeared as a guest on the podcast
of Teodrose Fikre, an activist who has promoted conspiracy theories about Freemasons and the Illuminati, and denounced 'those
fake Jews who pray in the synagogue of Satan'.[54]

On the British left, the popular website The Canary relies on conspiracy-theorist framing for much of its political analysis, especially about internal Labour Party matters. Its founding editor, Kerry-Anne Mendoza, has promoted the Zeitgeist films, and appeared as a guest on *The Richie Allen Show*: Allen is a protégé of David Icke, who has peddled Holocaust denial and spread dangerous misinformation about the Covid-19 pandemic via his digital radio broadcasts.[55] Political relations between former Labour MP George Galloway – now leading the Workers Party of Britain alongside the ultra-Stalinists of the CPGB (Marxist-Leninist), and, at the time of writing, advocating a vote for the Tories[56] – and figures such as Nigel Farage[57] and Steve Bannon[58] also show the potential for a pipeline between the left and the far right which could help conspiracy-theorist thinking spread.

Such a spread could toxify the very essence of what it means to be left wing, replacing materialist class politics with wild conspiracy theories that miseducate and disempower those they convince, and, ultimately, always identifying Jews – who stand at the centre of all historic reactionary-anti-capitalist conspiracy theories – as the hidden enemy to be exposed and defeated. With a crash worse than 2008 a near-inevitable follow-on from the pandemic, and with the pandemic itself having turbocharged new and dangerous conspiracy theories, the need to assert a materialist, class-struggle analysis remains acute.

# CHAPTER FOUR

# THE ANTI-IMPERIALISM OF FOOLS: THE STALINIST ROOTS OF LEFT ANTISEMITISM REVISITED

In 1955 Bohumil Doubek, one of the pre-trial interrogators in the 1952 Slánský Trial, recalled the instructions of the Russian bureaucrats present in 'Communist' Czechoslovakia, where the trial took place:

> They pointed out [...] the growing influence of Jewry in the international arena. They pointed out [prominent capital-ists] Rockefeller, Rothschild and Du Pont and put this in connection with what Slánský and the Jews were doing here, saying there's a danger that the Jews will end up as masters of everything. They also pointed out the role of the state of Israel and tried to prove [...] the Jews are the main represen-tatives of international imperialism. [...] One of the advisors even said that Jews are not interested in political offices in capitalist countries lest their intentions of mastering the world become apparent.[1]

Although it was presaged by earlier trends and develop-ments, the trial marked the major opening salvo of what would become a decades-long campaign, in the USSR and its satellite states, of 'anti-Zionism'. It was an anti-Zionism that was explic-itly antisemitic, explicitly conspiracy-theorist, and organised on an industrial scale. It provided the ideological fuel for campaigns of systematic repression and murder of Jewish dissidents and alleged dissidents.

Its central themes were that Zionism was a conspiracy organised by Jewish capitalists to colonise and plunder the Middle East, and that the Israeli state was the vanguard of world imperialism. This campaign is a seedbed of many of the key themes of contemporary left antisemitism. Many of the narratives and motifs of far-left discourse about Israel/Palestine and Zionism derive not from earlier Marxist critiques of Zionism but from this, Stalinist anti-Zionism, and the 'anti-imperialism of fools' which it expresses and encourages. This chapter discusses the role of Stalinism both as a system of state power and as the ideology informing movements and parties valorising that state power, as a source of left antisemitism. It will also explore how the influence of Stalinism has led left groups and figures who are not formally Stalinist – including various Trotskyist organisations and prominent left leaders such as Ken Livingstone and Jeremy Corbyn – to promote left antisemitic ideas.

Like all words associated with the name of an individual, Stalinism is a limited and imperfect term for the phenomenon it describes. It would be preferable if we had another word than Stalinism, which, as Martin Thomas put it, 'suggests only a school of thought, and probably one defunct'. Discussing the role and influence of an ideological trend can also risk reification, implying that an abstract force, made concrete only by its – inevitably contradictory – application by human beings, can act in a singular way. However, despite those limitations, as Thomas goes on to say, '"Stalinism" remains the best-available single word' for the bureaucratic dictatorship built on the ruins of the Russian Revolution, subsequent social and economic systems in other countries modelled on that in whole or in part (such as North Korea, China, Vietnam and Cuba), and the ideological tendencies that valorise those societies, and see them as a progressive alternative to capitalism.[2]

As such, Stalinism is therefore not merely an abstract ideological trend. Karl Marx wrote in 1845: 'The ideas of the ruling class are in every epoch the ruling ideas, i.e., the class which is the ruling material force of society, is at the same time its ruling intellectual force.'[3] That is as true for the Stalinist ruling classes as it is for the ruling classes of capitalist countries. During the years of the USSR's existence, official Communist parties in other countries acted as a conduit into their domestic labour and socialist movements for the 'ruling ideas' of the Stalinist ruling classes, albeit often adapted, on instruction from Moscow, for particular national conditions. From its emergence as a distinct social form in the 1920s, Stalinism's power allowed it to build ideological influence, which, while disrupted by the fall of the USSR, could not possibly be completely erased the minute its state power crumbled.

Even in countries like Britain, where Stalinism never supplanted reformist social democracy as the dominant current in the labour movement, its influence has not disappeared. On the contrary, in recent years it has undergone something of a limited but real revival. Despite the Communist Party of Great Britain having been weaker than many of its European counterparts, the *Morning Star*, the former CPGB organ now linked to its principal organisational descendant, the Communist Party of Britain (CPB), continues to enjoy sponsorship to the tune of tens of thousands of pounds from many major trade unions. It also receives patronage and support from several left-wing Labour MPs, most prominently Jeremy Corbyn, who has been a frequent columnist. It is distributed for free to all delegates at many trade-union conferences.

Corbyn's appointment of the *Guardian* journalist Seumas Milne and the former journalist and (unelected) trade-union official Andrew Murray to key roles in his office put into positions of political influence in the Labour Party two supporters of Straight Left, the CPGB's most hard-line and anti-revisionist tendency, founded in 1979. Milne was the business manager for Straight Left's newspaper. One of the issues on which Straight Left dissented from the CPGB leadership was the latter's opposition to the Soviet invasions of Czechoslovakia in 1968, and Afghanistan in 1979, both of which the activists who went on to found Straight Left had supported.

Central to the endeavour of renewing and reinvigorating a democratic, internationalist, revolutionary socialism in the twenty-first century is refuting the claim, made by defenders of capitalism and Stalinists themselves alike, that Stalinism in the USSR was the legitimate inheritor or inevitable outgrowth of the 1917 October Revolution, and that the societies subsequently modelled on Stalin's USSR, or aspects of it, including China, Cuba, North Korea, Vietnam and others, represent the alternative to capitalism.

Stalinism overturns the emphasis on liberty, democracy and equality that were central to the original Marxist project and replaces them with statism, bureaucratic hierarchy and, frequently, a profound conservatism on questions such as nation, gender and sexuality. The historic difference between Stalinism and democratic revolutionary socialism is not a theoretical or strategic dispute between distinct tendencies within a broader political category, but the difference between two irreconcilably opposed systems. As Leon Trotsky put it: 'Stalin revises Marx and Lenin not with the theoretician's pen but with the heel of the GPU [secret police]. [...] [There is] between Bolshevism and Stalinism not simply a bloody line but a whole river of blood [...] [and] not only a political but a thoroughly physical incompatibility.'[4]

Of the many poisonous legacies bequeathed to us by Stalinism, one of the most abiding, and the most relevant for consideration here, is what some writers call a 'campist' perspective on world politics.[5] Historically, the division was clear: there was a capitalist, imperialist camp and a socialist camp. As Gilbert Achcar puts it:

The main divide among anti-imperialists during the Cold War was rather caused by the attitude towards the USSR, which Communist Parties and their close allies regarded as the 'fatherland of socialism'; they determined much of their own political positions by aligning with Moscow and the 'socialist camp' – an attitude that was described as 'campism'. This was facilitated by Moscow's support for most struggles against Western imperialism in its global rivalry with Washington. As for Moscow's intervention against workers' and people's revolts in its own European sphere of domination, the campists stood with the Kremlin, denigrating these revolts under the pretext that they were fomented by Washington.[6]

The campist perspective was able to reconcile its obvious departure from Marxism – which sees the conflict between *classes, within* every society, as the key motor of social change – by claiming that the working class was, in some sense, in power in the socialist camp, and the conflict between East and West was therefore a clash not between rival systems of class exploitation but between capitalist imperialism and the socialist alternative to it. In his book *The Left in Disarray*, surveying the extent of Stalinism's influence over far-left thinking, the Irish socialist writer Sean Matgamna described how Stalinism distorted socialist internationalism:

> In international politics, the Stalinists emptied the terms 'imperialism' and 'anti-imperialism' of all 'objective' content. They presented predatory Russian imperialism, ruled over by a savage and sometimes crazily chauvinistic autocracy, as the expansion of the socialist revolution, and therefore, by definition, right on everything over which its rulers – not the imaginary working-class rulers, the real ones – clashed with the capitalist world, or were criticised in it.[7]

One might dissent from this or that action taken by this or that government in the socialist camp – some Communist Party leaderships, including Britain's, opposed the Russian invasions of Czechoslovakia and Afghanistan – but such missteps were never allowed to alter the overarching belief that what existed in the USSR and other states based on its model was an advance on capitalism.

Since the collapse of the Stalinist empire deprived it of a widespread model of allegedly 'actually existing socialism' to point to, campist perspectives have become somewhat more diffuse, but the essential structure remains: the anti-imperialist camp, now broad enough to encompass the governments of China, Russia, Syria, Iran, Venezuela and Belarus, as well as non- or semi-state forces such as the Islamist paramilitary parties Hamas and Hezbollah, is to be supported against the imperialist camp, which, without question, includes Israel.

Campism empties left-wing politics of any positive content – mere negative opposition to imperialism is sufficient to earn support. Anything harmful to imperialism, even if it means an advance for reactionary nationalisms or religious fundamentalisms, is to be welcomed. And if Israel and Zionism are understood as part of, perhaps even the leadership of, imperialism, then any form of anti-Zionism must, automatically, be progressive. The door is thereby thrown open to antisemitism.

## STALINIST ANTISEMITISM

Stalinist antisemitism predates the emergence of campist anti-imperialism. Stalinism trafficked in antisemitism since its inception. It was a central aspect in slanders against Bolshevik dissidents and opponents of the Stalinist counter-revolution, especially Leon Trotsky, as he himself suggested:

At the time of the expulsions of the [Left] Opposition from the party, the bureaucracy purposely emphasised the names of Jewish members of casual and secondary importance. This was quite openly discussed in the party, and, back in 1925, the Opposition saw in this situation the unmistakable symptom of the decay of the ruling clique.

After [Jewish Bolsheviks] Zinoviev and Kamenev joined the Opposition, the situation changed radically for the worse. At this point there opened wide a perfect chance to say to the workers that at the head of the Opposition stand three 'dissatisfied Jewish intellectuals'. Under the direction of Stalin, [the bureaucracy] carried through this line systematically and almost fully in the open.[8]

Stalinism's exploitation of the theme of Jewish conspiracy appealed to antisemitism as one of the strongest 'nationalist and chauvinist prejudices'[9] present in Russian society, which gave an easy frame to narratives about conspiracies of wreckers, saboteurs and foreign agents working to destabilise the socialist state. Antisemitism provided Stalinism with a channel into which to divert potential domestic dissent, and cohere nationalist loyalty to the state. It was deployed by Stalin against his internal enemies, and it would later be used both to explain the USSR's failures in the Middle East and to discredit efforts of reform within the Eastern Bloc, such as the 1968 Prague Spring and workers' uprisings in Poland.

Communist Party policy, directed from Moscow, also supported attacks against Jewish settlers in Palestine in the late 1920s. Criticising this policy at the time, the American Trotskyist Max Shachtman argued these attacks could not have a progressive character:

The Jew is pointed out to the Arab as the source of all evil. The reactionary Arab leaders have diverted the nationalist movement of the masses into Pan-Islamic and antisemitic channels and out of its natural current against British imperialism. [...] They are against all Jews as Jews. They set up the reactionary demand for the 'restriction of the Jewish immigration into Palestine'.[10]

Domestically, one of the specific charges levelled by Stalinist states against Jewish dissidents, or alleged dissidents, was 'cosmopolitanism', the claim that Jews were not rooted in whatever nation they were present but were instead connected and loyal to their own, Jewish, nation. After the foundation of the state of Israel, and despite, as will be discussed, Stalinism's initial support for that state, the charge of 'cosmopolitanism' became fused with, and eventually substituted for, the charge of 'Zionism' and support for Israel. According to Moishe Postone:

> All of the charges [...] were classically antisemitic charges: they were rootless, they were cosmopolitan, and they were part of a general global conspiracy. Because the Soviet Union could not officially use the language of antisemitism, they began to use the word 'Zionist' to mean exactly what antisemites mean when they speak of Jews.[11]

The Czech Communist politician Václav Kopecký, for instance, argued:

> Cosmopolitans should in principle not be posted in leadership positions. This truly is an issue of cosmopolitanism, not a racial question. There are people of Jewish origin who are firmly rooted in our nation. What we are concerned with here is those people who are strangers to us. [...] The people of this background mostly come from very wealthy strata. In many instances they also had a very religious upbringing, which

only fortified their Zionist tendencies. Today we know that the attitudes of many people of Jewish origin to the working class have changed. […] The Jews are drawn to Anglo-American imperialism, which is supporting Israel and using Zionism as a disintegrative agent within the parties of the popular demo-cratic regimes and within socialism.[12]

Readers may see parallels between Kopecký's insistence that it is only 'cosmopolitanism', and Jews with 'Zionist tendencies' he opposes, and contemporary denials of left antisemitism on the basis that those charged with it are only 'anti-Zionist', and have no quarrel with anti-Zionist Jews.

The late 1940s and early 1950s saw the USSR and its satel-lites pursue policies of systematic antisemitic violence. In 1948 the Jewish actor Shloyme Mikhoels, who had chaired the Jewish Anti-Fascist Committee (JAFC), was murdered by the secret police. The JAFC was destroyed by the state, accused of plotting to establish a Jewish enclave in Crimea that would serve as a base for US military incursions into the Soviet Union.

In 1949 the Hungarian government dissolved the Hungarian Zionist Union and stopped issuing passports to Jews wanting to emigrate to Israel. During the show trial of László Rajk, a former minister in the Hungarian government, the press wrote that 'Trotskyism, fascism and Zionism' were part of a 'family circle' that had informed Rajk's politics.[13] Between 1951 and 1953, Soviet state propaganda accused a group of mainly Jewish doctors of involvement in a plot to assassinate Stalin, on the orders of a 'Zionist spy organisation'.[14] A number of Jewish doctors were arrested and tortured.

In 1952 the Slánský Trial saw fourteen alleged dissidents in the Czech Communist Party, ten of whom were Jewish, accused of participation in a Zionist conspiracy. Eleven of the defendants, including Rudolf Slánský himself, the First Secretary of the Czech

Communist Party, were publicly executed on 3 December 1952. Eugen Loebl, one of the first defendants in the trial, was told:

> You are not a communist [or] a Czechoslovakian. You are a dirty Jew, that's what you are. Israel is your only real father-land and you have sold out socialism to your bosses, the Zionist imperialist leaders of world Jewry. Let me tell you, the time is fast approaching when we'll have to exterminate all of your kind.[15]

Thus, Stalinist antisemitism recycled the older themes of primitive antisemitism – the conflation of Jews with capital, Jews as a parasitic element on the national body politic, engaged in an international conspiracy to 'master the world' – and fused them with a new claim: that Jews, via 'the role of the state of Israel', were now 'the main representatives of international imperialism'. Thus, an antisemitic anti-Zionism was made a foundation stone of the campist anti-imperialism Stalinism promoted. It was one, too, that long outlasted Stalin himself: in 1983, in the final decade of its existence, the USSR established the Anti-Zionist Committee of the Soviet Public as a formal state institution.

This anti-Zionism was broadcast throughout the USSR and its satellite states via an industrial-scale production of propaganda. As the academic Izabella Tabarovsky wrote:

> In the course of the campaign, hundreds of anti-Zionist and anti-Israel books and thousands of articles were published in the USSR, with millions of copies entering circulation in the country. Many were translated into foreign languages – English, French, German, Spanish, Arabic and numer-ous others. In 1970 alone, the comparison between alleged Zionist and Nazi racism – just one of the campaign's numer-ous memes – merited 96 mentions. [...] Demonisation of

Zionism continued in films, lectures, and radio broadcasts. Anti-Zionist cartoons, many of an obvious antisemitic nature, were a regular feature of Soviet publications.

The campaign used the significant Soviet broadcasting and publishing capacity abroad, as well as front organisations and friendly communist and other radical left organisations in the West and Third World countries, to transmit its messages to foreign audiences.[16]

The anti-Zionist campaigns were taken up throughout the 'Communist' bloc, used by the bureaucratic rulers of Stalinist countries to shore up their own positions and ideological grip. In 1967–8, for instance, the Polish Stalinist state made antisemitic anti-Zionism central to its strategy for confronting dissent. In his book on Solidarność, the revolutionary workers' movement against Polish Stalinism, the writer Mark Osborn described how, in the 1960s: 'In the press and the party, intellectual dissent and the desire for freedom of expression became synonymous with support for Israel.' 'Zionist' became code for 'Jew', and, as in the 'anti-cosmopolitan' campaigns of the 1950s, Jews were accused of being 'anti-national' saboteurs and agents of foreign states – Israel, America or West Germany. A hundred and fifty Jews were expelled from the armed forces, and Leon Kasman, the editor of *Trybuna Ludu*, the main party newspaper, was sacked. All actual Zionist organisations had already been banned in 1949–50. As Osborn put it, 'the hunt for "Zionists" was taking place in a country without Zionists and where the remaining Jews were a very tiny minority'.[17] State-organised May Day parades in Poland in 1968 saw participants march with banners bearing slogans such as 'Down with Zionism, agency of imperialism', and 'Zionists to Israel'.

A similar approach was taken in Czechoslovakia. According to the academic William Korey, in his detailed survey of Russian and Stalinist antisemitism:

In the early summer of 1968, the theme of the world Zionist plot began to be employed in a new direction. The focus of Soviet concern was no longer only the Middle East, where a scapegoat was needed to explain the failures of Soviet policy. The basic fear of the Communist leadership in 1968 centred on Czechoslovakia, where [...] Alexander Dubcek's government threatened to burst the integument of Soviet totalitarianism. World Zionism would now be depicted as the spearhead of international capitalism engaged in an effort to subvert Communist states and harm relationships between them. A June 1968 article in the authoritative foreign policy journal *Mezhdunarodnaia zhizn* signalled the change in emphasis. Entitled 'Israel, Zionism and International Imperialism', the article by K. Ivanov recapitulated the international conspiracy thesis linking Zionism, Jewish capitalism, Israel, American imperialism, and West German revanchism in a gigantic plot to overthrow Communist rule.[18]

As studies such as Korey's have shown, Stalinist anti-Zionism also included a not insignificant anti-Freemasonry element, recycling a claim made in the *Protocols of the Elders of Zion* that Freemasonry was an instrument of Jewish domination. A study of the administration of US president Jimmy Carter by the prominent anti-Zionist writer Valery Yemelyanov 'found that virtually all of its key members were either Masons or Jews'. Yemelyanov 'considered the threat of "Zionist-Masonic" domination so immediate and palpable that he called upon the Kremlin for an all-out educational campaign to "unmask" Zionism'.[19]

Socialist activist Stan Crooke's seminal 1988 article 'The Stalinist Roots of "Left" Antisemitism' surveyed a cross-section of Stalinist anti-Zionist propaganda, showing that many of the historical claims, narratives and perspectives about Israel and

Zionism that were, and to a large extent remain, common on the far left, albeit sometimes in implicit forms, had their origins in Stalinist propaganda.

A number of key themes emerge, of which three will be examined here.

*First, the foundation of the state of Israel as a conspiracy of wealthy Zionist colonisers acting either in the service of imperialism or as its vanguard.*

Often recycling older themes conflating Jews with capital and finance, Stalinist anti-Zionism promoted a narrative that essentially reduced the history of Jewish immigration to Palestine, and the foundation of Israel, to a conspiracy of Jewish financiers. It was argued that 'Jewish capital' had become 'such a powerful force that it was able to participate independently in the colonial division of the world'.[20]

Some texts posited the existence of a distinct 'monopoly Jewish bourgeoisie', which had 'achieved an extension of colonial expansion in Asia and Africa', via their 'most important instrument [...] the state of Israel'.[21]

Elsewhere, the argument was made that the emergence and growth of Zionism was a result of the influential presence of individual Jews *within* Western capitalist ruling classes: 'The capitalists of England, the USA, France, Germany, and other countries, amongst them millionaires and multi-millionaires of Jewish origin, who had their eyes on the wealth of the Near East, helped the creation of the Zionist idea.'[22]

Israel was described as a 'parasite-state', reliant on 'financial-economic support [from] international Zionist circles'.[23] Israel's economy was 'controlled by the international Zionist corporation', which consisted of a specifically 'Zionist capital' within 'the USA, England, France, and a series of other countries'.[24]

*Second, Zionist collaboration with the Nazis, and Zionism itself as a form of antisemitism, or responsible for antisemitism; Zionism as racism, or comparable to fascism.*

Attempts to equate Zionism and Nazism, and claims of cooperation and collaboration between Zionists and Nazis, were highly prevalent, as were claims that powerful Jews had deliberately stoked antisemitism: 'hatred towards Jews was already very widespread in the West. The powerful Jewish bourgeoisie was far from being the least responsible for this.'[25]

It was argued that Zionism and antisemitism were 'two sides of the same coin – racism', and that 'Zionists greeted the antisemitic policies of Tsarism in its time and also the monstrous policies of genocide at the time of Hitler'.[26] Here again themes of shadowy conspiracies were common. It was claimed that 'antisemitic organisations have been set up with the resources dispensed from the secret funds of Zionism'.[27]

Zionists were accused of collaborating with Nazism against the USSR specifically: 'Cooperation between the Zionists and Hitlerites spread to the occupied territories of the USSR. The Zionists helped uncover those of Jewish origin who were hiding from the Gestapo and the police, handed them over to the fascists, and took part in the mass slaughter of Jews.'[28]

Straightforward equivalences were drawn between Zionism and Nazism, which were claimed to be 'akin' to each other,[29] and based on common ideas: 'As regards the theory of "racial purity", the treatises on "lower" and "higher" peoples, the concepts of the "Aryan" and the "superman", here there is really not a little in common between the Zionists and the fascists.'[30] A theme still common, that Israel's treatment of the Palestinians directly parallels Nazism, also emerged: 'Such is the irony of history: the Zionist rulers of Israel carry out the very same policies of genocide in relation to the Arabs as those which were carried out by the Hitlerites in relation to the Jews.'[31]

*Third, the central or leading position of the Israeli state in determining US, or world, imperialist policy.*

Despite Israel being a small state, one of several states of equivalent size and power supported by the US, Stalinist anti-Zionism insisted that Israel was, in fact, in the driving seat. 'The representatives of international Zionist capital', it was argued, 'openly aspire to world domination.'[32] Zionism was not a nationalist movement of Jewish people, arising from particular social conditions and historical experiences. Instead, 'the real masters of international Zionism' were 'the most powerful monopolies and banks of the USA and other countries, that is, the driving forces of contemporary imperialism.'[33]

Again, this was ascribed to the influential position of Jewish capitalists within imperialist ruling classes, especially in the USA:

> The existence in the United States of the most numerous grouping in the world of capitalists of Jewish origin [...] is the most important factor determining the specific nature of American Zionism. [...] About 20% of American millionaires are Jews, although, as is well known, the proportion of Americans of Jewish origin does not exceed 3% of the entire population of the USA.[34]

The old motif of Jewish conspiracy, a networked cabal behind the scenes of world affairs, exerting a controlling influence, was common:

> [It is] no exaggeration to say that the system of organisations of international Zionism (which extends throughout the entire world and, at the same time, is strongly centralised) united with a powerful financial-economic base in the shape of the monopoly bourgeoisie of Jewish origin [...] is the main source of strength and activity of Zionist influence on

the politics of a series of leading capitalist states. At present, international Zionism […] given the depth of its penetration into the most variegated spheres of political, economic, and social life of the capitalist countries, has no equal amongst the other bourgeois-nationalist and anticommunist currents and detachments of world reaction.[35]

In summary, as Crooke put it:

The Stalinist account sought to mobilise every sort of sentiment it could plausibly appeal to under 'Marxist' colours – anti-capitalism, anti-imperialism, anti-racism, anti-Nazism, and even opposition to antisemitism – against 'the Zionists', by way of portraying 'the Zionists' as in cahoots with, or as pulling the strings of, those responsible for all the evils appealed against. It was in fact tantamount to an updated and 'Marxist' version of the notorious *Protocols of the Elders of Zion*.[36]

The claim that Israel is in the vanguard of world imperialism was nonsensical at the time this Stalinist propaganda was produced, and remains so today. Israel is a heavily armed, regionally powerful state, imperialist in its expansionist policies and colonial in its occupation of the West Bank and blockade of Gaza. But in this, it is a power on the order of Turkey or Iran, not a global hegemon like the USA. It has supporters in other countries who lobby for its interests, as does more or less every other state on the planet. The claim of Israel's shaping position within world imperialism can only make sense as the product of another claim – that there is a conspiracy of Zionists at work behind the scenes of world affairs, powerful and effective enough to bring the foreign policies of much larger, more powerful nations under their sway.

According to this narrative, the Israeli-Jewish national community is an illegitimate presence in historic Palestine, the artificial implantation of a racist drive for colonial conquest. Supporting their national rights, their right to have a state, is necessarily inadmissible. After all, what 'rights' could the imperialist agents of 'Jewish capital' possibly deserve?

Given not only the Stalinist anti-Zionism of the 1950s onwards but also Stalinist support for attacks on Jewish settlers in the 1920s and 30s, the fact that Israel was, in the 1948 war, armed by the USSR's Czech satellite seems like an odd aberration. But understanding the campist framework of Stalinist policy makes sense of the oscillations. The Stalinist ruling class hoped that Israel might be drawn into its bloc, the so-called anti-imperialist and socialist camp. Therefore, in 1948, the *Daily Worker*, the newspaper of the CPGB, had, in line with the USSR's policy of the time, welcomed and celebrated the establishment of the state of Israel. It denounced the war against Israel as 'a reactionary war conducted by the chieftains of the Arab League under British control [and] entirely against the interests of the Arab masses'.[37] In the *Daily Worker*'s coverage of the 1948 war, according to the academic John Strawson, there was

> no suggestion that Israel is a colonial project. Quite the reverse in fact, Israel's Declaration of Independence is seen as blow against colonialism. What is also striking [is that] there is no coverage or discussion of Palestinian Arab displacement. [...] The sub-text of this silence is that the Arab suffering was a result of the pro-imperialist Arab leadership. For the Soviet Union and the communist parties, the world was divided into imperialism on one side and the forces of progress on the other. Israel is firmly placed in the latter camp. As a consequence, the suffering of the Palestinian Arabs is not the consequence

of the creation of the Jewish state but the result of those opposing it.[38]

Stalinist support for Israel in 1948 can clearly be seen, then, as motivated not by any consistent principle towards the Israeli Jews, but by campism. When the campist calculations changed, and it became clear that Israel would not align with the USSR and its bloc, it was deemed to have moved into the camp of imperialism, and the policy duly changed.

## STALINIST ANTISEMITISM AND THE LEFT IN BRITAIN

By 1952 the CPGB press was promoting the official Stalinist line on the Slánský Trial. An article in its *World News and Views* magazine said the trial 'revealed the now familiar pattern of American espionage and sabotage against the People's Democracies. […] The fact that eleven of the fourteen conspirators were of bourgeois Jewish origin […] proved beyond doubt the complicity of the Zionist organisation and Israeli government in the plot.'[39]

Surveying the CPGB and its press as a source for the transmission of Stalinist antisemitism into the British left and labour movement reveals a complex picture. The CPGB had a substantial Jewish membership base; a survey conducted by Whitechapel Public Library in 1939 found the *Daily Worker* was read by eighteen times more Jews than non-Jews. At least half the membership of the CPGB's Stepney branch, one of its largest, in the early mid-1940s was Jewish. In 1945 Jewish CP member Phil Piratin was elected to Parliament, representing the Mile End constituency, and supported by a substantial Jewish vote.[40] Many CPGB members, both Jewish and non, were dedicated and heroic fighters against far-right antisemitism, while also being convinced Stalinists.

As the historian Tony Kushner notes, the instinctive response of Jewish CP members to reports of antisemitic campaigns in the USSR and elsewhere was denial:

> Initially accusations of antisemitism in the Prague Trial and the [...] 'Doctors' Plot' from 1951–3 were strenuously denied by the Jewish Communists. The accusations were regarded as being part of American and British Cold War rhetoric. Jewish Communists attempted to turn the allegations on their head. The *Jewish Clarion* [a CP-supporting Jewish newspaper] published accounts of what it saw as antisemitism in Britain's 'own backyard' and claimed that hostility to Jews was the 'American way of life'.[41]

But although it was, in Kushner's phrase, a 'very slow process', by the mid-1950s there was underway what Kushner, quoting the historian Henry Pelling, called an 'agonising reappraisal' of the USSR by Jewish CP members.[42] In 1956, the same year that many Stalinists' worldviews were shaken by the USSR's suppression of a workers' uprising in Hungary, dissent burst into the open. In August of that year the Marxist academic Professor Hyman Levy raised questions in the *Daily Worker* about allegations of antisemitism in Russia that had been made in the Polish Yiddish newspaper *Folkstymme*. The *Daily Worker* editor replied that they were 'essentially correct', but refused to carry any further discussion. Levy conducted his own fact-finding tour of the USSR, and reported to the CPGB the following year that his investigations 'shook him to his foundations'.[43]

As historian June Edmunds recounts, in September 1956 the CPGB's International Department and members of the party's National Jewish Committee (NJC) held

an emergency meeting on the question of Soviet antisemitism, revealing a split between some Jewish members and
the leadership. Members of the NJC stated that the *Daily
Worker* had suppressed debate on antisemitism in the
Soviet Union and had given the impression that the party
condoned socialist antisemitism. The majority of the NJC
refused to accept [CP leader Rajani] Palme Dutt's defence of
the Soviet Union.[44]

Later, when the Polish Stalinist state began repressing Jews,
Jewish CP dissidents: 'accused the British party's leadership of
refusing to take seriously the possibility of antisemitism in Eastern Europe. In particular they attacked [prominent Jewish CP
leaders] Bert Ramelson and Maurice Lichtig for failing to provide
information on Poland's anti-Zionist propaganda.'[45]

As Kushner put it, 'the NJC believed that the *Daily Worker*'s
suppression of information and debate on the subject had "created
the feeling amongst many Jews that our Party was condoning evil
practices (including antisemitism) in a socialist country"'.[46] Some
Jewish dissidents, including Hyman Levy, were expelled from the
party. Many others left. 'Even for those Jewish members who did
not leave', writes Kushner, '[…] things would never be the same.'[47]

CPGB literature, although usually avoiding the worst excesses
of the propaganda being produced in the Eastern Bloc, sometimes
repeated elements of the conspiracy-theorist claims of Stalinist
anti-Zionism. In 1967 Ramelson authored a pamphlet that, while
recognising Israel's right to exist, also argued that its power rested
on 'Zionist-inspired financial, economic and "pressure group"
support from the widespread Jewish communities, conditioned
by years of Zionist propaganda to believe that they owe allegiance
to the Zionist state of Israel.'[48] He went on to argue: 'It is […] no
accident that the "new found" friends of the Jews and Israel during
1956 and 1967 are often the same ones who supported Munich

and the rise of Hitler and Mosley, and for exactly the same reasons – considerations of imperialist advantage.'[49]

A 1969 article in the CPGB-affiliated *Labour Monthly* magazine promoted the Khazar conversion theory, a canard claiming that Ashkenazi Jews are the descendants of Caucasian-Turkic people who some historians claim converted to Judaism, and therefore have no real ethnic connection to the original, Semitic, Jews of the Middle East: 'As for European and American Jews – a goodly proportion are not Semites at all but have the broad faces and wide noses of mongoloids, for their ancestors never knew Palestine: these derive from the mass conversion of the Khazar kingdom in South Russia a few centuries ago.'[50] The same article called Israel a 'racist, theocratic state', which was comparable to Nazi Germany and apartheid South Africa.[51]

## TROTSKYISM BETRAYED

In 1982 the *Morning Star* compared Israel's invasion of Lebanon to the Holocaust and said Israel had used 'Blitzkrieg tactics […] modelled on the military theories of Nazi strategists'.[52] Israeli leaders Menachem Begin and Ariel Sharon were portrayed as 'Nazi monsters', aiming to carry out a 'final solution' against Palestinians.[53] In an ugly instance of pre-modern antisemitism, the *Morning Star* wrote that 'the mark of Cain is clearly on Sharon's forehead'.[54] In a pamphlet on Israel/Palestine, the CPGB published a cartoon that depicted Begin 'salivating over skulls, with his mouth open and revealing the teeth of a vampire'.[55]

The claim suggested here, of Israel having consciously mimicked or become Nazis, is, along with the claim of comprehensive Zionist collaboration with Nazism, one of the motifs of Stalinist antisemitism that has proved especially durable. The claim was taken up by non-Stalinist organisations – in 1985 a *Socialist Worker* article asserted that 'Israel was founded on the

Nazi idea of "racial purity", only Jews have replaced Aryans'[56] – and has prominently reoccurred on the contemporary left. In 2017 Ken Livingstone attracted controversy with his claim, in a TV interview, that Hitler was 'supporting Zionism' before he 'went mad and killed six million Jews'.[57] Livingstone, and other propagators of the claim, extrapolate from incidental examples of certain Zionist leaders or organisations, usually from a position of desperation, seeking deals with the Nazi authorities, a much wider claim that 'Zionism', as such (which, again, is reified into a singular force), collaborated with Nazism in a comprehensive way. Thereby, a political-moral equivalence between Nazism and Zionism is implied. Like much of the far-left historiography of Zionism, the complexity and diversity of its history is entirely erased, and the actions of minorities are made to stand for the whole. The record of, for example, Zionist resistance fighters in the Warsaw Ghetto uprising is expunged from the historical page.

Livingstone's politics were not directly formed by involvement in the official CP tradition; his left antisemitism was consolidated via his collaboration with the Workers Revolutionary Party (WRP) of Gerry Healy, one of the key associations of Livingstone's political career. Along with the Socialist Workers Party, the WRP was a key wellspring of antisemitic ideas on the British left, perhaps even more so than the CPGB itself, although both the WRP and the SWP have an anti-Stalinist political provenance. That two of the primary sources of left antisemitism in Britain could be organisations from outside Stalinism, and even would-be opponents of it, speaks to a central tragedy of revolutionary socialism in the last eighty or more years: the substantial accommodation of even anti-Stalinist organisations with ideas and methods emerging from Stalinism.

The Trotskyist tradition from which both the WRP and SWP emerged was once much healthier in its thinking about Israel/ Palestine, and much more rational in its critique of Zionism.

Towards the end of his life, Trotsky himself advocated that the revolutionary socialist movement should support the right of Jews to self-determination and statehood. He believed the 'Jewish question', the issue of whether the Jews were a national people who could or should self-determine at the level of a national state, could not be resolved in a progressive way under capitalism, but believed that a socialist future would guarantee Jewish national rights – including in Palestine, if that is where Jews wished to exercise them:

> Once socialism has become master of our planet or at least of its most important sections, it will have unimaginable resources in all domains. Human history has witnessed the epoch of great migrations on the basis of barbarism. Social-ism will open the possibility of great migrations on the basis of the most developed technique and culture. It goes without saying that what is here involved is not compulsory displace-ments, that is, the creation of new ghettoes for certain nationalities, but displacements freely consented to, or rather demanded by, certain nationalities or parts of nationalities. The dispersed Jews who would want to be reassembled in the same community will find a sufficiently extensive and rich spot under the sun. The same possibility will be opened for the Arabs, as for all other scattered nations.[58]

Trotsky opposed Zionism as a 'utopian and reactionary' attempt to resolve the question of Jewish nationhood, and feared that 'the conflict between the Jews and Arabs in Palestine [would] acquire a more and more tragic and more and more menacing character'.[59] That fear has sadly come to be realised, but Trotsky's analysis shares nothing in common with the view that Jewish settlers were nothing more than imperialist colonisers undeserv-ing of rights.

His view was that socialism was the best guarantor of an equal right to self-determination for all peoples, to be arrived at via democratic accommodation, a promise socialism should make to the Jews and Arabs of Palestine equally. This is a view clearly at odds with the insistence on innately imperialist and anti-imperialist essences that Stalinism, and an increasingly Stalinised Trotskyism, would later come to confer on Israeli Jews and Palestinian Arabs respectively. What attitude Trotsky would have taken later, had he lived to witness the full unfolding of the horrors of the Holocaust and the flight of increasing numbers of Jews to Palestine, we will never know.

While all Trotskyist organisations sharply critiqued Zionism as a nationalist ideology, none supported the defeat and overrunning of the embryonic Jewish state in the 1948 war.[60] Throughout the 1930s, only one Trotskyist organisation, the Workers Party of South Africa, had dissented from the consensus of support for the right of Jewish immigration to Palestine and opposition to attacks on Jewish settlers.[61] In the 1948 conflict, many Trotskyist organisations supported neither side, and some, like the Workers Party (later the Independent Socialist League, ISL), the most consistently anti-Stalinist tendency within world Trotskyism, explicitly supported the Jewish side.[62] In 1948 Hal Draper, a leading figure in the Workers Party/ISL, wrote an article entitled 'How to Defend Israel', discussing how socialists could support the right of the Jewish national community to self-determination and self-defence without lapsing into apologism for injustices and atrocities committed by the fledgling Israeli state.[63]

Even some who would go on to be prominent exponents of left antisemitic ideas acknowledged the antisemitic potential of irrational critiques of Israel. As late as 1967, in the aftermath of the Six-Day War, SWP founder Tony Cliff wrote that 'an anti-Israeli campaign quite easily degenerates into a "jihad", in which the most reactionary regimes save themselves by channelling the struggle into racial channels'.[64] Even though the pamphlet's general perspective was campist, advocating an anti-imperialist 'Arab revolution', Cliff nonetheless also advocated 'a socialist republic, with full rights for Jews, Kurds, and all national minorities'. In this context 'full rights for national minorities' surely implies full *national* rights, a greatly different attitude from the admissibility of Israeli-Jewish national self-determination than the absolute anti-Zionist fervour the SWP would soon develop.

Cliff's views on Jewish immigration to Palestine, which he had initially supported, underwent a 180-degree reversal. As his biographer Ian Birchall puts it, 'in 1938 […] he's still in favour of unrestricted Jewish immigration into Palestine; by 1945 he's completely reversed that position. What nobody seems to remember is when exactly that reversal came and how it happened.'[65] Exactly what else Cliff believed those Jews, in the jaws of Nazism and then later as displaced refugees, were supposed to do, when much of the world was closing its doors to them, was not clear. As one reviewer of Birchall's biography wrote:

> Cliff came to oppose Jewish immigration into Palestine just as the extent of the Holocaust became clear. Cliff wrote off the Jewish working class as well as the possibility that Palestinian Arabs could win on their own. With no progressive force in the conflict, Cliff laid the basis for other substitutes – intellectually prefiguring the SWP's flirtation with Hamas and other Islamists.[66]

By 1973 any sensitivity to the origins of the Jewish national community in Palestine, or any notion that they might deserve national rights, seemed to have disappeared from the SWP's perspectives. The *Socialist Worker* was now arguing that the 'essence' of Zionism was that 'a "chosen people", the Jews, are superior to everyone else and should trample on the rights of others'.[67] In *That's*

*Funny*, Steve Cohen recounted the sorry tale of the incident in 1980 when the *Socialist Worker* printed, without critical comment of any sort, a letter from one Anthony Jones, commenting on a recent TV film about Saudi Arabia, which stated: 'Such is Zionist influence in Britain – particularly in the media ("Lord" Lew Grade, "Lord" Bernstein) – that this film was bound to be shown and therefore used to stir up anti-Arab feeling.' In fact, Jones was an organiser for the fascist National Front. As Cohen commented: 'Even if the SWP did not know this, then the nature of the letter should have alerted them. However, the *Socialist Worker* was seen to be quite unable to distinguish anti-Zionism from blatant antisemitism.'[68]

That was also evident in 1985, when the paper defended Sunderland Polytechnic Students' Union's banning of its campus Jewish Society. They said the ban was 'quite clearly not racist … One thing is clear – they are not racists, unlike the Zionists who oppose them.'[69] A subsequent article defined Zionism as 'the contention that the only hope for Jews throughout the world lies in an exclusively Jewish state in someone else's country,'[70] again collapsing the whole of historic Zionism, and implying all Jews who identified with Zionism were effectively Jewish chauvinists.

In 1986 the SWP published *Israel: The Hijack State*, a full-scale endorsement of a campist, and antisemitic, historiography of Israel/Palestine. The pamphlet described the Zionist Federation of Germany as having been a 'kindred spirit' of Hitler, and proclaimed that 'the Zionists' terrible attitude to the Nazis must never be allowed to hide or disfigure the tremendous courage shown by Jewish resistance fighters against the Nazis', again overlooking the fact that many leading Jewish resistance fighters, such as Abba Kovner, were themselves Zionists. According to the pamphlet, Israel's foundation was a matter of 'the Zionists' 'seizing' and 'hijacking' Palestine.

'Could the surrounding Arab countries not have done more?' the pamphlet asked. 'Certainly they went through all the motions of declaring "war". And the day after Ben-Gurion proclaimed the birth of the State of Israel on 14 May 1948, the Arab countries bound together through the Arab League "invaded". But it was a totally unreal exercise. There were military clashes – but key Arab governments were already in negotiations with the Israelis.' The pamphlet lamented that the Arab states 'had no stomach for a full-scale national war' against Israel.[71]

Abdul al-Rahman Azzam Pasha, Secretary General of the Arab League in 1948, was quoted as saying: 'It does not matter how many Jews there are. We will sweep them into the sea.'[72] Several historians have suggested that even more luridly exterminationist quotes attributed to Pasha were misquoted or taken out of context. Nevertheless, it is clear that the Arab League saw its war aims as territorial reconquest. The states that comprised the League included authoritarian dictatorships and repressive monarchies. Syrian historian Sami Moubayed describes the Arab leaders as 'promising to annihilate the Zionists by Christmas 1948'.[73] This – and not any democratic or anti-imperialist essence the SWP might have wished to project onto it – would have been the desired outcome of the 'full-scale national war' the SWP criticised the Arab states for having 'no stomach for'.

While an entire chapter in *Israel: The Hijack State* was given over to investigation of Zionist collaboration with Nazism, not a single mention was made of the collaboration between Hajj Amin al-Husseini, the Grand Mufti of Jerusalem and leading religious figure in the Palestinian Arab national movement, and the Nazis.[74] In 1946 Cliff had denounced al-Husseini as 'the organiser of attacks on Jews in 1920, 1921, 1929 and 1936–39'.[75] Forty years later his comrade John Rose's criticism of al-Husseini appeared to be that he had not organised enough.

Trotskyist perspectives on Israel/Palestine and Zionism were bent out of shape through the 1960s, 70s and 80s, and ultimately distorted beyond all recognition, via accommodation with the campist worldview. Orthodox Trotskyism saw an unfolding 'world revolution', of which forces as diverse as the IRA, Tito's Yugoslavia, Maoism, Arab nationalism, and the military and foreign policy of the USSR itself, could, according to the slant given by different tendencies, all be agents, and of which the wished-for 'Arab revolution' was the Middle Eastern expression.

Although they lamented the 'bureaucratic degeneration' that had occurred in the USSR, leading orthodox Trotskyist theorists such as Ernest Mandel insisted that the Stalinist states still embodied 'the revolution', and 'the contradictions in the Soviet economy' were merely 'those of any society in transition from capitalism to socialism'.[76] The Stalinist leaders of the socialist, anti-imperialist camp were criticised in the way one might criticise the bureaucratic leadership of a trade union or labour party – conservative and conciliating, but still heading organisations that were fundamentally working-class, and potentially socialist, in their class essence.

In the Middle Eastern context, campist dualism decreed that Israel, with its support from the USA, was the imperialist presence, and its opponents were therefore anti-imperialist. The consensus that had prevailed amongst Trotskyists, that the Jewish community in Palestine was a legitimate presence that was entitled to rights, and was itself a site of internal struggle with its own progressive potential, was abandoned. As historian Werner Cohn put it: 'When attacking Israel, it [was] no longer a question of Israeli rulers or Jewish capitalists but rather of Israel *tout court*.'[77]

Of course, material conditions in Israel/Palestine had changed too: the Israeli state consolidated itself as a military force and, in 1967, won a war of territorial conquest and became an occupying power. But those developments only justify a revision of the prior recognition of the legitimacy of Israeli-Jewish nationhood if one believes national rights are contingent on the military policy of a state, rather than a democratic entitlement.

On the British left, throughout the 1970s, 80s and 90s, it was often Trotskyist organisations that were most vigorous in the promotion of a campist, implicitly or explicitly antisemitic, anti-Zionism and anti-imperialism. In the 1960s and 70s the CPGB's *Daily Worker* and *Morning Star* were less shrilly anti-Israel than the *Socialist Worker* and the WRP's *News Line*. Once much of world Trotskyism had assimilated to the campist worldview, it took up claims originating in Stalinist anti-Zionism and Arab nationalism. Its critique of Stalinism often centred on the argument that it was too conciliating and conservative a force within a campist schema – that its geopolitical jockeying would hold back or sell out the 'world revolution', and the 'Arab revolution'. Rather than rejecting Stalinist-derived, campist anti-imperialism altogether, the critique of the role of Stalinism in world politics was that it wasn't vigorously anti-imperialist, in a campist sense, enough.[78]

A parallel and contemporaneous development helping to consolidate campist anti-imperialism and anti-Zionism, particularly in the 1960s and 70s, was the growth of what came to be called the 'New Left'. Tendencies within this milieu broke from what they saw as 'Old Left' orthodoxy that saw organised labour and class struggle as the historic agents of social change. Many young radicals began to view other forces, including anti-colonial and anti-imperialist revolts in the global south, as the key agents of progress. Despite 'Communist'-led anti-colonial movements relying on the USSR for financial and political support, national liberation leaders like Che Guevara and Ho Chi Minh had a radical appeal, and a genuine courage, that the stuffy bureaucrats of the Eastern Bloc did not.

For some on the New Left, the Jewish – or 'Zionist' – presence in Palestine was no different from the American presence in Vietnam: a colonising invasion that should be militarily repulsed. Thus, Jewish communal institutions were legitimate targets for anti-imperialist struggle because of their links to

Zionism and Israel. Prominent West German New Left activist Dieter Kunzelmann criticised the 'Jew hang-up' of the wider West German left, and in 1969 Kunzelmann's organisation, Tupamaros West-Berlin, an anti-imperialist cell committed to military tactics, carried out a failed bombing of a Jewish community centre.[79] And although influenced by Maoism, much New Left thinking saw itself as anti-Stalinist, or at least non-Stalinist. Nevertheless, the spread of such thinking, and the retreat from class politics it expressed, helped strengthen a two-camps worldview.

Much of orthodox Trotskyism shared the New Left's enthusiasm for the radical Stalinist-nationalists, and other anti-imperialist nationalist movements. The book *50 Years of World Revolution*, published in 1968 by the printing press of the Trotskyist Fourth International, then represented in Britain by the International Marxist Group (IMG), was dedicated to, amongst others, Che Guevara.[80] In the 1970s, enthusiasm for Arab nationalism, especially as a carrier of world-historic anti-imperialist progress, led the WRP to seek formal links with, and patronage from, Muammar Qaddafi and Saddam Hussein.

The WRP published pamphlets that lauded Qaddafi, Hussein and the regimes they led, paid for with funds from those regimes. It denounced 'Zionist' opposition to those regimes, and even sent photographers to a demonstration in London organised by left-wing Iraqi dissidents to take photos of the attendees, which were then passed on to the regime.[81] It saw the appointment of Stuart Young, who was Jewish, as chair of the BBC's board of governors, as evidence of a Zionist conspiracy. *Labour Herald*, the newspaper the WRP had launched with Ken Livingstone, published cartoons showing Menachem Begin in SS uniform, giving the Nazi salute. The Labour MP Reg Freeson, a rival of Ken Livingstone's in Brent East Labour Party, was frequently referred to by the WRP simply as 'the Zionist Freeson'.[82] Freeson was indeed a Zionist – a left-Zionist, who chaired the Labour-affiliated British section of Poale

Zion, a predecessor of today's Jewish Labour Movement. Freeson also opposed much Israeli policy, including Israel's 1982 invasion of Lebanon. The WRP's badging of him as 'the Zionist Freeson' was not a rational critique of his politics, but a euphemism for 'the Jew Freeson'.

Formally, the SWP rejected the orthodox Trotskyist view, held by the WRP, IMG and others, that the Stalinist states were workers' states, and the campist view that the world could be understood as divided into imperialist and anti-imperialist blocs. But it also saw an anti-imperialist, and implicitly cross-class, Arab revolution, rather than a working-class, socialist revolution, which could comprise Jewish workers as well as Arab, as the agency for progress in the Middle East. These tensions were eventually resolved in favour of a thoroughgoing campism when the SWP pivoted to a more explicitly two-camps view of world imperialism. In 1987 it junked its prior policy of opposition to both states in the Iran–Iraq war, and switched to a policy of support for Iran, on the basis that Iraq was backed by the US and was therefore the 'imperialist' side in the conflict, saying 'we have no choice but to support the Khomeini regime'.[83]

## THE STOP THE WAR COALITION, JEREMY CORBYN, AND CAMPISM

Campist anti-imperialism continued to dominate much far-left thinking on international issues into the 1990s and 2000s, in conflicts such as Serbia (1999), Afghanistan (2001), Iraq (2003), Syria (2010 onwards), the Crimea (2014) and others. That campism frequently saw sections of the left act as apologists for explicitly antisemitic political forces, including various political Islamist movements, the Islamic Republic of Iran and the Ba'athist regimes in Iraq and Syria.

The core leadership of the Stop the War Coalition (StWC), founded in 2001, consisted of an alliance between the SWP and

Andrew Murray – self-proclaimed Trotskyists conducting their primary political activity in close collaboration with Stalinists, on the basis of a shared two-camps worldview.[84] Jeremy Corbyn was an initial sponsor of the StWC, and its chair from 2011, working closely with Murray and with Counterfire, the group founded when the main SWP leaders involved in StWC split from the SWP in 2010. A clear indication of its campism came in 2013, when it invited Mother Agnes Mariam de la Croix, a Melkite nun and prominent supporter of the Assad regime, to address a conference, prompting other speakers, including the journalist and activist Owen Jones, to withdraw.[85]

In 1946 Tony Cliff had called the Muslim Brotherhood, one of the oldest Islamist movements, 'clerical fascist'.[86] But in 2003 the StWC allied with the Muslim Association of Britain (MAB), a British group linked to the Brotherhood, previously politically marginal and helped to much greater prominence by the leg-up given them by the SWP. The SWP subsequently launched Respect, an electoral coalition based substantially on appeals to Muslim communalism, again in alliance with figures from MAB. Respect was headed by George Galloway, famous for saluting the 'strength, courage, and indefatigability' of Saddam Hussein, with whom Galloway proclaimed he was with 'until Jerusalem'. In 2012 the *Socialist Worker* called for a vote for the Brotherhood's Mohammed Mursi in the Egyptian presidential elections.[87]

In 2006, on StWC-organised demonstrations against Israel's bombing of Lebanon, banners, placards and chants proclaiming 'we are all Hezbollah' were widespread. Richard Seymour, then a prominent SWP member, reporting on one such demonstration, wrote:

> Israel is a terrorist state, and we will support the Lebanese resistance, including Hezbollah. [...] It was a real pleasure to hear thousands of people yelling ['we are all Hezbollah']

outside the American Embassy. [...] George [Galloway] said
Hezbollah is not and never has been a terrorist organisation.
I endorse that. [...] Hezbollah was formed to resist Israel,
which it has done admirably over a couple of decades, finally
driving Israel out of the south of Lebanon in 2000. I did not,
I regret to say, get footage of Andrew Murray reading out an
address from Hezbollah.[88]

The positive content of Hezbollah's social programme is
reactionary religious sectarianism, for which 'clerical fascism',
Cliff's label for the Brotherhood, is not hyperbole. This did not
trouble Seymour. The mere fact of its opposition to Israel was
enough to position Hezbollah in the camp of anti-imperialist
resistance and progress, and justify support. This vignette – a
prominent SWP member deriving 'real pleasure' from chants
of 'we are all Hezbollah', and regretting that they failed to film
Andrew Murray, a Stalinist, reading out an address directly from
Hezbollah – provides as succinct and clear an expression of the anti-
imperialism of fools as one could possibly wish to find.

Campist anti-imperialism, so mechanical as to be ahistorical,
continues to inform assessments of Israel/Palestine that are prominent on the far left. In 2020, an article in the *Socialist Worker*
argued that 'the British Empire decided to back the Zionist movement – settlers who moved to Palestine to establish an exclusively
Jewish state – in 1917. Those settlers helped the British Empire
keep control of Palestine in the first half of the twentieth century.'[89] Elsewhere, another *Socialist Worker* contributor has written
that 'the British signed a declaration supporting the creation of a
Jewish state in Palestine – knowing this would mean the expulsion of Palestinians'.[90]

Significant historical elisions are taking place here. In 1917,
at the time of the Balfour Declaration, the British Empire did
not control Palestine, so was hardly in a position to gift it to the

Jews. The declaration supported a 'national home', not a 'state'. It is not that the Balfour Declaration played no role in the creation of Israel; clearly it did. But the drawing of a straight line from the Balfour Declaration and the creation of the Israeli state, without taking account for changes in British colonial policy, or, indeed, what happened to the Jews of Europe in the meantime that might have made them eager to emigrate to Palestine, has the effect of ripping the development of Israeli-Jewish nationhood out of its actual historical context.

We have here a version – paler, but bearing the same essential shape – of the old Stalinist idea that the creation of Israel and the expulsion of Palestinians was an imperialist plot – rather than the result of conflict between competing nationalist claims, both of which were, at various times, sponsored, and played off against each other, by the rival imperialisms of big powers. In the SWP's version, the plot was hatched by British imperialism in 1917 and eventually reached fulfilment in 1948 – even though British imperialism, by that time, was militarily opposing the Zionists. In this view, history becomes not a matter of conflict between forces representing contesting interests – not only states but classes, national groups and political movements – but a process driven conspiratorially by 'imperialism', a somehow singular and historically transcendent force.

During Jeremy Corbyn's 2015 leadership campaign, and following his victory, many leftists who had quit Labour during the New Labour years, or become inactive, were drawn back to membership and activity, and others who had never previously oriented to the Labour Party now did so. These were older activists, with long-standing, if sometimes interrupted, experience on the organised left, with all its biases and accumulated common sense. A demographic study of the 'Corbyn surge' showed that 93.6 per cent of those rejoining the party after 2015, and 69.1 per cent of those joining it for the first time, were over forty-six years old. The average age of returning members was sixty-one; for new joiners the average was fifty-two.[91]

It was a surge in which both returners and new joiners were motivated by sincere aspirations for progressive change, and which contained enormous potential for opening up new political horizons. But it also meant that people whose views were likelier to have been to some degree shaped by campist anti-imperialism, including absolute anti-Zionism, were now a more vigorous element within Labour Party political life, in meetings and in online discourse, than previously.

Jeremy Corbyn himself can hardly be called a Stalinist: in 1984 he co-signed a letter denouncing the Polish regime's supplying of coal to Britain during the miners' strike, and its repression of the mass independent workers' movement Solidarność.[92] In 1989 he signed an Early Day Motion welcoming 'the magnificent movements in Eastern Europe for full democratic control over what happens in society', and recognising 'that this outburst of discontent and opposition in East Germany and Czechoslovakia, in particular, reflects deep anger against the corruption and mismanagement of the Stalinist bureaucracy'.[93] In February 2021 he lent his support to campaigning against the Chinese state's repression of the independent labour movement in Hong Kong.[94]

But Corbyn has also been a consistent supporter of the *Morning Star* and a regular guest on the Iranian state's Press TV, on which he asserted, in 2012, that he suspected 'the hand of Israel' was behind terrorist attacks in Egypt.[95] He said he hoped to welcome the Palestinian Islamist Raed Salah, to Parliament, and called Hamas and Hezbollah 'friends'.[96] In 2007 Salah gave a sermon in which he said people 'should ask what happened to some of the European children whose blood was mixed with flour for use in holy bread', widely interpreted as an endorsement of the 'blood libel' claims of Medieval Christian antisemitism that Jews used the blood of Christian children to make matzah, the unleavened bread eaten during the festival of Passover.[97] In 2011 Corbyn wrote in his *Morning Star* column that Salah's was a voice 'that needs to be heard', and said 'it's time that Western governments stood up to the Zionist lobby which seems to conflate criticism of Israel with antisemitism'.[98]

Without question, Corbyn's thinking on international issues is substantially shaped by campist anti-imperialism. And, as noted by David Renton, in office he chose to 'surround himself with a number of people whose politics were […] campist'.[99] Given contemporary left antisemitism's intrinsic link to the anti-imperialism of fools, it was therefore little wonder that Corbyn proved unable to consistently confront it – or, often, even recognise it.

## LOOKING AHEAD

Although it is rarely clear from the tone and emphasis of its writing on the topic, the formal policy of the CPB, the most prominent and influential surviving splinter of official Stalinism, is to support a two-states settlement in Israel/Palestine.[100] The CPB is linked to Maki, the Israeli Communist Party, whose electoral front Hadash is an important force on the Israeli left, and which supports equal national rights for Israeli Jews and Palestinians.[101] The historic role of official Stalinism in Israel itself, and how Israeli-Jewish Stalinists attempted to reconcile their support for the USSR with its shifting policies on Israel and Zionism and its antisemitic propaganda campaigns, are matters worthy of specific consideration and about which there is a significant literature.[102]

While the overwhelming majority of the *Morning Star*'s coverage of antisemitism in Labour has been denialist in tone and has sought to downplay the issue or present it as a smear, prominent CPB members Mary Davis and Phil Katz have spoken out against left antisemitism.[103] Nevertheless, it is clear that the key themes of contemporary left antisemitism have their origins in

Stalinism's anti-Zionist campaigns of the 1950s onwards, and sit within the geopolitical framework of campist anti-imperialism. Moreover, the historical record shows that, although its anti-Israel agitation was sometimes less shrill than that of the WRP, IMG and SWP, the CPGB variously either reproduced, in part or in full, arguments from those campaigns, suppressed criticism of them or simply ignored them. Leftists who maintain an affinity with the official Communist Party tradition but are critical of left antisemitism need to reckon with this ugly truth about their own tendency's history – and, hopefully, draw some practical conclusions, just as the Jewish dissidents who broke from the CP in the 1950s over the issue of antisemitism did.

Burying the legacy of Stalinism, and definitively rejecting campist anti-imperialism, is necessary for transforming the left into a movement capable of making effective solidarity with struggles for freedom across the world. Although US imperialism remains dominant, the world is increasingly multipolar, with China challenging the US on the global stage and states like Russia, Iran, Turkey and Saudi Arabia increasingly influential as regional-imperialist powers. A consistently anti-imperialist policy means opposing *all* imperialisms, not designating smaller-power, regional imperialism as relatively progressive against global imperialism. It means supporting movements fighting for democratic freedoms and social equality, rather than lauding antisemitic clerical-fascists or authoritarian nationalists as anti-imperialist heroes. The key fault line in our world is not between imperialist and anti-imperialist camps, but between labour and capital *within* every nation and globally.

Rival states, and rival imperialisms, are not all equally powerful – US capital remains largely hegemonic – but challenges to the hegemonic powers by smaller powers are contention between rival ruling-class forces, not the clash of competing world systems representing progress and reaction. National oppressions, whereby a state suppresses the national rights of an entire national group, still exist, and struggles against such oppression therefore embody a progressive democratic potential. But there is no campist, imperialism versus anti-imperialism, framework into which those oppressions can be slotted. Is Israel's oppression of the Palestinians an 'imperialist' national oppression, because Israel is backed by US imperialism, but China's policy towards the Uyghurs and Tibetans, or Russia's policy towards the Chechens, somehow 'anti-imperialist' because China and Russia challenge US hegemony?

The idea that mere negative opposition to a hegemonic system, such as capitalism or big-power imperialism, is enough to give something a progressive character was anathema to classical Marxism. Marx and Engels dedicated an entire section of the *Communist Manifesto* to a strident critique of various other forms of 'socialism' – 'reactionary socialism', 'petty-bourgeois socialism' and others – which opposed capitalism in the name of a *worse alternative*.[104] Campist anti-imperialism is in essence a form of reactionary anti-imperialism, including a reactionary anti-Zionism. It is a 'nameless, classless, "anti-imperialism", specifying only what it is against'.[105] As Marcel Stoetzler put it: 'It is imperative that those who use "imperialism" as a category of analysis make any support of anti-imperialism dependent on what the specific *social content* of any particular anti-imperialist struggle is: *in the name of which societal goals and to which effects is the struggle being conducted*?'[106]

In the campist worldview, the 'specific social content' of a given anti-imperialist struggle or movement is irrelevant. Its incidental position relative to Western imperialism, of which Zionism is understood either as a wholly contained subset or as the driving force, is all that is required to support and celebrate it. The US *Socialist Worker* can therefore declare: 'We unconditionally support Hamas when it is engaged in military or non-military struggles against Israel, because it weakens the Zionist state.'[107]

The UK *Socialist Worker* can laud Hamas's 'history of resistance',[108] describing it simply as 'an organisation dedicated to defending the right of Palestinians to exist', as if it has no wider political or social programme.[109]

Hamas's 'societal goal' is the construction of a highly repressive, theocratic state, whose use of force is, on a day-to-day level, directed far more against other Palestinians than against Israel. Thus, campism leads its advocates into cheerleading for social and political forces which are explicitly, militantly antisemitic, and whose programme is utterly antithetical to socialism.

A confrontation with left antisemitism's roots in campism is inseparable from a wider confrontation with Stalinism's other enduring legacies – on questions of party, state, nation and more. The Third Camp tradition that proclaimed 'neither Washington nor Moscow, but international socialism', can be a source for theoretical renewal, including in its clarity on Israel/Palestine: opposition to Zionism expressed as chauvinism towards the Palestinians, but support for Israeli-Jewish self-determination as a democratic right.[110]

A left that has meaningfully reckoned with the legacy of Stalinism would be vastly better able to recognise and confront antisemitism. It would also be a more effective force for solidarity not only with the Palestinians, but with the Uyghurs, Chechens, Hong Kongers, Tibetans and other peoples oppressed by allegedly anti-imperialist states, as well as with democratic struggles in countries like Syria and Belarus. Those peoples and movements are surely no less deserving of leftist solidarity than the Palestinian national liberation struggle, their struggles no less expressive of a democratic, emancipatory potential. Expanding the horizons of solidarity can only serve to reinforce it. And a consistently democratic internationalism, which opposes all oppressions and imperialisms on the basis of support for equal rights for all peoples, is a far surer foundation for that solidarity than the anti-imperialism of fools which the left inherits from Stalinism.

# CHAPTER FIVE

# TOWARDS AN 'ANTI-ZIONIST ZIONISM'

In 2019 The Canary responded to the BBC *Panorama* documentary 'Is Labour Antisemitic?' by 'exposing' the fact that several of the Jewish contributors were members of the 'anti-Corbyn' Jewish Labour Movement (JLM). One contributor's previous job at the Israeli Embassy, and another's job working for the Board of Deputies of British Jews, the main Jewish communal organisation in Britain, were similarly 'exposed'.[1]

The positioning of the JLM on the centre-right of the Labour Party's internal political spectrum is no secret. Undoubtedly, some of its members did and do have a more generalised opposition to Corbyn and the left. But the claim that this means that whatever they have to say about antisemitism can be dismissed out of hand is dangerous and wrong. The argument was, in effect, that Jews must pass a political loyalty test, and be deemed sufficiently 'pro-Corbyn' and anti-Zionist, before they are permitted to speak about antisemitism without being immediately accused of ulterior, conspiratorial, motives. This is a political trap that renders the vast majority of Jews, who are not left-wing anti-Zionists, essentially fair game: say whatever you like about the – bad, Zionist – Jews, because if they object or complain, that will merely confirm their malicious, anti-left scheming.

If there is an approximate equivalent to this in recent political discourse, it is the demand sometimes levelled at Muslims that they publicly disavow Islamism before being granted social permission to talk about anti-Muslim discrimination and prejudice. The left has rightly called this out, but sections of it replicate exactly the same logic when it comes to Jews. We, the left, *should* oppose Israel's oppressive policies, and oppose Islamism, and seek to persuade others – including Jews and Muslims – to disavow them too. But this should be because of positive commitments to values to which those things run counter, not as a loyalty test demanded before people will be listened to when speaking about bigotry they face.

The need to assert Jews' right to speak on antisemitism without being interrogated about their views on Israel is sometimes presented as an argument that tackling antisemitism must be strictly decoupled from *any* political discussion about Israel/Palestine, Zionism or anti-Zionism. The impulse is understandable. A reflexive insistence that every discussion of antisemitism *must* become a discussion of policy for Israel/Palestine can be part of the problem, linked to notions of collective Jewish responsibility for the policies of Israel, which Jews must first performatively disavow or apologise for before being allowed to speak about antisemitism.

However, while the idea of collective Jewish responsibility for Israel must certainly be rejected, including when implied by the Israeli government itself, a strict separation between a discussion of the history and politics of Israel/Palestine and a discussion of antisemitism on the left is, ultimately, not possible. As the place of origin of Judaism as an ethnic religion, Jews have had a cultural and religious connection to what is now Israel/Palestine for centuries and, as we have seen in Chapter Four, left antisemitism since the 1950s has been so closely bound up with narratives about Israel/Palestine and Zionism that the issues cannot be considered in abstraction.

Indeed, the history of European antisemitism has flowed into the history of Israel/Palestine. The Palestinian poet and activist Mahmoud Darwish, widely regarded as Palestine's national poet, said, in an interview with the French-Israeli-Jewish actor Sarah Adler:

> Do you know why we Palestinians are famous? Because you are our enemy. The interest in us stems from the interest in the Jewish question. [...] We have the misfortune of having Israel as an enemy because it enjoys unlimited support. And we have the good fortune of having Israel as our enemy because the Jews are the centre of world attention. You've brought us defeat and renown.[2]

The questions are not identical. But, as the Lebanese writer Joey Ayoub has said, history has substantially 'interlinked' the Jewish question, which is in large part the question of how to respond to antisemitism, and the Palestinian question.[3] This does not mean that antisemitism must be viewed through the prism of Israel/Palestine; antisemitism far predates the modern concepts of both 'Israel' and 'Palestine'. Nor does it mean that antisemitism is a 'response' to events in Israel/Palestine, or that the struggle for Palestinian national rights must be viewed through the prism of antisemitism. But it does mean that consideration of each question must involve consideration of the other.

This chapter will argue that a politics of equal rights, including equal national rights, and consistent solidarity can overcome the antisemitism implicit in some far-left thinking about Israel/Palestine, and thus take an approach to both the Jewish question and the Palestinian question consistent with socialist principles of equality and democracy.

It is necessary at the outset to state some fundamental perspectives – not as qualifications or caveats required to gain permission to discuss antisemitism, but so readers are absolutely clear about the principles that inform and underlie my analysis. I hope that this book will be read by people who bring to it widely differing beliefs about Israel/Palestine – both those with some affinity with Israel, especially in Jewish communities, and those whose thinking is shaped by the absolute, unqualified forms of anti-Zionism prevalent on the far left.

If it does not sound too grandiose an aim, I hope to persuade both to question those beliefs. In both cases, they may proceed from understandable impulses: a sensitivity and opposition to historic antisemitism in the former, a vigorous opposition to the oppression of the Palestinians in the latter. Both of those impulses are legitimate; they are not mutually exclusive, and neither support for Israeli policy nor absolute anti-Zionism serves them well.

Two peoples – Palestinian Arabs and Israeli Jews – inhabit the territory of historic Palestine. Both these peoples are national groups – a group that speaks a shared language, has a shared culture and collective history, inhabits a discrete territory, is internally class-differentiated and sees itself as a nation. As argued in Chapter One, nationhood is a construct, an 'imagined community', but it is a construct that cannot simply be wished out of existence.

Between those two national peoples there exists a gross disparity of rights. The fundamental relation of power is not a conflict between equally matched sides, but one of national oppression, with the Israeli state blocking the full expression of Palestinians' right to national self-determination. The endeavour of socialist politics as it relates to Israel/Palestine must be to support a levelling up of rights, including national rights, between the two peoples, so that unity and common struggle between Israeli-Jewish and Palestinian-Arab workers, a necessary condition for the ultimate success of socialist politics, can be built free from the toxifying influence of colonialism and national oppression.

This is the approach most consistent with the attitude of the majority policy of the pre-Stalinist revolutionary socialist tradition to questions of national oppression, summarised in Karl

Marx's phrase 'a nation that oppresses another forges its own chains'. Lasting peace, security and freedom for Israeli Jews is possible only within a framework that guarantees those same rights to Palestinians. Leon Trotsky also expressed the classical socialist attitude to national oppression when he wrote:

> The removal of any, even disguised, even the most refined and practically 'imponderable' national oppression or indignity, must be used for the revolutionary unification rather than the segregation of the workers of various nationalities. Wherever national privileges and injuries exist, nations must have the possibility to separate from each other, that thus they may facilitate the free unification of the workers, in the name of a close rapprochement of nations, with the distinct perspective of the eventual complete fusion of all.[4]

## FOR EQUAL RIGHTS

Contemporary national oppression in Israel/Palestine is neither 'disguised' nor 'refined'. It is not an abstract constitutional arrangement, but a concrete, material reality that has scarred the lives of generations of Palestinians, towards whom the state of Israel has been a brutal power. In the course of the war surrounding its foundation, the Palestinians suffered ethnic cleansing and displacement, refugees from which, and their descendants, have often continued to live in desperate conditions, an injustice for which both Israel and the cynical politicking of neighbouring authoritarian regimes, which have denied equality to Palestinian refugees, share responsibility.

Since 1967 Palestinians have been subjected to direct military occupation and blockade. The Palestinian minority inside pre-1967 Israel has faced intense racism and discrimination. For decades, via such mechanisms as the sponsoring of settlement expansion, house demolitions in the West Bank and bombardments of Gaza, Israeli policy has sought to atomise the material basis for a viable Palestinian national entity. In May 2021, Israeli bombing of Gaza killed 256 people, including sixty-six children. In all of this, the Israeli state has been motivated by what Edward Said called 'an utter refusal to accept the sovereign existence of a Palestinian people that is entitled to rights over […] the West Bank and Gaza'.[5]

The left must support the Palestinian people's struggle to claim those rights. Nothing written in this chapter, or elsewhere in this book, is an argument for tempering that support, which must be full-throated and active. On the contrary, this chapter in particular aims to affirm that necessity. A politics of solidarity that does not license antisemitic variants of anti-Zionism as legitimate forms of opposition to Israeli state oppression will be more effective than one that does, as well as more consistent with socialist aims and principles. Despite its 'pseudo-emancipatory' claims, antisemitism – like all forms of chauvinism, bigotry and racism – cannot be made to serve genuinely emancipatory ends, including the Palestinian struggle for self-determination and equality. Instances of antisemitism within movements of solidarity with the Palestinians are not merely bad PR, they are politically disorienting and toxifying. Oppression cannot be fought on the basis of a politics that advocates the oppression of others.

Socialists, as people seeking to develop a worldview, have a duty to assess history in its totality, in all its complexity. Abstracting the history of Israel/Palestine from the history of world events, and from the historical experiences of both the Jewish and Arab peoples, cuts against the development of an egalitarian politics and feeds a politics based on, usually vicarious, chauvinism. Socialist opposition to national oppression must be motivated by the principle that all peoples and communities are entitled to equal rights, and that justice comes from the levelling up of rights.

Left antisemitism arises not from vigorous opposition to Israeli state policy, but from an abandonment of consistent democracy, and its replacement with campist historiographies, which are used to inform reactionary political conclusions.

The prevalent historical-political perspective towards Israel across much of the far left is summed up by the statement 'There can be no peace while the state of Israel continues to exist.'[6] In other words, Israel is an illegitimate presence. Although it can be given a different twist depending on the context, the popular slogan 'from the river to the sea, Palestine will be free' can also imply that it is not Israel's policies of occupation or anti-Arab discrimination that make Palestinians unfree, but Israel's very existence – on *any* territory 'from the [Jordan] river to the [Mediterranean] sea', i.e. the whole of historic Palestine. There is no place for a national entity based on the Jewish population – or, in some extreme versions of the position, for Jewish presence in the region at all.

Nahuel Moreno, an Argentinian Trotskyist leader whose political descendants are a relatively significant force on the far left in some South American countries, encapsulated this position clearly, advancing the slogan 'Zionists out of Israel'. What should happen to 'the Zionists' if they refused to leave was strongly implied: 'Arab racism against Israel is progressive: it destroys the Zionist state.'[7] In May 2021 an article on the Left Voice website, which has origins in the 'Morenoite' tradition, suggested 'Free swimming lessons for Zionists!' should accompany the 'from the river to the sea' slogan on demonstrations.[8]

The Socialist Workers Party in the UK opposes the existence of Israel. It says it supports 'a single, secular state with equal democratic rights for all its citizens'.[9] But if the right to national self-determination, surely a 'democratic right' in itself, is denied to either one of the two national peoples in Israel/Palestine, a single state will not be 'equal'. It is also not clear how the SWP reconciles its professed support for a 'secular' state with its support for

Hamas, a party with a foundational hostility to secularism, which aims to create a theocratic state.

Underlying the claim of the essential illegitimacy of Israel is the idea that it is an artificial creation or implantation of imperialism, rather than a state based on a legitimate national community entitled to democratic rights. Often, British imperialism is held accountable, usually because of the Balfour Declaration, and sometimes Zionism itself is claimed to have manipulated imperialist policy, owing to the presence of 'multimillionaires of Jewish origin' amongst the imperialist ruling classes.[10] Chapter Four examined the essentially Stalinist origins of this perspective. This chapter seeks to further explain what is antisemitic about those arguments, and argue for an alternative political perspective based on solidarity and advocacy of equal rights.

The state of Israel was not created by Britain. British policy oscillated on the question of Jewish immigration to, and settlement in, Palestine, initially supporting and encouraging it. British colonial authorities were often the direct agents of the displacement of Arab communities who lived on land that had been sold to Jewish settlers, who had been promised they would receive the land empty.

But in 1929 an Arab attack on Jews in Hebron mobilised under slogans including 'The British are with us!' By the 1940s, keen to maintain its own colonial interests and gambling that the semi-feudal Arab ruling classes might be more reliable partners than Jewish settlers, British policy had shifted decisively to opposing unrestricted Jewish immigration and taking measures to limit it. British colonial authorities blocked shiploads of Holocaust refugees attempting to reach Palestine and detained them in camps on Cyprus. In 1947–8, British intelligence services went as far as to organise the bombing of ships docked in Italy, which were preparing to bring Holocaust refugees to Palestine. British officers led regiments in the Arab armies in the 1948 war.

This is not to suggest that the Arab side in the 1948 war was merely a cat's paw for British imperialism, or that British imperial policy played no role in the process of Israel's national formation. The period of British colonial support for Jewish immigration undoubtedly contributed to the establishment of a viable Jewish national community in Palestine. But narratives that see Israel as having been directly created by the reified agency of imperialism, and British imperialism specifically, are simplistic and imbalanced. They erase from the picture the national aspirations of the Jews of Palestine – which, whatever one thinks about their legitimacy, cannot be dismissed as merely an imperialist plot.

In considering this history, both campist anti-Zionists and those who believe reformist social democracy represents a pristine alternative tradition, untainted by the left antisemitism held to be the preserve of the revolutionary left, should question their assumptions. The campist anti-Zionist should see that British imperialism, far from directly 'creating Israel', acted in its own interests, playing national communities against each other, attempting classic colonial tactics of divide-and-rule, and behaving foully towards Jewish refugees from Nazism.

The true – complex, contradictory and shifting – nature of Zionism's relationship with imperialism and colonialism, similar to that of many other national movements, can thus be brought into the light, affirming its status as a genuine nationalism, rather than a hyper-imperialist conspiracy. National movements of both Jews and Arabs have, at various points throughout history, been both allies and opponents of competing imperialisms – British, American, Russian and others. That fact does not give either people an 'imperialist' or 'anti-imperialist' essence, nor negate their basic entitlement to democratic rights.

The social democrat, who claims to uphold a mainstream Labour tradition from which the bogey figure of Corbyn was held to be deviating, should remember which party oversaw

Britain's colonial policy at the time of Israel's foundation. As John Strawson put it:

> Many of those in the Labour Party who opposed Jeremy Corbyn's leadership lionised [Clement] Attlee. Corbyn has sided with Israel's military opponents such as Hamas and Hezbollah and oversaw Labour antisemitism that caused Jewish members of the Labour Party great discomfort and discrimination while poisoning political discourse. However, he was never in a position to prevent Holocaust survivors from reaching safety, to arm states waging war against the Jewish state, or to refuse to support Israel's UN membership. That was the role that Clement Attlee played.[11]

The existence of the state of Israel is a product of *the effects of imperialism on Jews*, as much, if not more than, a product of the shifting colonial policies of any then-existing empire. As such, the primarily culpable imperialism is Nazism, and arguably Tsarism before it. Had it not been for those acts of violent oppression, displacement and attempted extermination, the material basis for the state of Israel – large numbers of Jews emigrating or fleeing to Palestine, convinced of the need to exercise their right to self-determination there – could not have existed. Who does not wish it otherwise? As the Polish-Jewish leftist Isaac Deutscher, best known as the biographer of Trotsky, wrote, 'it would have been better had Israel remained unborn and the six million Jews stayed alive'.[12] But the history of the twentieth century unfolded as it did, not as internationalist leftists would have wished.

The denial of this reality has the effect of erasing from the historical page one of the most traumatic experiences any people has ever suffered. It reduces the Holocaust to the status of a 'virtual fact', the occurrence of which is acknowledged, but the impact of which on subsequent events, or the consciousness of those affected, is denied.[13] A politics which demands that Israel cease to exist as a precondition of any form of progress must first account for how it intends to transport us to a world in which the Holocaust did not happen. Israel's existence, and the very existence of the Israeli Jews as a national people, is so bound up with a history of persecution and genocide that a politics which insists on Israel's innate illegitimacy is almost inevitably heard by many Jews as an insensitivity to that history. When the shriller, but in some ways more honest, advocates of the anti-imperialism of fools fantasise about rerunning the war of 1948 with the outcomes reversed, what else will Jews hear but support for antisemitism?

Many on the left seem incapable, or unwilling, to acknowledge the reasons why their experiences of persecution might have led many Jews to reach nationalist, statist and even militarist conclusions about their own safety. But one way in which some on the left *do* connect Israel and the Holocaust is by comparing its conduct with that of Nazis. As well as being inaccurate, these comparisons often either implicitly or explicitly claim that Jews should somehow 'know better' than to oppress Palestinians because of their own historic experiences of oppression. In May 2021, for example, veteran leftist Tariq Ali used his speech at the rally of a mass pro-Palestine demonstration to proclaim that Israelis 'had learnt nothing from what happened to them in Europe. Nothing.'[14] The idea that the experience of attempted genocide is a form of moral instruction from which one should learn certain lessons, and then be held to a higher moral standard if one fails to do so, is particularly obscene.

Although there has been a continuous Jewish presence in historic Palestine for millennia, Jewish incomers to the territory during the twentieth century were not merely immigrants seeking citizenship in some other state. Zionism was a settler nationalism, rather than one that aimed to found an independent state in a territory with an existing Jewish-majority population. Jewish immigrants to Palestine frequently acted as all settlers throughout history have, and displaced communities already living in the territory they arrived in. But, unlike the French in Algeria and the British in India, there was no imperial metropole to which these colonists, many of them survivors of pogroms and death camps, could return. In this history, the distinction between 'settler' and 'refugee' is blurred. Jewish immigrants to Palestine were, in essence, both.

The origins of Zionism, and the state of Israel, in Jewish experiences of oppression do not justify the ethnic cleansing that took place as part of Israel's formation, or the Israeli state's contemporary oppressive policies. Nor do they imply that the Palestinians must give up the struggle for their own rights because the forebears of their oppressors were themselves oppressed. But a left which aims to transform consciousness cannot do so without an understanding of existing consciousness. As the Palestinian writer Iyad el-Baghdadi put it, responding to an interlocutor describing Israel as 'the epitome of hate': 'Israel is the epitome of hurt. You will not understand Israel without understanding how a Jewish person felt in 1945. Two third[s] of all Israeli soldiers who expelled us from our homes in 1948 had either survived or fled the Holocaust just a few years earlier.'[15]

The acute asymmetry of the contemporary relationship between Israel and the Palestinians – a heavily armed regional power with an essentially first-world economy versus a subjugated and dispossessed people – can lead to an understandable instinct to baulk at the idea that the left should have any consideration of both sides in our perspectives towards the issue. 'We can't "both sides" colonialism', the argument goes.[16] That is true on its own terms; in the immediate situation of national oppression, the left should be on the side of the Palestinians against the oppressive power, the Israeli state, in their struggle for independence and self-determination.

But this does not mean the left should be against the *people* of Israel, and their right to self-determination, in some intrinsic, essential sense – to move from opposition to Israeli nationalism, chauvinism and colonialism to straightforward 'anti-Israelism'.[17] Opposition to Israeli policy no more necessitates opposition to Israeli-Jewish self-determination than opposition to the oppression of, for example, the Tamils necessitates opposition to Sinhalese rights, or the existence of Sri Lanka. When the left takes sides on the basis of the existing relationship between a state and a national group it oppresses, we are not required to extrapolate from that that the people of that state are transhistorically 'bad', or have given up their own entitlement to democratic rights because their state has acted oppressively. Nor are we required to endorse nationalist arguments that insist entitlement to rights derives solely from who was in a territory first, or who has been there for longest. The construction of categories of 'good' and 'bad' peoples, whose status as good or bad determines whether they deserve rights, is a form of anti-materialist mysticism that belongs to a politics of national and communal chauvinism, not international socialism.

For rights to be meaningful, they must be universal. Keith Kahn-Harris emphasises the importance of this universalist, rather than particularist, advocacy of democratic, including national, rights, with reference to Palestine:

> Pro-Palestinian campaigners understandably try and demonstrate why Palestinian society and culture is worth fighting for. Yet to make the case for Palestinian liberation in terms of the excellence of their poetry, their heroic resilience, and the worthiness of their political movements, is ultimately to weaken the Palestinian cause. The corollary of such arguments is that if the Palestinians were culturally uninteresting, hate-filled extremists they would be unworthy of liberation

– which is, in fact, a common argument made by some defenders of Israel.

Rights, in other words, are not afforded on the basis of whether a group is 'good' or 'bad'. As Kahn-Harris continues:

Liberation is not a reward for good behaviour but a human right. [...] This also acts as a paradoxical guarantee to Palestinians: that they will not be abandoned when they become politically inconvenient (like Palestinians in Syria have) and that if a future Palestinian state was to oppress certain kinds of people, they would not be forgotten.[18]

In its attitude to Israeli-Jewish self-determination, much of the left reduces national rights to precisely the status of a 'reward for good behaviour', to which Israeli Jews are not entitled because of the oppressive policies of their state, or the injustices perpetrated in the process of their state's foundation.

The formation of a Hebrew-speaking Jewish national community in historic Palestine and the foundation of a state based on that community was both a process of settlement that displaced an existing population *and* a flight of oppressed people seeking refuge from persecution and attempted extermination. That flight for refuge did not include only Ashkenazi Jews fleeing Europe, but Mizrahi Jews fleeing Middle Eastern and North African countries. In the Nakba, the ethnic cleansing and displacement that took place during the 1948 war around Israel's foundation, 750,000 Palestinians fled, or were driven out of, their homes. In the years around the state of Israel's foundation, a similar number of Jews fled, or were expelled from, Arab countries.

Neither reality justifies or diminishes the other; Palestinian refugees from the Nakba are not responsible for the expulsion of Mizrahi Jews from Middle Eastern countries, any more than they are responsible for the displacement of Ashkenazi Jews from European countries. Nor is this to argue that the Nakba and Jewish flight and expulsion from Arab countries are directly parallel or equivalent events. But these histories reconfirm that both Jewish and Palestinian experience in the Middle East has involved ethnic cleansing and displacement. As Spencer Sunshine put it:

> The important thing here is not to say, 'Israel is not as bad as other countries, so it needs to be let off the hook,' nor is it to say, 'Since some Mizrahi Jews were expelled by Arab countries, it's okay that Palestinians were expelled in the Nakba.' But the question is, 'Why is Israel on the hook when other countries are not?'[19]

In other cases of ethnic cleansing and displacement in the context of wars and inter-communal violence, the left advocates a broad programme of restorative measures, including reparations, repatriation (i.e. return) and demands for full equality in the countries in which refugees and exiles now live. But for the Nakba, much of the far left insists that justice is possible only via a maximal 'right of return', not only for the still-living Palestinian refugees but for all of their descendants, to what is now Israel. This policy belongs to a different discourse than a general advocacy of free movement and open borders, and pits the children and grandchildren of Palestinian refugees from the Nakba against the children and grandchildren of Jewish refugees from the Holocaust and expulsions from Arab countries. It also serves to deflect criticism from governments such as Lebanon's and Syria's, which have denied Palestinian refugees full equality and, in Syria's case, bombed refugee camps.

Amongst Palestinians themselves, the notion of 'return' has, according to polling, a variety of meanings and applications.[20] As with all the injustices of the history of Israel/Palestine, ultimate settlement and redress are possible only via democratic accommodation between the peoples of the region. Without question, lasting peace and justice requires Israeli acknowledgement of the Nakba and a settlement based on meaningful material redress for its victims. As Ayman Odeh, a Palestinian socialist and member of the Knesset (Israeli Parliament) has written: 'True Jewish-Arab partnership begins with mutual recognition of the right of the two peoples, Jewish and Palestinian, to self-definition. Only through recognition and amending the historical injustice can we build together a future of justice, equality, democracy, peace and partnership.'[21]

Internationalists and anti-racists in Israel/Palestine have sought to develop policies that acknowledge the trauma of the Nakba and advocate meaningful redress, without revanchism. The 'Two States, One Homeland: A Land for All' initiative, a joint Israeli-Jewish/Palestinian campaign for a democratic and egalitarian two-states settlement, argues:

> Ignoring [the Palestinian refugee question] is not an option. However, one of our basic principles is that two wrongs don't make a right. Jews will not be driven out of their homes so that their original Palestinian owners may be housed in them.
>
> The wrong will be corrected in two ways. The first: Refugees will receive appropriate monetary compensation. If possible, efforts will be made to rebuild towns or villages in areas that are at present unpopulated. The second: Palestinian refugees, after becoming Palestinian citizens, will have freedom of movement throughout the homeland they have been exiled from. They will be allowed to make long-term visits and work there. A certain percentage of them will receive residential rights even in the first phase, and our vision is that in the future they will all enjoy this right.

But the next stages will be implemented gradually and in agreement.[22]

Instead of endorsing such approaches, many left groups insist on a kind of maximalism, applying to Israel policies and perspectives they have not advocated for similar situations throughout history. As the academics Sina Arnold and Blair Taylor put it:

State foundation and expansion are frequently accompanied by forced population transfers, yet the demand for the right of return for Palestinians is almost exclusively directed at Israel. Although this has been a persistent sticking point holding up negotiations for Palestinian statehood, it is rarely a condition for other partitioned states, for example India and Pakistan. Left discourse also seldom discusses the treatment of Palestinian refugees by other states like Syria and Egypt, or mentions the hundreds of thousands of Jewish refugees exiled from neighbouring Arab countries in the wake of 1948. None of these examples serve as justification for Israeli crimes or any other occupation; rather the lack of attention and activism around them illustrates a profound double standard operating within left political discourse, one that happens to resonate with historical patterns of antisemitic exceptionalism.[23]

## ISRAELI-JEWISH NATIONAL SELF-DETERMINATION: A RACIST ENDEAVOUR?

The argument that Israel's very existence, rather than any particular act or policy, is essentially racist, and should, by implication, therefore be undone, was the political substance underlying much of the largely unedifying debate over the Labour Party's endorsement of the International Holocaust Remembrance Alliance's

(IHRA) 'working definition of antisemitism', which generated a great deal more heat than light. Much of the opposition to endorsement has focused on one particular example in that guidance, that 'claiming a state of Israel is a racist endeavour' could, 'taking into account the overall context', be an example of antisemitism.[24]

Agreeing with the IHRA on this point does not preclude description of Israeli policies as 'racist'. It does not even preclude description of *the* – i.e. the current, existing – 'state of Israel' as 'a racist endeavour'. It merely suggests that arguing that '*a* state of Israel' – that is, *any* state of Israel, *any* expression, at the level of statehood, of Israeli-Jewish national self-determination – *is*, necessarily, automatically, 'a racist endeavour' *could be* antisemitic. And yet a great deal of leftist energy in Labour Party circles has been expended in furious opposition to this clause, demanding the right to denounce Israel as 'a racist endeavour' without ever having to think through the implications of the claim or acknowledge that it *could*, in the context of certain critiques, imply antisemitism.

Israel has racist policies – not only that of occupation in Palestinian territories, but via discrimination against the Palestinian minority within Israel itself. The right to describe those policies as such, the right to name the injustices committed in the process of Israel's foundation as ethnic cleansing, and the right to critique exclusionary and chauvinist conceptions of Israeli nationhood, must be protected as matters of free speech. That means resisting attempts to use IHRA guidance to close down debate about Israel/Palestine, and to turn it from its original intention – guidance – into a statutory code of conduct used to criminalise speech.

But the broader argument here is more than semantic hair-splitting over definite and indefinite articles. The claim that *any* expression of Israeli-Jewish national self-determination is necessarily a 'racist endeavour' implies there is some racist essence to Israeli-Jewish nationhood that exists in abstraction from any concrete racist policy a state of Israel may pursue, or constitutional form it might take. Tony Greenstein, a left-wing activist and prominent denier of even the possibility, let alone the existence, of left antisemitism, has said of Israel: 'There are many repressive states in the world [...] but *there is only one racist state*, there's only one apartheid state.'[25] This statement succinctly encapsulates the claim, key to left antisemitism, that Israel is a unique and singular expression of racism at the level of a nation state. The logical extension is that the vast majority of Jews internationally, who have some level of affinity with Israel, however diffuse or critical, must also therefore be tainted by or complicit in that unique and singular form of racism.

This claim, of an innate, essential illegitimacy, is not a claim the far left generally makes of other national groups, even those whose states have colonised or oppressed other peoples. One proffered justification for this apparent discrepancy is that the Israeli Jews are not, in fact, a national group that should, like all other national groups, be entitled to national self-determination. They are a settler caste, equivalent to whites in apartheid South Africa, by which any expression of self-determination is *necessarily* racist and exclusionary.

Israel's occupation regime shares many operational features with South African apartheid, and the Palestinian minority inside Israel itself faces intense discrimination. Some human rights groups have argued that Israel's policies meet international legal definitions of 'apartheid', given that, despite notional Palestinian self-rule, Israel is the de facto ruling power over an entire territory within which people are formally discriminated against on the basis of their ethnic or national origin.[26]

But on the left, a much more general equivalence between Israel and apartheid South Africa – between Israeli Jews and white South Africans – has frequently been drawn. That equivalence obscures important differences between the two situations.

South African apartheid was a particular social form: the white South Africans were relatively economically homogeneous and a small minority, around 13 per cent at the time of the fall of apartheid, whose rule relied on the exploitation of the labour of the Black majority. Israeli Jews, by contrast, are a fully class-differentiated populous, not a narrow caste, and although many Palestinians work in Israel, the Israeli economy has never relied solely on the exploitation of a Palestinian majority in the way apartheid rested on the backs of Black workers. Indeed, the early Israeli economy was based on an *exclusion* of Arab labour, rather than an exploitation of it – an exclusion that was, shamefully, actively facilitated by the mainstream Israeli labour movement.

A white South African 'nation' could not have survived without the exploitation of Black labour. Therefore, any notion of a distinct form of self-determination for white South Africans, *as* white South Africans, was, indeed, necessarily racist. But an Israel that surrendered its occupation of the West Bank and blockade of Gaza, recognised an independent Palestinian state and granted full civil rights and equality to the Palestinian minority within its own borders, would still be a viable national entity.

The implied democratic solution to South African apartheid was to smash the apartheid state, and institute a democratic system based on equal rights between Black and white South Africans. But a democratic solution based on equal rights in a situation where there are two distinct *national* groups, both with a strong will to self-determine, as opposed to a majority community exploited by a minority caste, must involve equal *national* rights, up to and including the right to an independent state.

It should be noted that there are leftist traditions that reject the principle of national self-determination altogether, and view demands for independent national statehood as reactionary detours that obstruct and divert class struggle. Consistent adherents to these traditions oppose all national claims equally, seeing them as inherently nationalist, and viewing anything other than workers' struggle to overthrow capitalism as a blind alley.[27] One tendency even summarises its position as 'neither Israel nor Palestine'.[28] This perspective, which does not make an exception of Israeli-Jewish nationhood and sees demands for Palestinian statehood as equally distracting from the need to build revolutionary working-class consciousness, is not logically antisemitic, but these traditions are highly minoritarian, and none of the most prominent tendencies on the left that stridently oppose Israeli-Jewish national rights belong to them.

## BOYCOTT ISRAEL?

The aforementioned comparison with apartheid South Africa is what gives the demand to boycott Israel, now dominant across much left-wing and even liberal opinion, its emotional power and apparent logic. If Israel is the contemporary equivalent of South Africa, it can only be right to isolate and boycott it, as part of an ultimate effort to get rid of it. But if the Israeli Jews are a national group, rather than a racial-supremacist minority caste, then the Jewish working class, and internationalist and anti-racist forces within Israeli society, have progressive potential – and not merely in the sense that courageous white South African supporters of Black struggle were progressive, but in the sense of being an agency for transformative change within a distinct national group. They should be made a focus for support and solidarity, not opposed as part of an allegedly illegitimate people, lumped in with their own ruling class, or sacrificed as the acceptable collateral damage of a root-and-branch boycott policy.

Certain targeted boycotts of particular companies have their place in the tactical arsenal of international solidarity movements. Some campaigners advocate targeted boycotts of produce from settlements, the direct outposts of Israeli colonialism. Those are matters of tactical assessment – a different premise entirely from making a comprehensive boycott policy – what Edward Said called an 'unselective boycott of even the name "Israel"'[29] – a non-negotiable political starting point of solidarity.

Palestinian socialist Maisam Jaljuli wrote of her struggles in the left-wing movement Omdim be'Yachad (Standing Together), which organises Israeli Jews alongside Arabs:

> We're affected by BDS [Boycott, Divestment and Sanctions] movements which tell people it's wrong to make direct links with anyone in Israel – which, as a Palestinian citizen of Israel, really makes me sad. We're the people on the ground who are fighting the right wing in Israel, who are opposing the occupation. It's a shame when people refuse to acknowledge us and stand in solidarity with our struggles.[30]

The multinational orchestra, including both Israeli-Jewish and Palestinian-Arab musicians, which Edward Said co-founded with Israeli musician Daniel Barenboim, has also been targeted by BDS activists.[31]

The strong Palestinian support for BDS as the baseline political stance towards Israel is understandable. Neither armed uprising nor diplomatic negotiation has moved the Palestinians much closer to meaningful equality and statehood. BDS provides a clear formula for international supporters of Palestinian rights to take action against Israel. Attempts by various governmental authorities and public bodies, now underway in several countries, to censor and even criminalise advocacy of BDS are grave affronts to free speech, that must be resisted. But defending the right to advocate BDS also means defending the right to contest 'boycott Israel' as a politically and strategically useful starting point.

Demands for sanctions such as arms embargoes, a policy which the left absolutely should advocate, must be separated from a blanket boycott stance. Here, too, the left makes an exception of Israel. No socialist group proposes 'boycott China' as a response to China's oppression of the Uyghurs or its occupation of Tibet, perhaps in part because some on the left have yet to accept the reality of those oppressions, and no group proposes 'boycott India' as the necessary response to Modi and Hindutva. While some Kurdish solidarity groups have proposed a 'boycott Turkey' strategy, this has gained little traction on the left. The contradictions were neatly illustrated by a November 2020 tweet from Jewish Voice for Labour, a group set up to deny and downplay allegations of left antisemitism, which said: 'If you want to celebrate [the Jewish festival of] Chanuka and support BDS, these candles are made in China – we can't certify the working conditions unfortunately.'[32]

My intent here is not to argue for the expansion of boycotts – rather the reverse. In the case of Turkey, India and China, a boycott strategy would counterproductively refocus activity away from practical solidarity with labour movement, left-wing and democratic forces resisting oppression and towards the pursuit of an impossible ethical consumption. It would also make Chinese, Indian and Turkish communities in Britain, who are themselves victims of racism, and for whom boycotting China, India and Turkey would be simply inoperable, objects of suspicion and hostility because of their links to the country targeted for boycott and isolation. Similarly, making a comprehensive boycott of Israel, and the breaking of any and all links with it, a precondition of support for the rights of the Palestinians creates an unnecessary and artificial political test that the vast majority of the world's Jews will almost automatically fail, and therefore risks turning 'boycott Israel' efforts into campaigns that target Jews.

Socialist internationalists might well look forward to a future when a clear separation can be drawn between the Israeli-Jewish nation and diaspora Jewish communities, but the diffuse cultural affinity most Jews undeniably feel for Israel cannot be overcome at will. If the left tells Jews that Israel, flight to which might have been the difference between members of their own families' survival and their murder – but not other states that practise similar policies of national oppression – must be boycotted and isolated, that is far more likely to reinforce nationalist consciousness than help dismantle it.

Some on the left argue that, because BDS is the majority policy of the Palestinian national movement, it is somehow anti-democratic, racist, or even an act of 'scabbing' to oppose it. But supporting a national liberation movement's democratic goals – such as independent statehood – does not compel socialists to support every policy or strategic orientation that movement adopts. Indeed, given that the majority formal policy of the Palestine Liberation Organisation has, since 1993, been for a two-states settlement, any leftist advocating a one-state solution already implicitly accepts the right to dissent from particular policies that a given national liberation movement supports.

In 2006 a proposed motion at a conference of the National Association of Teachers in Further and Higher Education (NATFHE, now part of the University and College Union) called for a boycott of all Israeli individuals and institutions 'that do not publicly disassociate themselves from' Israeli policy. Steve Cohen wrote in response:

> The issue here is loyalty tests. It is being forced into making an open and public political statement not out of principle but out of blackmail. […]
>
> The NATFHE resolution refers to boycotts of individuals and institutions – with the loyalty test applying to both. The Palestinian Campaign for the Academic and Cultural Boycott of Israel (PACBI) has said in support of the boycott 'no Israeli academic body or institution has ever taken a public stand against the military occupation of the West

Bank and Gaza'. This I am sure is true. But it is equally true that in the UK no academic body has taken a stand against the institutionalised racism of immigration control. [...]

Why does not NATFHE campaign for a boycott (not a loyalty test) against UK college institutions for compliance with such racism? In reality NATFHE has for years been accepting the loyalty test set by UK colleges and universities – 'Are you or have you ever been of full immigration status?' It would be interesting to know if NATFHE as an employer demeans itself by complying with immigration legislation (legislation which incidentally would prevent it employing Palestinian asylum seekers fleeing Israeli repression). Perhaps NATFHE should start boycotting itself.[33]

The antisemitic potential of the 'boycott Israel' default is further illustrated by the historic focus of much such activity in Britain on Marks and Spencer (M&S), which has been regularly picketed by the Revolutionary Communist Group and others. M&S sells some Israeli produce, like every other retailer of its type, and has commercial operations in Israel, like every almost every major high-street corporation.

The particular focus on M&S originates in the fact that its former chairman, Israel Sieff, was a prominent Zionist. Michael Marks, one of the co-founders of M&S, was Jewish, and his son Simon appointed Sieff, a childhood friend and business associate, as chairman. Sieff has been dead since 1972, Simon Marks since 1964, Michael Marks since 1907. But these historic associations are enough to make M&S a target, even though, since 2008, M&S has explicitly refused to stock goods from occupied Palestinian territories.[34]

In a Revolutionary Communist Group article justifying M&S as a target for 'boycott Israel' agitation, no event later than 1972 is cited as justification for the focus on M&S. No explanation is given as to how boycotting M&S will make any contribution towards any material improvement in conditions of life for the Palestinians, or exert any pressure on the Israeli government, to which M&S has no links.[35] And if the only qualification necessary to be a target for this agitation is 'historical support for Zionism',[36] then that too is a net wide enough to catch almost all Jews alive.

## ON ANTI-ZIONISM

The far left has not, in general, felt it necessary to express its opposition to specific nationalisms via a discrete political label, still less one that is made a general point of departure, in the way much of the left now does with 'anti-Zionism'. As Martin Thomas puts it:

> [This] implies that there is some political force in the world, 'Zionism', which is such a great and compact power that just to be 'anti' says enough to outline a whole political programme. All the 'Zionists', from the young idealist [...] getting herself or himself arrested for street protests against Israel's recent killings on the Gaza border, to the foulest Israeli chauvinist, to the Jew who does no more than refuse to commit to hating Israel, are bundled together as components of that great and compact power.[37]

Using anti-Zionism as a general political label, implying that there is some way to take an anti-Zionist approach to *all* politics, including those unconnected to the national question in Israel/ Palestine, has an unavoidably antisemitic logic. It inflates Jewish nationalism specifically to the status of a world-shaping power – a status it has only ever held in the antisemitic imagination.

Zionism has been heterogeneous since its emergence as an organised movement in the late nineteenth century. Its various wings were united by the common belief that the Jews constituted a national people, which should self-determine in a national home – and, later, that that national home should be in Palestine. The contemporary far left understood Zionism, broadly, as a Jewish expression of the equivalent forms of nationalism emerging amongst numerous national and proto-national peoples, politically hegemonised by bourgeois elements that aimed to establish a capitalist nation state, but arising from genuine social grievances on the part of an oppressed people. Different strands within the socialist movement took different attitudes to the possibility and desirability of Jewish national self-determination, with some, including the General Jewish Labour Bund (known simply as 'the Bund') arguing that Jews should aspire to cultural autonomy rather than national statehood, and others, while opposing antisemitism and supporting Jewish rights, advocating a form of integrationism that they believed would, in time, resolve the Jewish question.

Early on, Zionism developed a far-left wing, shaped by Poale Zion, an explicitly Marxist party, founded in 1897, which would itself undergo a number of splits along broadly left/right lines. Poale Zion's theorists saw the oppression of Jews as inherent to capitalism, and therefore viewed the struggle for independent Jewish nationhood and the struggle for socialism as fused. Poale Zion members organised detachments to fight in the Bolshevik Red Army during the Russian Civil War, and the left wing of Poale Zion sought affiliation with the Bolshevik-led Third International. Poale Zion supporters staffed a bureau of Jewish affairs, effectively a unit of the civil service, that advised the Bolshevik government on issues affecting Jews, along with supporters of the Bund.

In 1934 Poale Zion supporters in Palestine advocated 'Jewish-Arab workers' solidarity', and argued: 'There is no place [...] for those who are an enemy of Arab workers and their advancement in this land. [We] aim to forge in this land an anti-fascist force against all forms of fascism and chauvinism among the Jewish and Arab publics. We provide brotherly help to victims of fascism and antisemitism.'[38] Today's JLM is connected, via distant political genealogy, to the original Poale Zion: JLM was founded in 1902 as a British section of Poale Zion, which affiliated to the Labour Party in 1920.

There were also binationalist tendencies within Zionism, which advocated a unitary Jewish-Arab state, or confederal models, rather than an independent Jewish state. Zionism also developed a far right, coalescing from the 1920s around Ze'ev Jabotinsky, who was sympathetic to Mussolini, which advocated an aggressively national-chauvinist policy towards Arabs. Partisans of this wing of Zionism committed brutal massacres against Arab communities. Zionists from across the political spectrum were involved in displacements of Arab communities, and the exclusion of Arab labour from the new society they built.

But for increasing numbers of Jews throughout the twentieth century, and especially following the rise of Nazism, Zionism appeared as an ideology of national liberation, the only apparent solution to generations of persecution and oppression. For many others, particularly during and after the Second World War, whether or not they were ideologically convinced nationalists, emigration to Palestine seemed the only way to bid for safety in a world that had witnessed their slaughter, then frequently closed its doors in their faces.

In 1954 Isaac Deutscher encapsulated this feeling:

> For the remnants of European Jewry (is it only for them?) the Jewish state has become an historic necessity. It is also a living reality. [...] From a burning or sinking ship people jump no matter where – onto a lifeboat, a raft or a float. The jumping is for them an 'historic necessity', and the raft is in a sense the basis of their whole existence.[39]

The far left of prior generations, closer to the lived experience of the Holocaust, understood this better. As the US socialist writer Barry Finger puts it, it was a left 'rooted in the intellectual shadow of pre- and post-Holocaust immediacy, where no one […] denied the elemental legitimacy of the Israeli state'.[40] As mentioned in Chapter Four, no prominent tendency on the international far left supported the victory of the Arab armies in the 1948 war. It was understood that the overrunning of the fledgling Jewish nation by an alliance between Arab quasi-feudalism and British colonialism would be a reactionary outcome, and not in the interests of the poor and working classes of either the Arab or the Jewish nations.

The Revolutionary Communist League, the small Trotskyist group in Palestine, denounced what it saw as the Arab League's 'racial war against the Jews of Palestine'. Although they opposed partition – i.e. the creation of separate Arab and Jewish states – they supported 'full national minority rights for the Jewish community', accepting the Jewish presence in Palestine as legitimate and deserving of rights.[41]

The National Liberation League, a Palestinian-Arab communist (i.e. Stalinist) party that emerged from a 1943 split along communal lines in the Palestine Communist Party, also supported mutual national rights and in fact explicitly advocated partition. Although this was in part because of its loyalty to the dictates of Moscow, according to the academic Musa Budeiri in his study of the Palestinian communist movement, 'the same reasons adduced for the adoption of this new line could have been made convincingly a number of years earlier and would have followed quite consistently from the NLL's characterisation of the situation'.[42] This makes clear that opposition to Israeli-Jewish national rights, and insistence on the incompatibility of Israeli-Jewish self-determination with Palestinian-Arab self-determination, has by no means been the unquestioned position amongst left organisations, including left organisations in Palestine.

Much of the far left now categorises Zionism as a subset of white-supremacist European colonialism. Although all analogies are limited, a better parallel for Zionism in the 1920s, 30s and 40s is with tendencies within Black nationalism and pan-Africanism – a parallel noted by several Black radicals. In 1919 the American sociologist and civil rights activist W. E. B. Du Bois said: 'The African movement means to us what the Zionist movement must mean to Jews.'[43] Much later, the Black Panther leader Eldridge Cleaver wrote:

> The parallel between the situation of the Jews at the time of the coming of Theodore Herzl and the present situation of black people in America is fascinating. The Jews had no homeland and were dispersed around the world, cooped up in the ghettos of Europe. Functionally, a return to Israel seemed as impractical as obtaining a homeland for Afro-Americans now seems. [...] The facts of history show that the Jews were able to do precisely the same thing that Afro-Americans must now do.[44]

The academic Brian Klug expressed the contradictory dualities of Zionism, and the blurring of categories of refugee and settler, when he wrote:

> Zionism belongs to two opposite histories at one and the same time. On the one side, it saw itself as a movement for self-determination by (or on behalf of) the Jews, the 'inside outsiders' of Europe, a people with a long history of persecution. On the other side, it was itself part of a European expansion into non-European territory. [...] Zionism spoke the language of colonisation – but for the sake of emancipation, not empire. Seen from this side, Zionism historically was a flight from Europe, not an extension of the European homeland. But seen from the other side,

the Jews who came as settlers were Europeans by any other name. And they were. They were both. They were Jewish as distinct from European, and European as distinct from Arab.

As Klug goes on to say, when the left promotes historical narratives insensitive to these dualities and 'simply folds the Jewish story into a larger narrative of Western imperialism', then 'Jews, whether Zionist or not, are liable to feel marginalised and excluded all over again. It is understandable that this feels like antisemitism, even when it isn't.'[45]

As Spencer Sunshine points out, if those sections of the left insisting that 'Zionism is racism', and a form of white suprem-acism, were serious about the implications of those arguments, they would argue for the left to treat almost all mainstream Jewish communal organisations – which are all, to some degree, 'Zionist' – the way the left would treat the National Front or the Ku Klux Klan: 'The left accepts violence against fascists, so – following its logic – if Zionism is white supremacy, why aren't leftists burning down synagogues and attacking most Jews? [...] Either Zionism should be treated like any other form of white supremacist politic, or it should not be described this way at all.'[46]

This is not to endorse the claim that 'anti-Zionism *is* antisem-itism', or to argue that *any* expression of support for Israel, or any form of Zionism, must simply be excused or justified as an inevitable product of Jewish experience. Like any nationalism, when elevated to the level of military and state policy, Zionism has had oppressive consequences for other peoples. For Pales-tinian Arabs, Zionism is the nationalism of their oppressor, the ideological impulse behind their dispossession and colonisation. Whether or not individual Zionists have been conscious racists, as some certainly have and others clearly have not, Zionist policy has frequently been racist in its effects. Thus, like Jewish Zionism,

Palestinian anti-Zionism has to be understood in the context of the historical experiences that have generated and shaped it.

In another parable of Isaac Deutscher's, Jewish settlement in Palestine was described as the act of a man leaping from a burning building and landing on someone in the street below, breaking their arms and legs. If the one who leapt 'behaved rationally', Deutscher wrote, they, 'having recovered, would have tried to help and console the other sufferer; and the latter might have realised that they were the victim of circumstances over which neither of them had control.' Instead, the one who leapt brutalises the one onto whom they fell, 'insults them, kicks them, and beats them up whenever they meet. The kicked person again swears revenge and is again punched and punished.'[47]

We do not need to draw crude equations between experiences, or repeat the claim that Israeli policy towards the Palestinians mirrors or is based on Nazi policy towards the Jews, to see that, just as historic antisemitism became a fertile ground for Jewish nationalism, so the historic and ongoing treatment of the Palestinians by Israel is also fertile ground for nationalism.

Although he was addressing Palestinian, and wider Arab, national sentiment, rather than the socialist left, leftists should learn from the spirit of radical egalitarian humanism that informed Edward Said when he wrote:

> In our situation as Arabs, it has been a stupid and wasteful policy for so many years to use phrases like 'the Zionist entity' and completely refuse to understand and analyse Israel and Israelis, on the grounds that their existence must be denied because they caused the Palestinian Nakba. History is a dynamic thing, and if we expect Israeli Jews not to use the Holocaust to justify appalling human rights abuses of the Palestinian people, we too have to go beyond such idiocies as saying that the Holocaust never took place,

and that Israelis are all, man, woman, and child, doomed to our eternal enmity and hostility.

Nothing historical is frozen in time; nothing in history is immune to change; nothing in history is beyond reason, beyond understanding, beyond analysis and influence. [...] There must always be room for dissent, for alternative views, for ways and possibilities to challenge the tyranny of the majority and, at the same time and most important, to advance human enlightenment and liberty.[48]

An understanding of history as 'a dynamic thing', capable of having contradictory effects on consciousness, must be consistent, applied to all communities and reject the idea that any national people is transhistorically good or bad. It is only by understanding Zionism as containing both racist and anti-racist impulses that we can arrive at a comprehensive understanding of it, which avoids insensitivities to Jewish history that will, in Klug's phrase, 'feel like antisemitism' whether or not anti-Jewish bigotry is consciously intended. It is only such an understanding that can provide the basis for a worked-out socialist perspective, a perspective that must be both 'for' Zionism, in Deutscher's sense, and against it, opposing all national oppression and chauvinism on the basis of a consistent internationalism.

## ANTI-ZIONIST ZIONISM

How, then, to fulfil these apparently contradictory requirements?

Labour Party members were treated to a real-time effort to respond to some of these complexities in February 2020, when candidates for the party leadership were asked, at a hustings organised by the Jewish Labour Movement (JLM), if they were Zionists. Lisa Nandy, Rebecca Long-Bailey and Emily Thornberry said they were; Keir Starmer said that, while 'sympathetic' to Zionism, he wasn't one himself.

In the context of the left's debates on both Israel/Palestine and antisemitism, it was positive that the candidates gave clear statements of support for Israeli Jews' right to self-determination. None of them was a supporter of Israel's policies: Lisa Nandy, whom JLM subsequently nominated, chairs Labour Friends of Palestine, and both Starmer and Thornberry had spoken at Palestine Solidarity Campaign events. Their answers showed, then, that support for Israeli-Jewish rights, or even self-identification as 'Zionist', does not make one a supporter of the occupation.

For Rebecca Long-Bailey, widely acknowledged as 'the left candidate' in the election and supported by the outgoing Corbyn leadership, to proclaim herself a 'Zionist' made it harder, if only momentarily, for the left to claim that Zionists were akin to racists or fascists, or that Zionists should be no-platformed or driven out of the labour movement and left spaces.

But by proclaiming themselves Zionists, Nandy, Long-Bailey and Thornberry did more than express support for the right of Israeli Jews to self-determination. They explicitly aligned themselves with a form of nationalism – one that has historically been, and continues to be, associated with severe injustice.

Had the candidates brushed up on their Cohen before commencing the debate, they might have been able to answer the question with more nuance. And, while it would have represented a challenge to most JLM members in the audience, it is one they would hopefully have been familiar with, as they would all have received a complimentary copy of *That's Funny*, distributed by JLM itself, only a few months previously. Steve Cohen gave us the way out of this apparently intractable problem, with his concept of 'anti-Zionist Zionism'.

When Cohen wrote *That's Funny*, he said: 'The distinction between anti-Zionism and antisemitism is absolute. Methodologically there is no question of anti-Zionism 'merging into' or 'becoming' antisemitism.'[49] But later in his life he acknowledged that there had indeed been a process of 'merging'. In 2007 he wrote: 'Anti-Zionism and antisemitism should and could be distinct yet they have in many respects merged. [...] The immediate political task is to separate them.'[50] He began writing of himself as an 'anti-Zionist Zionist' from 2005, as a provocative way of challenging this 'merging', and used the description in an introductory essay for the 2005 republication of *That's Funny*, which was reprinted in the 2019 edition.[51]

My usage of the label, like Cohen's, is ironic and provocative, not a straight-faced descriptor for my politics. I do not demand that all Jews immediately declare themselves anti-Zionists, nor that Palestinians embrace Zionism. I do not propose that anyone on the left launches the 'League for Anti-Zionist Zionism', or emblazons 'Both for and Against Zionism!' on a banner to take on a demonstration ... although doing so would, undoubtedly 'confuse the bastards', to use Cohen's phrase.

While there are good reasons for avoiding the term anti-Zionist as a political point of departure, consistently democratic socialist internationalism *is* unavoidably anti-Zionist in the literal sense of opposing Zionist ideology in the context of a consistent opposition to nationalism. My use throughout this book of the phrase 'absolute anti-Zionism' as a shorthand for the policy perspective of left antisemitism towards Israel/Palestine is not an argument that the left should not oppose Zionism. It is an argument that, for socialists, 'anti-Zionism' cannot be an unqualified political label, implying a historically rigid attitude to Israeli-Jewish self-determination. Socialist opposition to Zionism should be contextualised by sensitivity to its historical origins (i.e. the reality of the oppression that impelled its growth), and should support the levelling up of rights between Israeli Jews and Palestinian Arabs as the democratic alternative to Zionism.

While Marxists have historically drawn distinctions between nationalisms of the oppressed and of the oppressor, Jewish nationalism – Zionism – perhaps more than any other form of nationalism, shows that these categories are unstable, geographically variable and historically traversable. Jewish nationalism was a nationalism of the oppressed in pre-war Europe, and in the Stalinist states after the Second World War, even while it was in the process of becoming an oppressor nationalism in Palestine. That history should also give pause to leftists who advocate the realisation of Palestinian national rights via the extirpation of the national rights of Israeli Jews – merely reversing the poles of oppression rather than achieving equality.

As Martin Thomas wrote:

> It is true that the nationalism of an oppressed nation is different from the nationalism of an oppressor nation. The demand for free speech from those socially bred to deference and self-effacement is different from the same demand from those educated in the voice of command. Yet free speech is only free speech, not a guarantee that what the previously self-effacing say must be true. National rights are only national rights, not a guarantee that what the previously oppressed nation does with those rights must be ideal. Nationalism of any stripe, putting nation above class, is alien to socialism.[52]

What, then, did Steve Cohen – a thoroughgoing revolutionary, an internationalist opponent of borders and a determined advocate of international solidarity – mean when he called himself an 'anti-Zionist Zionist', and how might the thinking behind this tongue-in-cheek description help us today?

Cohen described his anti-Zionist Zionism like this:

> On the one hand Zionism is undoubtedly, unquestionably racist towards the Palestinians. Which is why I'm an anti-Zionist. On the other hand it is seen, and I think correctly

seen, by most Jews as anti-racist. It is anti-racist in that it was and is a response by Jews to extricate themselves from the racism of antisemitism. Maybe not your way of fighting racism. Maybe not mine. But anti-racist nonetheless.

And the majority of Jews in the world today view Israel as a 'bolt-hole' were Nazism to arise again. It is in response to this political contradiction that I have started to assume the somewhat novel self-description of being an 'anti-Zionist Zionist'. I am an anti-Zionist like no other (maybe I exaggerate) in that I refuse to accept anti-Zionist myths and untruths. I am a Zionist unlike no other (here I don't exaggerate) in that I am opposed to the state of Israel. The only way out of this contradiction – a political contradiction, not one of my personal pathology – is the unity of Palestinian/Jewish workers within Palestine/Israel, combined with a relentless fight against antisemitism internationally.[53]

Anti-Zionist Zionism in this context is a way of confronting the contradictions of history that an unqualified anti-Zionism, or Zionism, blur out. Cohen allows us to express solidarity with two conflicting historical experiences at once, and discharge elementary duties of solidarity to both Jews and Arabs. The spirit of Cohen's anti-Zionist Zionism suggests a leftism that seeks to integrate into its historical analyses the perspectives and consciousness of *both* the Jewish refugee from the Holocaust, confronting British colonialism to demand their right to immigrate to Palestine and self-determine as part of an established Jewish community there, *and* those of the Palestinian displaced and later subject to occupation as part of that process of national formation and state foundation. From a specifically Jewish perspective, the spirit of anti-Zionist Zionism offers the potential for a recasting of Jewish identity that integrates solidarity with the Palestinians while continuing to uphold a Jewish right to self-definition and self-determination.

Cohen did not share my programmatic conclusions about Israel/Palestine. Reading his work reveals a utopian, semi-anarchist streak, and he preferred what he called a 'no-state solution' to both a two-states settlement and the 'smash Israel' programme of left antisemitism. But his way of thinking about the issue, which presupposed that the left should be in historic sympathy with the experiences that impelled Jewish immigration to Palestine, while also resolutely opposing Israel's oppression of the Palestinians and advocating equality between Palestinian Arabs and Israeli Jews, provides a clear antidote to left antisemitism. To return to Deutscher's analogy of the burning building, Cohen's anti-Zionist Zionism implies a politics that preaches hostility to the people who set the fire, but equality and solidarity between the one who jumped and the bystander they injured.

To anyone stirred by instinctive emotional opposition to oppression, either their own or someone else's, it can seem like pettifogging unreasonableness to insist on particular parameters for the form and content of criticism of Israel. What does it matter, one might ask, if the Palestinians and their supporters sometimes go a little overboard? Isn't that understandable? Surely it is the Israeli state that needs policing, not people's criticisms of it? So what if some Jews get offended? Doesn't their possible offence pale into insignificance compared with the material suffering of the Palestinians?

Yes – in one sense, it does. And it is indeed understandable that a Palestinian victim of Israeli occupation would be especially intense in their hostility to the Israeli state. But if our aim is not merely opposition – any opposition – to Israel, but the advancement of a democratic socialist internationalism, then some critiques will hinder, not help. To embrace 'smash Israel'-type absolute anti-Zionism because it expresses maximal opposition to the Israeli state, and can thus energise more determined solidarity with the Palestinians, is a trap. As well as needlessly pitting the cause of Palestinian solidarity against the vast majority of Jews, it binds any advancement for Palestinian rights to an outcome that, barring a mass collective disavowal of national rights by Israeli Jews, unprecedented throughout all of human history, could be achieved only by bloody force. It would be a contemporary rerun of the 'racial war on the Jews of Palestine', and as such would undoubtedly amplify antisemitism across the region and beyond. The fact that such a sequence of events is extremely unlikely does not make it any less reactionary. It is rare for lasting equality and justice to emerge from ashes. More usually they are fertile ground for ongoing cycles of nationalist resentment and revanchism.

Socialist internationalism is a class politics. It cannot be nationalist – neither Jewish or Israeli-Jewish, nor Arab or Palestinian – even while it supports the right of national groups to self-determination and, if they wish, to statehood. The socialist perspective is not merely for the realisation of the national aspirations of oppressed peoples, but for the construction of a working-class movement capable of overthrowing capitalism, necessarily involving workers in oppressor nations as well as oppressed ones. If the left cannot construct an active support for Palestinian self-determination on the basis of consistent democracy and equal rights, which advocates transnational workers' unity rather than revanchist counter-nationalism, our politics are doomed.

The starting point of an approach informed by Cohen's version of anti-Zionist Zionism would be active campaigning for equality between Israeli Jews and Palestinian Arabs. In the first instance this means vigorous opposition to both the Israeli occupation and racism against Palestinians. It would make practical solidarity in that cause, supporting left-wing and labour movement forces organising in both Israel and Palestine, and especially those seeking to organise across national and communal divides, and build Israeli-Jewish/Palestinian-Arab unity on a class basis, such as Omdim be'Yachad, WAC-Ma'an (the Workers Advice Centre), and others. It would oppose attempts to close down legitimate criticism of Israeli policy by claiming that *any* such criticism is necessarily antisemitic.

An anti-Zionist Zionist approach would involve such things as opposition both to blanket boycotts of Israel and to attempts to treat Zionists like fascists, no-platform them or drive them out of left-wing spaces. Supporters of this perspective would fight for genuine free speech in the labour movement and on the left, for all political factions and tendencies, including both supporters and opponents of BDS. It would acknowledge that there are organic Zionist tendencies within our own movement, broadly defined, that have as much right to organise and express themselves as any other tendency, including anti-Zionist ones.

This perspective recognises that some affinity with the *idea* of Israel, if not the state itself, amongst Jews, whether or not this is labelled as Zionism, is an understandable product of historic Jewish experience. It seeks to give Jews the ideological tools to overcome particularist, nationalist instincts, and move towards a universalist political perspective and consciousness. It can celebrate and promote revolutionary universalist political traditions within Jewish history, but does not demand of Jews that they overcome the entirety of historically accumulated consciousness on pain of being damned as racists and driven out of the left.

Anti-Zionist Zionism does not make support for political outcomes that presuppose the non-existence of Israel – which are at best utopian and at worst wholly reactionary and antisemitic – a precondition for political legitimacy. It makes support for universal human and democratic rights, and support for the material advancement of the rights of the Palestinian national community, its litmus test for judging politics on Israel/Palestine, not whether a person or group calls themselves Zionist or anti-Zionist. Anti-Zionist Zionism is, in fact, a call for a renewed political discourse on the left that can leave the terms 'Zionist' and 'anti-Zionist' behind altogether, or at least return them to their proper proportions.

Human rights activist Iyad el-Baghdadi wrote:

> From my many conversations and interactions with Israelis I can now see that there are two Israels. One is an Israel that is a safe haven and cultural homeland for the Jewish people. Another is an Israel which is a sophisticated, well-oiled machine of institutional repression. [...] Peace is only possible with the first Israel. No peace is possible with the second Israel.[54]

This is the contradiction and duality I believe Cohen's anti-Zionist Zionism aimed to express, acknowledging that a democratic confrontation with the 'second Israel', based on internationalist unity between Palestinian Arabs and Israeli Jews, and centrally between Arab and Jewish workers, required an understanding of the first. In 2007 Cohen wrote: 'There can be no liberation through any movement infected with antisemitism. And there can be no struggle against antisemitism which articulates a position detrimental to the Palestinians. One struggle! One fight!'[55]

He was right, I think. He was also right that, on much of the far left, anti-Zionism and antisemitism have 'merged'. As paradoxical as it may seem, the only way to decouple them is to consciously fuse the imperative for solidarity with the Palestinians with an active struggle against antisemitism, including and perhaps especially on the left, in order to construct a politics based on consistent democracy and struggle for equal rights. That is the radical, emancipatory potential of the provocation of anti-Zionist Zionism, the way out of the ideological trap set by left antisemitism.

It is up to us to fulfil that potential.

# CHAPTER SIX

# THE LEFT AND JEWISH COMMUNITIES: SOME RECENT TRENDS

On 25 November 2019 Chief Rabbi Ephraim Mirvis wrote an article in *The Times* that asked the question: 'What will become of Jews and Judaism in Britain if the Labour Party forms the next government?'[1] Although Mirvis wrote that it was 'not [his] place' to tell people how to vote, the article was in essence an impassioned plea not to vote for the Labour Party in the upcoming 12 December election, arguing that Labour was a site of 'anti-Jewish racism' in which its leadership was 'complicit'.

Mirvis's opening claim was that 'the overwhelming majority of British Jews [were] gripped by anxiety' about the election, and the prospect of a Labour government. The data backed this up: polling from March 2019 showed that 87 per cent of Jews viewed Jeremy Corbyn as antisemitic, 42 per cent said they would consider emigrating if Labour won and 61 per cent believed there were 'high levels of antisemitism' within the Labour Party.[2]

Any leftist, or even secular liberal, should be alarmed by a direct intervention into politics of any clerical figure. But any serious leftist should also be alarmed by those statistics.

I campaigned for Labour in the 2019 election. I think Mirvis was wrong, and I think the anxiety he was speaking to, while undeniably real, was misplaced. These issues, around Jewish fears about the election, were explored in my exchange with the writer and activist Rabbil Sikdar, which appears as an appendix in this book. For the Labour-supporting left to ease this anxiety required sensitivity to its origins, and an acknowledgement that it was grounded in inherited cultural memory of historical experience, and that it was a response to actually existing antisemitism in the Labour Party. It required sensitivity to the fact that, as much as we on the left might wish it were otherwise, when Mirvis made his statement, he was, as far as could reasonably be ascertained, speaking for most Jews in Britain – at least in the sense of expressing opinions that it seemed most Jews shared.

The required sensitivity was not universally forthcoming. In a tweet that was later deleted, a staff member for the Labour left group Momentum responded to Mirvis by suggesting: 'Chief Rabbi Ephraim Mirvis is a Boris Johnson supporter. He's also an uncritical supporter of Netanyahu + the violent oppression of Palestinians by Israel. Labour is promising to recognise a Palestinian state + end arms sales to Israel. His comments must be taken in that context.'[3] Other responses, on websites such as Counterpunch, Vox Political and The Canary, made similar arguments.[4]

The first instinct was thus not to address the substance of Mirvis's claims, but to allege he was making them essentially *because of* his desire to perpetuate the oppression of the Palestinians, ensure the continuation of arms sales to Israel, and return a Tory government. This is the rhetorical sleight of hand that allows much of the left to avoid any serious engagement with antisemitism at all: if a Jew supports Israel, then what they say about antisemitism must have the ulterior motive of deflecting criticism of Israel. And since the vast majority of Jews do have some affinity with and support for Israel, then the vast majority of Jewish concerns about antisemitism can be ruled out and dismissed.

Mirvis may well have been politically motivated to oppose Corbyn and prevent a Labour government. He is, after all, the Chief Rabbi of the United Hebrew Congregations of the Commonwealth, an establishment figure if there ever was one. He may well be a Tory. But does this mean the issues raised in his article can be automatically dismissed? Does the fact that he might also have other reasons for opposing Labour mean the one at the centre of his article, concerns about antisemitism, is necessarily not 'real'?

## SELECTIVE PHILOSEMITISM

The pro-Corbyn website Skwawkbox, which had a famously close relationship with Corbyn's office throughout his leadership, responded to Mirvis's statement by publishing a letter from United European Jews, a Charedi (ultra-Orthodox) organisation, that 'totally rejected and condemned' the Chief Rabbi's statement.[5] This represented a continuation of a peculiar sort of selective philosemitism – that is, an ostentatiously pro-Jewish attitude, performed by non-Jews, based on notions of an essential Jewishness – it had developed, mobilising the opinions of a small layer of vocally pro-Corbyn Charedi figures against the criticisms levelled by more mainstream communal voices.

The left has frequently taken sides in political, social and especially class struggles within ethnic and religious communities. Traditionally this has been to support socialists, secularists, feminists, LGBT+ people, workers in struggle and other dissidents within those communities, fighting for greater freedom against the frequently conservative values of the community leadership. In Skwawkbox's selective philosemitism, a surreal adjunct to contemporary left antisemitism, we find that tradition inverted, and a section of the left boosting some of the most reactionary – misogynist, homophobic and patriarchal – elements of Jewish life. The nearest thing we find to this phenomenon in recent leftist history is the episode, stretching from around 2001 to 2005, where sections of the far left opportunistically courted right-wing communalists within Muslim communities in the Stop the War Coalition and the Respect electoral initiative, much to the vocal dismay of some secularists and leftists from Muslim backgrounds.[6] Steve Cohen denounced this approach, whether in relation to Muslim communities or Jewish ones, as 'reliance on a self-appointed leadership', which, he argued, was an 'apolitical disease which needs to be challenged and destroyed – instead, sections of the left are cultivating it at its most dangerous points'.[7] Although Skwawkbox promoted, in the United European Jews, an *alternative* 'self-appointed leadership' to the mainstream Board of Deputies, their approach expressed the same communalist logic.

Skwawkbox made a particular hero of Shraga Stern, a Charedi activist aligned with the Union of Orthodox Hebrew Congregations, who was especially outspoken in his denial of Labour antisemitism, and who particularly endeared himself to some of the left with his plan to organise a protest at a dinner organised by the Board of Deputies of British Jews, the most prominent cross-denominational Jewish communal organisation, in November 2018. The other primary focus of Stern's activism is educational issues, where he campaigns vigorously against LGBT-inclusive education. In 2019 he donated £500 to campaigns by some Muslim parents to end such education in a Birmingham primary school.[8]

By boosting Charedi claims that mainstream communal bodies like the Board of Deputies are not representative, Skwawkbox and others found another way to discredit claims of antisemitism without having to engage with their substance. If the Board of Deputies and the Chief Rabbi don't *really* represent Jews, they cannot be trusted when they say Jews are concerned about antisemitism in Labour. The implication of this promotion of ultra-Orthodox voices is that *these* Jews – black-hat-wearing and bearded, sporting peyos (the sidelocks worn by ultra-Orthodox men), zealously devout – are the *real* Jews, and those Jews who are secular, or at least not immediately identifiable as Jews, and whose Jewishness may consist in a complex cultural consciousness more so than the performance of religious ritual, are less authentic, less legitimately Jewish.

Steve Cohen wrote that 'the left's advice to Jews' was 'assimilate and stop being Jewish'.[9] His argument was that the non-Jewish left could not cope with the complexities and contradictions posed by historically accumulated Jewish culture and experience, and advocated a kind of blank assimilationism in the hope of making the problem go away. In a peculiarly inverted form, his argument serves as a pointed rebuttal to selective philosemitism of the Skwawkbox type. In that particular case, 'the left's advice to Jews' appeared to be: '*don't* assimilate: express your Jewishness in an authentically sanctioned, purely religious form'. Thus, this particular variant of left antisemitism is able to keep Jews where it can see them: in the immediately, visibly identifiable status of the marginalised outsider, without muddying the waters with complicated ethnic identities that might not be expressed through clothing or religious belief, but through attitudes to collective history.

It was an abject position for would-be leftists to take, and was colluded in by people who ought to have known better. Historically, the primary sphere of political conflict for many Jewish leftists, including those from non- and anti-Zionist traditions such as Bundism, would have precisely been against the equivalents of Shraga Stern, and the forces of religious ultra-reaction within their communities. And yet Jewish Voice for Labour (JVL), which claimed to stand in the tradition of non-Zionist Jewish leftism, boosted and recirculated Skwawkbox's philosemitic tokenising of Stern,[10] affirming the central criticism levelled at them – that, far from being a group promoting labour movement organisation and socialist politics within Jewish life, their primary purpose was to provide a Jewish-branded denialist chorus to deflect allegations of antisemitism.

Jewish political opinion, and indeed Jewishness as a broad cultural category, is, of course, diverse. There is no default identity and viewpoint to which all Jews should be expected to conform. And there is nothing wrong with promoting highly minoritarian and marginal voices and political elements within a community *because you agree with them*, and because you hope the minority may one day be able to convince the majority. That is what any of us on the left are doing whenever we promote the struggles of small socialist groups in other countries.

But is that what Skwawkbox and JVL were doing with Shraga Stern? Do these leftists really hope Charedi and Hasidic sects become the majority in Jewish life, with all that would entail for women's rights, LGBT+ rights and more? Indeed, with all it would entail for secularist and leftist Jewish currents? A committed Charedi activist might well dismiss the entire notion that the overwhelmingly secular JVL could possibly represent a legitimate 'Jewish voice'. Thus, JVL, desperate to amplify arguments insisting that antisemitism in Labour was not an issue, assisted in the promotion of people who quite probably deny JVL activists' right to speak as Jews.

The point here is not to downplay the importance of Jewish diversity, or to claim that Shraga Stern's unquestionably reactionary wider politics automatically invalidate what he has to say about antisemitism in the Labour Party. His claims should be judged on their substance. But the denialists judged neither Stern nor Mirvis on this basis: Mirvis was dismissed out of hand, and claims about his reactionary politics were used to invalidate everything he had to say, while Stern was lauded despite his reactionary politics (which are quite considerably *more* reactionary than Mirvis's), because he affirmed what the Skwawkbox/JVL milieu already believed about antisemitism on the left, and allowed them to promote a figure who conformed to an ultra-authentic image of Jewishness whose pronouncements could be used to salve the conscience of the majority non-Jewish left.

Here, too, we find unavoidable crossovers with the politics of Israel/Palestine. Shraga Stern is explicitly anti-Zionist. He calls mainstream Jewish communal groups such as the Board of Deputies and the Jewish Leadership Council 'extremist

Zionist' groups.[11] But his form of ultra-religious anti-Zionism has reactionary, rather than progressive, motivations. The religious-fundamentalist critique of Israel is, in essence, that only divine will and the coming of the Messiah can establish a Jewish state, and that the establishment of the modern nation state of Israel, on the basis of a largely secular nationalism, is a crime against God's will. It has nothing to do with support for Palestinian rights, or opposition to national oppression motivated by advocacy of equal rights. But for a section of the left, the mere label 'anti-Zionist' is enough to bestow political legitimacy, regardless of whether the alternative in the name of which Zionism is opposed is any better from a left-wing point of view. It allows left antisemitism to maintain its implicit claim that 'Jews' and 'Zionists' are, in Kahn-Harris's phrase, 'two entirely separate categories of persons'.[12]

The lauding of the marginal ultra-Orthodox sect Neturei Karta (NK) by some leftists is an expression of the same phenomenon.[13] Like Stern, NK provide those keen to deny or downplay left antisemitism with a seemingly authentic expression of Jewishness, which proclaims itself as such, that they can point to in their defence. NK refer to themselves as 'Torah true Jews', and use slogans such as 'Authentic Judaism opposes Zionist aggression'. As the Israeli academic Eldad Levy, writing in the radical Israeli/Palestinian +972 *Magazine*, put it, 'the fact that a rigorous Jewish sect officially denounces the existence of Israel and joins efforts with the Palestinian national struggle has a symbolic political gain. [...] The use of Neturei Karta as "Jews opposing Israel" is heavily tokenised to achieve a political goal'.[14]

When not attending pro-Palestine protests, NK members have participated in Holocaust denial conferences hosted by the Iranian state,[15] mobilised in London to support the leader of the Hungarian fascist group Jobbik (which NK admires for its anti-Zionism)[16] and have been photographed performing the *quenelle*, the inverted Nazi salute popular amongst antisemites in France.[17] In 1991 an NK rabbi sat down for a convivial, sympathetic interview with Patrick Harrington, a far-right political activist and sometime member of the National Front.[18] As Spencer Sunshine rightly put it, NK is 'the Jewish equivalent of the Westboro Baptist Church'.[19] But for some of the left-wing arbiters of authentic Jewishness, none of this is enough to put NK off limits.

Sunshine points out:

> The left would never hold up the 8% of Black voters who supported Trump as representing the Black community. In fact, when Trumpists put Black supporters front and centre, the left understands their opinions are not those of the majority of Black Americans. So, since the Jewish community as a whole appears to not want Israel to be abolished, why does the left hold up the tiny minority of anti-Zionist Jews as representative of the Jewish community? They are being used as tokens by the larger left that refuses to engage in Jewish issues or to confront antisemitism.[20]

## BLAMING JEWS FOR ANTISEMITISM

A common theme of recent denialist discourse on left antisemitism, additional to arguments that deny or downplay antisemitism entirely, are arguments that acknowledge its existence and significance, but lay the blame for it at the feet of Jewish communities and institutions themselves. Sometimes this has been expressed in the hoary claim that Israel's actions are the 'root cause' of antisemitism. As a *Morning Star* article, later withdrawn and apologised for by the paper's editors, put it:

> Surely the Jewish organisations and individuals who lately were protesting about growing antisemitism in Britain must

see that, as advocates of Israel's historical and still unremit-
ting brutality against the Palestinians, they will inevitably be
regarded by some other British nationals as directly complicit
in that country's actions [...] no amount of protestations
about the symptoms of rising antisemitism [...] will end the
problem until its root cause – Israel's criminal behaviour – is
dealt with.[21]

This repeated an old theme of left antisemitism, that antisemitism was a perhaps tactically ill judged but ultimately understandable
response to Israel's actions, while advancing a straightforward lie
that 'the Jewish organisations and individuals [...] protesting growing antisemitism' were, in a direct and unqualified sense, 'advocates
of Israel's [...] brutality against the Palestinians'.

In fact, the formal policy of most mainstream Jewish
communal organisations is against the occupation of Palestinian
territories, and for the establishment of an independent Palestinian state. The Board of Deputies' policy is: 'Promote peace projects
that unite communities and resist boycotts that divide communities, advocating for a permanent and comprehensive solution to
the Israeli-Palestinian conflict that results in a secure Israel alongside a viable Palestinian state.'[22]

It is surely fair to criticise it for failing to actually advance
that policy, which effectively exists on paper only, and does not
seem to inform the Board's official responses to events in Israel/
Palestine, which often express knee-jerk defences of Israel. In May
2020, for instance, an open letter from thirty-eight deputies did
just that, when they urged the Board to take a firm stance against
the annexation of Palestinian territories.[23] The following year,
numerous deputies pressed the Board to oppose Israel's bombing of Gaza, and criticised the Board's president for speaking at
a pro-Israel rally.[24] Describing mainstream Jewish communal
bodies as 'advocates of brutality against Palestinians' is not only

inaccurate, it erases and undermines the efforts of progressive voices within such bodies. And even if it were the case that every Jewish organisation protesting antisemitism *was* a direct 'advocate' of Israel's policy, that would not mean the antisemitism they protested did not exist – still less that it was justified. Bigotry is not an acceptable or legitimate response to bigotry.

Some on the left go further and argue that antisemitism is not only *fuelled* by Israel's actions, but *created* by them. Tariq Ali's May 2021 speech at a protest against Israel's bombing of Gaza argued: 'Every time they bomb Gaza, every time they attack Jerusalem, that is what creates antisemitism. Stop it! Stop the occupation, stop the bombings, and the casual antisemitism will soon disappear.'[25]

Ali's formulation is a gross caricature of Mahmoud Darwish's sentiments, discussed in Chapter Five, about the interrelation between the Jewish and Palestinian questions. Ali jettisons the whole history of pre-1948 antisemitism and sees Israel, conceptually fused with the Jews, standing outside of history, with 'antisemitism' something that is only 'created' in response to Israel's actions, with no internal dynamics of its own.

As Kahn-Harris responded:

> Even if you assume that antisemitism is simply a reaction to things Jews do and believe – which, rest assured, I do not – no social phenomenon is simply 'reversible'. Racism has its own dynamic that persists beyond its origins. That, after all, is why the antisemitic 'Christ killer' trope persists amongst people who are not Christians. And that's why, if Israel and Zionism were 'defeated' (whatever that would look like) the antisemitism it 'provoked' (again, a simplistic assumption) would persist.[26]

An additional 'blame-the-Jews' angle came from those who worried about the prospect of Labour voters turning on the Jewish community for having sabotaged the prospect of a Corbyn-led government. 'What if Corbyn loses by a narrow margin? How will the millions who voted for him see the Jewish community and its three-year campaign to brand him toxic?' asked Robert Cohen, in an article entitled 'The Jewish Establishment's "War Against Corbyn" Risks Bringing Real Antisemitism to Britain'. The argument was that while the antisemitism currently being complained about was substantially not 'real', the antisemitism provoked as a backlash might be … but it would be 'self-inflicted': 'We are […] on a path that risks turning fake antisemitism into real antisemitism. What we are witnessing could be an on-coming, self-inflicted tragedy for the Jewish community in Britain,' Cohen wrote. The article also asserted that the Jewish community leadership 'only have one issue on their mind – Israel, and how best to protect it from criticism'.[27]

This assertion reflected an attitude sometimes encountered on the left towards Jewish communal organisations that sees them all as part of an interconnected and monolithic effort to advance Israeli state interests. This thinking starts from the institutional connections between some Jewish communal organisations and bodies linked to the Israeli state, and extrapolates an argument that those bodies function solely as instruments of an Israeli power that aims to, as the sociology professor David Miller, previously mentioned in Chapter One, argues, 'impose its will all over the world'.[28]

A diagram produced by Miller encapsulated this view. It included entries for most major mainstream Jewish communal bodies, including the Board of Deputies, which was described as a 'key Israel lobby group'. Numerous prominent Jewish individuals were also included, with linking labels such as 'donor', 'affiliate' and 'within', with 'the Israeli government' and its 'quasi-state institutions' sitting atop the whole web.[29] As stated in Chapter One, Miller even saw interfaith activities that brought Jews and

Muslims together to make chicken soup as an effort to promote Israeli power and 'normalise Zionism'.

As Keith Kahn-Harris wrote in response, this approach 'constructs a kind of "flatland"; a world in which networks of power and influence are so intricately connected that they form a seamless system'.[30]

Any attempt to draw a distinction between 'Zionists' and 'Jews' is meaningless when anyone connected to the principal infrastructure of Jewish communal life can be seen as an agent of an Israeli state project for world domination. This wild conspiracy-mongering does nothing to advance the struggle for Palestinian national rights. All it trains activists to do is to engage in a Jew hunt, targeting Jewish individuals and organisations to reveal the promotion of Israeli power for which even something as seemingly innocuous as interfaith chicken soup preparation must be a vehicle.

Even those organisations more directly linked to the actual prosecution of Israeli state policy are the equivalents of political and cultural organisations that most, if not all, states use to pursue their geopolitical interests. Only for the Jewish state do conspiracy-theorist anti-Zionists see in such activity a compact network pursuing a project not merely to advance interests but to achieve global domination and control, to 'impose its will all over the world'. As argued in Chapter Two, Zionism is thus reified into a singular entity capable of embodying agency. As the socialist activist Cathy Nugent wrote, 'reification is at the heart of conspiracy-theory thinking, and that often brings left antisemitism into alignment with "traditional" antisemitism'.[31] Had David Miller been an academic in the USSR or its satellites in the 1950s, 60s or 70s, his work might well have been celebrated and amplified by the state, whose campaigns of conspiracy-theorist anti-Zionism it resembles.

Responding to the 2021 controversy around Miller's work, an article on the left-wing Jewish website Jewdas said: 'Miller's writings on Jewish institutions contain few outright falsehoods, but they are embarrassingly conspiratorial, significantly overstating the influence and aims of various organisations.'

The article continued, 'It's tempting to blame the ills of the British government on a small, powerful group of people manipulating our politicians,' but counselled the left to 'remember that the UK isn't pro-Israel and anti-Muslim because of a well organised Jewish lobby', but rather because of the British state's own imperialist policy and state-sanctioned racism.[32]

## JEWISH LEFT TRADITIONS

Like many leftist Jews, I find wrangling, often conducted vicariously, over questions of Jewish communal representation, leadership and identity highly unseemly. In many ways it represents a miring of debate on terrain the left has no business occupying in the first place, but has allowed itself to become bogged down in by much of its own accommodations with forms of identitarian politics. If you accept an identitarian logic, wherein the identity of the sayer can confer validity on an argument, in abstraction from the substance of what is actually being said, you utterly inhibit your own ability to assess and intervene in political discourse on an independent basis, and necessarily limit yourself to an unseemly quest for an appropriate token person, who will allow you to argue that *your* Jew is the really authentic 'Jewish voice'.

I oppose communalism. I believe the idea of a unitary interest for ethnic groups is dangerous, and I believe the social role of official community leaderships, especially in faith groups, is often reactionary. I contest the claims of the Chief Rabbi or the Board of Deputies to represent Jews not because I don't believe they are authentically representative, or because I have an allegedly more representative alternative to supplant them with, but because I contest the idea of communal representation *as such*. I am also a secularist and an atheist. As much as I defended the necessity to engage seriously with the contents of the Chief Rabbi's article, I was also alarmed by the fact of it: direct interventions into politics by unelected clerics have necessarily anti-democratic implications. I believe organised religion should play no role in political life.

In all of this, I identify with the rich secularist, anti-clerical and antitheistic traditions present in historic Jewish leftism. In the Jewish East End of London of the late-nineteenth century, radical Yiddish newspapers like *Arbeter Fraynd* (*Workers' Friend*) were part of a vibrant Jewish anarchist and socialist milieu. Individuals and groups from this milieu frequently had an ostentatiously irreverent attitude to the bourgeois communal and rabbinical establishments, and to organised religion itself.

*Arbeter Fraynd* mounted a 'non-stop verbal assault on religion and its institutions'; in 1889, on Yom Kippur, one of the holiest days in the Jewish religious calendar, when believers spend the day fasting and at prayer, supporters of the paper organised a mass meeting, followed by a ball. At the meeting, lectures on 'The Absurdity of Religion' were given, and *Arbeter Fraynd* journalist Benjamin Feigenbaum, who had been educated in a yeshiva (religious college) but became a dedicated free-thinker and secularist, gave a lecture entitled 'Is There a God?', which he concluded by proclaiming: 'If there is a God and if he is Almighty as the clergy claims he is, I give him just two minutes' time to kill me on the spot, so that he may prove his existence!' When the time elapsed, he exclaimed, 'See, there is no God!', a band struck up 'La Marseillaise' and the ball began.[33]

Jewish leftists in other cities, including New York, also organised Yom Kippur balls, 'a gesture of contempt for ancient superstitions'[34] that allowed for the expression of a Jewishness that was irreligious and radical. Some young Jewish anarchists went as far as to 'march in column to the Spitalfields Great Synagogue

(*Machzikei Ha Dath*) in Brick Lane, smoking or brandishing ham sandwiches as gestures of defiance and rejection' of religion.[35] While it should be noted that many in the movement at the time felt these anti-religious provocations were counterproductive, such vignettes communicate a sense of the bombastically irreverent and iconoclastic attitude towards the official clerical and communal leaders that pervaded much of the Jewish radical milieu.

I will not be so presumptuous as to mobilise Benjamin Feigenbaum in support of all of the arguments I make in this chapter; he might well have been far more scathing and dismissive of the Chief Rabbi than I have been. But I feel confident that, were he alive today, he would react with contempt to people who claim to occupy the radical left wing of Jewish life celebrating the likes of Shraga Stern and Neturei Karta, and with disgust at the spectacle of non-Jews implicitly telling Jews that they should look to Stern and Neturei Karta for political leadership.

The agitation of Feigenbaum and others took place in a particular social context: a far-left milieu that was embedded in an immigrant community, made up of people from that community, competing with bourgeois community leaders and the religious establishment for ideological hegemony over that community's working class. Our context is different. A compact Jewish working class, with an organised left, no longer exists in Britain in the way it did in the late nineteenth and early twentieth centuries. The intervening years have wrought significant changes on Jewish demography, socio-economic status, identity and consciousness. Despite having been known to enjoy a bacon roll of a Saturday morning, I do not advocate that anyone today, Jewish or not, 'brandishes ham sandwiches' outside their local synagogue. I invoke the spirit of Feigenbaum and the *Arbeter Fraynd* not to advocate the direct replication of their methods – although I will happily collaborate with any comrades interested in organising a Yom Kippur ball in the future – but to show that there is an alternative framework for thinking about ethno-religious communities than those currently prevalent on the left.

That framework understands communities neither as 'flat-lands', nor as having an essential, unitary interest that can be expressed if only the purest, most 'authentic' representative can be identified. Rather, it sees them as sites of struggle and ideological conflict, riven by differences of class, and oppression along lines of gender and sexuality, in which the left should intervene to support those fighting for freedom. That framework has largely receded from left-wing common sense. Significant sections of the left have, in the past two decades, opportunistically accommodated to communalism – directly and explicitly, via the 2001–5 alliance with the Muslim communalist forces already mentioned, and in an indirect way in the 2015–19 period, contesting the claims of the Chief Rabbi and the Board of Deputies on behalf of a *more reactionary* communalist alternative. Conversely, those in the Labour Party and beyond who insisted that whatever the Chief Rabbi and the Board of Deputies said was beyond question or challenge, because they spoke for Jews, in an immutable way, were also expressing a communalist logic.

While there are no direct modern analogues of the *Arbeter Fraynd* and similar publications and organisations, and while there is not a combative Jewish workers' movement engaged in direct class struggle, there are live struggles, and a political left, inside the Jewish community that could benefit from solidarity and amplification from the wider, predominantly non-Jewish, left. Non-Jewish leftists may be aware of the Jewish Socialist Group, which identifies with Bundism, and the politically heterogeneous cultural collective Jewdas, already mentioned in this chapter. Both of these have done valuable and respectworthy work, although both have tended to downplay left antisemitism, and in particular the possibility of a link between it and anti-Zionism.

There is a small British supporters' group of Meretz, a left-Zionist party in Israel, which has hosted events with Husam Zomlot, the Palestinian ambassador to the UK. Even the Jewish Labour Movement, generally on the right of the Labour Party, is itself a site of ideological conflict, and hosted Palestinian activist Ghadir Hani at its 2020 conference. Although the JLM is a frequent target for left antisemitic ire, and appears on David Miller's diagrammatic representation of Israel's alleged plot for domination, it has its own left wing, which competes ideologically with more conservative elements. Uncritically pro-Israel elements are by no means hegemonic in JLM. In May 2021 JLM issued a clear statement of condemnation of Israeli 'brutality' towards Palestinians on Temple Mount, and said:

> The tensions in Israel have been heightened due to the threatened evictions of Palestinian families from Sheikh Jarrah. We are entirely opposed to efforts to expand settlements, demolish homes and evict Palestinians and will continue to work with all who promote peace, human rights, security and dignity for Israelis and Palestinians.[36]

A left that sees even critical-minded people within the JLM as beyond the pale, enemies, even agents of Israeli domination, but will laud the likes of Shraga Stern, is a left that has utterly lost its political bearings.

Beyond what might be termed the organised Jewish political left, there are charities like Mavar and GesherEU, which help Charedi Jews escape the frequently highly oppressive conditions of ultra-Orthodox communities, and campaigning networks such as Yachad and Na'amod, which organise predominantly young Jews to protest the Israeli occupation. All of these, and others, do their work in the face of suspicion, hostility and harassment from right-wing and reactionary elements within Jewish communities.

The politics of these groups are often liberal, rather than socialist, and in each case there will be aspects of their perspectives and approach with which, depending on their own particular point of view, leftists may disagree, for a number of reasons. They have a variety of political approaches to communal representation, Israel/Palestine and other questions. Some, like the JLM, Meretz-UK and Yachad, self-identify as Zionist. But all, in different ways, are engaged in struggles to advance values and ideas the left should fundamentally support. The status of some such organisations as charities makes a direct relationship between them and more formally political bodies difficult, but the left can and should amplify and support their work, critically where necessary, and seek to engage their supporters in discussion about wider left-wing ideas.

As the 2020–21 anti-occupation and anti-war agitation by Board deputies showed, even more official and establishment communal organisations can be sites of political contestation. In April 2021 Noam, the official youth wing of the Masorti movement, one of the branches of organised Judaism in Britain, protested the Masorti leadership's hosting of Tzipi Hotovely, the Israeli ambassador to the UK, and boycotted a meeting with her, over Hotovely's history of racist remarks towards Palestinians and her reactionary attitudes on some religious and social questions. Noam's statement said: 'We are a Zionist youth movement. We believe in the importance of engaging with Israel as it is, with all the joys and challenges which come with that. Despite this, we feel that Hotovely's comments are beyond the pale.'[37]

Masorti Judaism, to which Noam is formally linked, is affiliated to, or represented on, several of the bodies that appear on Miller's diagram, including the Board of Deputies and the Jewish Leadership Council. So, too, is Liberal Judaism, whose youth wing, LJY-Netzer, another Zionist organisation, took a strong stance against war and occupation and for equality during Israel's bombardment of Gaza in May 2021. In doing so, they explicitly and vocally challenged the Board of Deputies, the Zionist Federation and the Jewish Leadership Council's responses. The Board of Deputies had promoted the hashtag #NoToRocketsYesToPeace, without saying anything explicit about Israel's bombing.[38]

Perhaps, for Miller and his supporters and co-thinkers, anti-racist and anti-war protests by the Zionists of Noam and LJY-Netzer – which, in the context of Jewish communal organisation as a contested terrain, were courageous and laudable stands – were not really anti-racist and anti-war at all, but merely further attempts to extend Israeli influence and 'normalise Zionism' by suggesting Zionists could oppose anti-Palestinian racism, occupation and war. A left that upholds Miller's conspiracy-theorist 'flatland', even in diluted forms, will inevitably fail in its duty of solidarity to those engaged in progressive struggle within the Jewish community.

The left could also boost left-wing voices inside international Jewish life by promoting solidarity with the labour movement and internationalist left in Israel itself, including groups like Omdim be'Yachad, Koah LaOvdim (Power to Workers) and the Workers Advice Centre WAC-Ma'an, who struggle in extremely adverse circumstances. Much of the left is inhibited from such solidarity because of its implicit rejection of any progressive potential from within Israeli society, and its refusal to see any Israel other than that of Netanyahu and Hotovely.

## SOLIDARITY: A CHALLENGE FOR THE LEFT

The left should heed the words of the Palestinian socialist activist Maisam Jaljuli, who said:

> We need to convince Jewish citizens, including Zionists, that
> the only way to change the regime in Israel – to change the

government, to change society – is as part of a class-based alliance with not only Arabs, but which also includes Ethiopian communities, poor Jews from the former Soviet states, and other marginalised groups. They all need to be part of the struggle to change the regime. That's the basis for building a new left.[39]

Supporting those efforts, and encouraging diaspora support for leftist and progressive struggles in Israel itself, would be a far better intervention into Jewish communal life than promoting a religious-fundamentalist anti-Zionist fringe, or, wilder still, by implicitly designating the entire Jewish community as an 'enemy' agent of a conspiracy for world domination.

As a movement aspiring to political hegemony, the left is necessarily required to contest existing hegemonic politics, including in minority communities. This often also involves contesting the existing political construction of minority identities. But without sensitivity to the roots of those political constructions, the door is opened to bigotry. As Kahn-Harris puts it:

It is not intrinsically racist to oppose the politics of a particular minority or section of a minority. What *is* racist is denying that such political identities exist; to refuse to recognise the ways in which Jews and others treat Zionism and other political projects as part of their very being. That doesn't mean accepting or supporting that politics; it means finding a form of civility that can somehow balance a recognition of the nexus of politics and identity with advocating an alternate politics.[40]

The left gains the ability, and in a sense the right, to effectively intervene in and contest the politics of minority communities only when it defends those minority communities from bigotry, and consistently supports the right of those communities to free speech – even when that speech is used to make claims with which we on the left disagree. On the whole, the left, and especially the Skwawkbox wing of the Labour left, has not fulfilled these duties of solidarity, instead amplifying only those Jewish voices that served a denialist narrative – shamefully including, in the form of the likes of Shraga Stern, some of the most reactionary elements in Jewish life.

A frequent refrain from opponents of antisemitism throughout the recent debates has been to 'listen to Jews', emphasising the idea that people who experience oppression or persecution should be the ones to define that oppression, and, ultimately, that if a person from a marginalised group says an idea or action is – or, conversely, is not – bigoted, they should be believed.

Amplifying and centring the voices of people from marginalised groups in discussions about that marginalisation is, clearly, vital. 'Listen to Jews' is the beginning of good sense. But it cannot be the sum of it, given the obvious disagreements *within*, and indeed *between*, historically marginalised groups, including Jews, about their experiences. Without attempting to independently assess arguments on their substance, the exhortation to 'listen to Jews' cannot help anyone assess the conflicting arguments of Ephraim Mirvis and Shraga Stern, the numerous positions in between, and the entirely alternative arguments also from Jewish sources. If 'listen to Jews' was as far as the discussion went, all we would be left with is a grubby game of tokenising, selective-philosemitic chess, where predominantly non-Jewish political factions wield 'their' respective Jewish tokens against each other. This is the game much of the left and the centre/ right within the Labour Party have played during recent years; it has added nothing to a serious understanding of antisemitism, except perhaps by providing an object lesson in how not to fight it.

Some of the contradictions of this approach were highlighted by a 2018 video from Momentum, featuring an undoubtedly well-meaning presentation from left-wing Jewish activist Tania Shew giving her view on antisemitism on the left. In it, she rightly argues that tackling antisemitism on the left can't be allowed to curtail freedom of speech, particularly for Palestinians. She goes on to say that Palestinians have an absolute right to 'describe their oppression in whatever terms they see fit'. On strict freedom-of-speech grounds, which are themselves no small matter, this is indisputable. But whether that means the 'terms' Palestinians or Jews, or anyone else, use to describe their experiences of oppression, cannot be challenged is another question. For example, the view that the oppression of the Palestinians is part of a world Zionist conspiracy by Jews to dominate other peoples is an antisemitic calumny, whether it is uttered by a Palestinian or anyone else. They have a 'right' to say it, to 'describe their oppression' in such terms if they wish. But socialists also have a responsibility to challenge such 'terms'.

And, conversely, Jews have historically understood and described their oppression in all sorts of different 'terms', some religiously rooted, some based on a variety of political analyses, and drawn vastly differing conclusions from these various descriptions and understandings. Some Jews today see the Palestinian struggle for national liberation as inherently antisemitic, even claiming that the entire social construction of Palestinian national identity is anti-Jewish. A left that responds by saying, 'all of these descriptions are equally valid, and it's not for anyone else to question the terms in which oppressed people describe their own oppression' will not be much use when it comes to confronting oppression or bigotry as it actually exists. 'Listen to Palestinians' and 'listen to Jews' are necessary, but not sufficient, dictums for the left in the effort to arrive at comprehensive, historically rigorous analyses of Zionism, Israel/Palestine and antisemitism that can inform effective socialist politics.

The instruction to 'listen to' members of a group is intended to affirm the agency of that group. But it can also end up erasing that agency if it simply reduces the group to a politically undifferentiated 'flatland'. Once you have listened, it is still incumbent upon you to process what you have listened to, bring the arguments into critical engagement with other arguments you have heard and read, and reach your own conclusions.

The question, then, is how the left can engage with the political claims made by historically and currently marginalised communities about their marginalisation – and how, where necessary, we can politically critique and contest those claims. That can only be done on the basis of sensitivity to and understanding of the history that shaped the identity from which those claims arise. Kahn-Harris writes: 'True anti-racism [...] requires fighting for the right of Jews to be Zionists, the right of Muslims to be Islamists, and so on. That is the only way that there is even the slightest chance they will see their political choices as political choices, their foundational beliefs as politically contestable.'[41]

In other words, sections of the left must abandon their demand of Jewish individuals and organisations that anti-Zionist political tests be met as a precondition to being listened to – not automatically agreed with, but merely listened to, and not dismissed out of hand or automatically accused of ulterior motives – on the issue of the bigotry they face in society. This makes leftist solidarity against antisemitism conditional on prior political agreement with leftist common sense, an approach that can neither build a robust movement against bigotry nor stand any chance of persuading a significant number of Jews to become organised socialist activists.

Worse still, when sections treat Zionism as a 'flatland' or 'seamless whole', functioning as a reified, networked project for political domination, capable of manipulating the domestic politics of any state, they designate the majority of Jews as the enemy.

If such things as David Miller's uncritical republication of writing by the neo-Nazi Kevin MacDonald are anything to go by, this thinking can lead its adherents into some extremely ugly places.[42]

The left, if we aspire to genuine egalitarianism and anti-racism, has a responsibility to relate sensitively to anxieties within Jewish communities about antisemitism, and within other historically and currently marginalised and oppressed communities about bigotries they face. Conspiracy mongering, the presumption of ulterior motives and vicarious identitarian and communalist approaches must all give way to a working-class anti-racism that stands with minority communities, whatever their hegemonic politics, against racism and bigotry, but also understands those communities as sites of struggles in which the left should seek to intervene. If we cannot do that, we risk abdicating both our responsibility to seriously and critically analyse the world around us, and basic duties of solidarity.

# CHAPTER SEVEN

# LEFT ANTISEMITISM, RACISM, AND OPPRESSION

There is an ostensible clarity to defining antisemitism as anti-Jewish racism, or even to dispensing with the term antisemitism altogether and putting anti-Jewish racism in its place. This labelling has much to recommend it. It situates antisemitism within a wider nexus of bigotry and prejudice against people on the basis of assumed racial characteristics, and embodies an implicit potential for solidarity between Jews and other victims of racism.

The latest wave of the Black Lives Matter movement has carved out additional social space for discussion of how contemporary racism operates, and how racial inequality is structurally reproduced. Building anti-racist solidarity between Jews and other historically racialised and oppressed peoples is a necessary task. The construction of such solidarity will require some political courage and self-reflection, including the acknowledgement of anti-Black and anti-Muslim racism in some Jewish communities and movements, and of antisemitism in some Black and some Muslim communities and movements, while also stamping out the idea that expressions of antisemitism by Black and Muslim people are qualitatively worse than other expressions or forms of antisemitism. It also requires an acknowledgement of the relative degree of privilege that has accrued to many Jewish people owing to their substantial integration into whiteness, a racial category of relatively recent construction, while recognising that integration as both recent and precarious.[1] Finally, it will require an amplification of the voices of Jews of colour, who often face multifaceted forms of marginalisation, within and between the multiple communities to which they may belong.

As Kahn-Harris puts it, without integrating the fight against antisemitism into a wider struggle for equality and liberation:

> [Jews] allow ourselves to be used as a stick to beat other minorities [...] fighting the antisemitism of marginalised Western Muslims as though it were the same as the antisemitism of the white majority. We can be blind to the connotations of singling out minority women of colour [...] as antisemitic folk devils. And at the other end of the Jewish political spectrum, we can collude in the message that other minorities can behave as they wish towards Jews, that their antisemitism will not count.[2]

A similar argument has been advanced by the Black Jewish writer Nadine Bachelor-Hunt, who has suggested: 'Black people and Jewish people need to stand together more than ever in the face of rising far-right populism—and the only way to do that is to actively dispel and debunk myths and tropes that may exist in each community. Only then can we move forward to a point of true and constructive solidarity.'[3]

Understanding of and opposition to antisemitism therefore has to be built into a wider anti-racist politics, both because of the historic position of Jews as a racialised other and because of the position of antisemitism as the 'theoretical core' of contemporary white nationalism, especially in the USA. As Eric Ward put it, in the white supremacist mindset, 'some secret cabal, some mythological power, must be manipulating the social order behind the scenes. [...] What is this arch-nemesis of the white race, whose machinations have prevented the natural and inevitable imposition of white supremacy? It is, of course, the Jews.'

Ward writes that the antisemitism at the core of white nationalism is 'a particular and potent form of racism so central to white
supremacy that Black people would not win our freedom without
tearing it down'. [4]

## IS LEFT ANTISEMITISM RACISM?

Thinking about antisemitism in total abstraction from racism
would therefore be a serious error. Certainly we cannot say,
'antisemitism is *not* racism'. Probably we can say, 'antisemitism is *often* – even *usually* – a form of racism'. But can we say,
without qualification, that antisemitism is *always* racism? Is left
antisemitism, in particular, racism, and are those who express left
antisemitic ideas therefore racists? This chapter will argue that
understanding left antisemitism as racism is counterproductive,
and that antisemitism more generally cannot always be nested
neatly under the general header of racism.

This assessment does not represent a moral value judgement.
Believing left antisemitism is not best understood as form of
racism does not mean it is somehow more acceptable than other
bigotries that can be understood as such. A form of bigotry can
be dangerous without being racist. Conversely, believing that
antisemitism has specificities which distinguish it within, and in
some cases *from*, the generic category of racism does not mean it
is worse than racism in general. But if we set out to understand
the particular functioning of different bigotries, and especially
in understanding how antisemitism manifests specifically on the
left, collapsing it into a general category of racism sets us back.

Many expressions of antisemitism are clearly, classically
racist. They assert the existence of a Jewish race, one of a number
of racialised collectivities, which is presumed to have particular
characteristics somehow derived from biology and passed on via
heredity. But, unlike in many other forms of racism, where the

imagined racial characteristics are used to inform simplistic binaries, antisemitism contends that Jews use these characteristics to achieve dominance. As Postone wrote:

> The way in which antisemitism is distinguished, and should be distinguished, from racism, has to do with the sort of imaginary of power [sic], attributed to the Jews, Zionism, and Israel, which is at the heart of antisemitism. The Jews are seen as constituting an immensely powerful, abstract, intangible global form of power that dominates the world. There is nothing similar to this idea at the heart of other forms of racism.[5]

Antisemitism is also distinguished by its age. As Martin Thomas puts it:

> Antisemitism is much older than racism. It is possible, of course, to stretch the term racism by back-defining it to cover many phenomena from centuries before the term existed. But to do that blurs rather than clarifies. In particular, it blurs the ways in which antisemitism operates quite differently from general racism (or, if you insist on putting it that way, from other racism).[6]

Stretching the definition of racism, a category that presupposes the social construction of the concept of 'race', to cover any instance of bigotry, prejudice or chauvinism on the basis of religious, ethnic, national or communal difference throughout history also serves to blur what is historically distinct about modern racism. Modern racism has particular roots in the white-supremacist ideological scaffolding placed as justification around the economically driven enslavement of Black Africans, and the colonial expansion of the seventeenth, eighteenth and nineteenth centuries. These are not its sole roots, but they are key ones. The origins of modern racism therefore overlap and intertwine with the origins of capitalism, giving developing capitalism, at the global level, a racialised character that, notwithstanding the widespread achievement of formal legal equality and other gains of anti-racist struggle, it substantially retains.

Antisemitism has parallels with that, with modern antisemitism forming partly in the development of capitalist modernity, including via the enforced role of Jews in mercantile trades, and the exclusion of Jews into ghettoes or prescribed territories. This often forcibly placed Jews in a position that was simultaneously at the centre and on the margins of developing capitalism. The historic racialisation, in which a group is socially ascribed the status of a 'race', of Jewish immigrants to Britain was also closely linked to an economically rooted imperialist prejudice, which also found expression in the labour movement and on the left via agitation for controls on immigration.[7] The protectionist-nationalist arguments of socialist antisemites in the late nineteenth and early twentieth centuries persist in the contemporary labour movement through arguments designating migrant workers as a threat to the economic conditions, or even the way of life, of the local working class.[8] As Steve Cohen showed in *That's Funny*, nationalist, anti-migrant racism, especially in the labour movement and would-be left, took shape substantially in an antisemitic agitation. An overemphasis on the distinctions between antisemitism and racism can, therefore, obscure their shared features.

Nonetheless, narrowing the definition of racism to refer only to phenomena directly traceable to the European colonial subjugation of peoples of colour can also be analytically limiting, failing to meaningfully process 'the anomalous position Jews sometimes occupy within an anti-racist imaginary focused on whiteness and empire'.[9] As Camila Bassi writes: 'The colonial model of racism, as prevalent in US and British academia (and indeed on the wider political left), is not able to explain the combination of events, circumstances, and social relations in which certain populations have been racialised and excluded without being colonised.'[10]

An insistence on the 'colonial model' as racism's only form is particularly damaging in the context of left antisemitism, as it erases the specificities and complexities of the history of Jewish immigration to Palestine, the formation of a Hebrew-speaking Jewish national community there and the foundation of the state of Israel. It substitutes in their place a simplistic binary – white colonisers oppressing non-white colonial subjects – that somehow renders Jews fleeing genocide, or post-Holocaust refugees in displaced persons camps, the agents of a straightforwardly white-supremacist colonial project, with no internal contradictions of its own nor any relationship to Jews' own experiences of racism.

At the time, the contemporary far left rejected that view. As discussed in Chapter Five, in 1948 the Palestinian Trotskyists denounced as a 'racial war' not Jewish immigration to Palestine but the Arab League's assault. As also noted in Chapter Five, Black radicals such as W. E. B. Du Bois and Eldridge Cleaver saw parallels between Zionism and their own struggles, a perspective which thoroughly complicates claims that Zionism is an extension of empire-building, European white-supremacist colonialism. Brian Klug wrote that Zionism 'spoke the language of colonisation – but for the sake of emancipation, not empire'.[11]

Some Zionists undoubtedly did, and do, see Arabs as a racialised inferior other. There can be racism between racialised subjects, and even *within* racialised groups. And although the oppression of the Palestinians by the Israeli state is in essence a *national*, rather than racial, oppression, the barriers between categories of 'nationality', 'ethnicity' and 'race' are often permeable. As Frantz Fanon noted, it is possible to pass from nationalism 'to ultra-nationalism, to chauvinism, and finally racism', which, as Martin Thomas puts it, 'can take markers other than skin colour to tag the group to be denied equal rights'.[12] Conversely, as noted in Chapter Five, some left antisemites have recognised 'Arab racism against Israel', in order to celebrate it as progressive.[13]

We must acknowledge, then, the possibility of types of racism that do not fit neatly into the 'colonial model', with racialised others who are not necessarily historic colonial subjects. But wholly defining all variants of antisemitism as racism blurs the specificity of antisemitism as a pre-racial bigotry which often has distinct ideological characteristics, even when expressed in racial terms. At the same time, this extends the definition of racism backwards into history, to include all forms of ethnic or communal chauvinism, and risks blurring what is distinct about modern racism.

Understanding antisemitism as only and always a form of racism can blunt our analysis of forms of antisemitism, historic and contemporary, that are not linked to racialised categories. The prejudice, hostility and potential bigotry that left antisemitism implies towards the vast majority of Jews is on the basis of assumed *political*, rather than racial, biological, characteristics.

Those on the left who baulk at the suggestion they might be carriers of some implicitly antisemitic ideas often reflexively defend themselves by insisting that they are opposed to racism. Insisting in response that left antisemitism *is* racism necessitates a psychological interrogation as to whether their professed opposition to racist antisemitism, to the idea that Jews should be discriminated against on the basis of heredity and assumed racial characteristics, is really sincere. That would be fruitless.

As Martin Thomas has written:

Much better to say to those with political antisemitic views: yes, of course, I know you abhor racist antisemitism as much as anyone. I know you think your views are only [...] opposition to a sort of politics, Zionism, and a state with that sort of politics. But here is something special about your political opposition to what you call 'Zionism' – a quality different from that of your political opposition to neoliberalism [...] or whatever – and that 'something special' has implications which may make you want to reconsider.[14]

Camila Bassi argues that left antisemitism *is* a form of a racism, as it

involves a process of signification that defines the Other by real and imagined cultural features [and] marks out a group of people in relation to Israeli/Zionist Jewishness – and assigns this categorised group of bodies with negative characteristics and as giving rise to negative consequences. This Jewish Other is generalised with a singular and static understanding of Israel and Zionism: that this Jewish collective has uniquely world domineering and tyrannical power.[15]

Bassi is right to identify that left antisemitism involves a form of 'othering' of Jews, avoidable only by performative disavowal of any affinity with Israel. However, this perversely – and, as Sean Matgamna noted in his 1988 open letter to Tony Cliff, the founder of the SWP – has, in formal terms, more in common with pre-racial Christian antisemitism than with racist antisemitism.[16] Christian antisemitism offered its victims an escape from itself, by conversion to Christianity. Similarly, Jews can escape the implied hostility of left antisemitism by 'converting' to an absolute anti-Zionism, boycotting Israel, eschewing any sympathy or support for historic Jewish immigration to Palestine or the rights of the contemporary Israeli-Jewish national group, denying the possibility of antisemitism on the left and accepting a geopolitical narrative that 'identifies Israel as the world's hyper-imperialism'.[17] If Jews can pass these 'loyalty tests', as Steve Cohen called them, they are welcomed into the community of the good, and frequently aggressively tokenised as evidence that antisemitism cannot exist on the left – because look, here is a Jew who also demonises Zionism and Israel!

States often attempt to discipline racialised minorities into the belief that if they act in a certain, state-sanctioned, way, they will be able to escape racism. But the material constitution of racism in relations of power means it cannot be, ultimately and definitively, escaped, regardless of how many loyalty tests the racialised minority passes. The relations of power must be overthrown.

But Jews on the left really *can* escape the political hostility of left antisemitism by passing the loyalty tests set for them. Indeed, some prominent standard-bearers of left antisemitism are themselves ethnically and/or religiously Jewish. Insisting that such people are – presumably 'self-hating' – anti-Jewish racists adds nothing to our understanding of left antisemitism, and makes it harder, not easier, to confront it.

Some critics of left antisemitism have preferred to designate antisemitism as an oppression. In an explanatory note in the introduction to her excellent 2007 pamphlet *The Past Didn't Go Anywhere*, April Rosenblum defines antisemitism succinctly as 'oppression against Jews'.

I believe that for the concept of oppression to have meaning, it must refer to something structural and systemic – a relation of power, not only speech or ideas. It implies institutional discrimination, structural inequality in areas such as jobs and housing, and, invariably, violence against a group of people with a shared characteristic such as gender, sexuality, disability, ethnicity, nationality or religion. Oppression is often directly state sponsored, or, in instances where a state may be formally committed to equality, state-tolerated, or perpetuated by failures to enact that commitment to equality.

Much historic antisemitism has clearly been spectacularly oppressive, in this structural sense. The discrimination that Jews experienced under Stalinism was also undeniably oppressive, and as such left antisemitism could be said to have roots in the ideological buttressing of anti-Jewish oppression. But flatly describing all forms of contemporary antisemitism as 'oppression against Jews' is misleading.

To argue that I, as a white Jew in modern Britain, am 'oppressed' by antisemitism is to dematerialise what oppression is. I am highly unlikely to be denied a job, or a tenancy, or a place at an educational institution because I am Jewish. I am not paid less, on average, than my non-Jewish workmates. I am not more likely to be harassed or brutalised by the police because I am Jewish, or deported because of my Jewishness. Some Jews do face what might be termed structural or systemic social barriers: Charedi communities in Britain have higher rates of poverty than the average, and some Charedi Jews face access barriers related to language. It is, however, highly debatable whether these are instances of a specifically antisemitic systemic oppression, rather than the consequences of systemic state discrimination against non-English-speaking, migrant-heritage people in general.

## IDEOLOGICAL BIGOTRY

There are dangers here. Some on the left use the fact that Jews are not targeted by state racism or subject to systemic oppression to dismiss the possibility of racist antisemitism entirely, arguing, for instance, that: 'Jews are a prosperous, privileged section of the white community. There's no racism that I can discern. [...] Racism is experienced by Black and Asian people [in Britain], not Jewish people.'[18] The fact that Jews are not systemically oppressed by the state does not mean they cannot 'experience racism', including racist violence. This attitude ignores racist antisemitic attacks by non-state actors such as the white supremacist far right or Islamists, and is also highly complacent about the possibility of regressive developments. The dematerialisation of antisemitism, from a materially constituted oppression to a primarily ideological bigotry, is not fixed. It could change, perhaps sharply and rapidly. As April Rosenblum rightly notes, 'in some of the most famous examples of anti-Jewish expulsion and mass murder (i.e. medieval Spain or modern Germany), just prior to the attacks, Jews appeared to be one of society's most successful, comfortable, well-integrated minorities'.[19]

As stated, most Jews' integration into whiteness is both recent and precarious. Just how precarious is evidenced by Donald Trump's explicit use of antisemitic dog-whistle phrases and imagery in his campaign adverts, and the use of similar dog whistles, such as 'globalists', a term used by many on the far right to refer to the so-called 'financial elites'. Further evidence is provided by references to 'Cultural Marxism' – a far-right conspiracy theory that posits an effort by Frankfurt School Marxists, prominently including several Jewish figures, to subvert Western culture through infiltration of academic institutions – by Viktor Orban's government in Hungary, or senior Tory politicians such as Jacob Rees-Mogg and Suella Braverman.[20] These people are not members of marginal neo-Nazi sects; they are presidents and ministers, leading political representatives of a section of their respective national ruling classes.

Nor has antisemitic violence disappeared. It especially threatens Jews whose Jewishness is outwardly visible, for example through religious clothing, and Jewish religious and communal institutions such as synagogues. The Community Security Trust, which collects data on antisemitic incidents, recorded three incidents of 'extreme violence' in 2020, compared with one in 2019, and ninety-seven incidents categorised as 'assault'.[21] Incidents spiked against the backdrop of intensifying violence in Israel/Palestine in May 2021, and included a convoy of cars that drove through areas of north London with significant Jewish populations shouting slogans such as 'Fuck Jews, rape their mothers, rape their daughters'.

And as incidents such as the 2018 shooting at the Tree of Life synagogue in Pittsburgh showed, murderous white supremacist far-right violence against Jews remains a particular threat. It is plausible that, given certain conditions, the exploitation of antisemitic ideas by ruling parties in Britain and America, or figures within them, could license more widespread anti-Jewish violence and discrimination that, over time and via links with elements of state power, might harden into structural oppression. Those dangers are real and the left must be alive to them.

Rosenblum refers to antisemitism as 'the amazing disappearing oppression', parodying the idea that 'antisemitism is over' because Jews are no longer structurally discriminated against in the ways traditionally associated with oppression. She is absolutely right to argue that antisemitism is not 'over' because of Jewish integration into whiteness, or the relative social prosperity of Jews in a country like Britain. But understanding oppression as constituted in relations of power and structural inequalities, and therefore not seeing Jews in Britain or America as a currently oppressed group, in that material sense, does not require us to contend that antisemitism is 'over', only to understand that it has changed.

In a sense, it is antisemitism that has dematerialised, and is expressed now at the level of attitudes and ideas rather than structural relations of power. Those attitudes and ideas can impel physical violence, but that is not the same as a system of oppression. Denying that, and insisting that antisemitism currently, and always, constitutes oppression, risks making us less sensitive to regressive developments, and sensing the moments when antisemitism might, to adapt a phrase from Marx and Engels, 'descend from language into life',[22] and once again become a systemic oppression. Indeed, acknowledging that the functioning of antisemitism has changed should, by rooting us in an understanding that the dynamics involved are not fixed, make us more aware of the reality that it could change back.

Failure to distinguish between the different ways racism and antisemitism are expressed and structured in society, as well as their overlapping and shared features, can also lead to Jews of colour being especially marginalised, and having their 'identities pitted against each other', particularly if they are assertive in confronting both antisemitism with Black communities, and anti-Black racism within Jewish communities.[23] When some right-wing political forces, such as Trumpism, attempt to tokenise a politically constructed version of Jewish identity based on uncritical support for Israel and hostility to Muslims, leftist critique of that will be sharper if we are able to identify the distinctions between categories of racism, antisemitism and oppression, as well as the points at which they might touch or overlap.

Left antisemitism in particular has even less connection to anything that might be understood as structural oppression than contemporary antisemitism in general. Reading social media posts, or hearing comments in meetings from fellow leftists about the assumed power of Israel and Zionism might make me angry, upset, wearied. I may *feel* oppressed, in the sense of being put upon and overwhelmed, but does this amount to oppression in a concrete, structural sense? I would suggest not.

I acknowledge that I speak from a position of privilege and relative comfort in that, as a white, cis-gendered, heterosexual male, I have no direct experience of structural oppression. I am also someone with, at the time of writing, nearly twenty years of close encounters with the various ideological maladies of the far left behind me, and a (hopefully) unshakeable conviction that they can and must be confronted and changed. Perhaps all of that inures me to the oppressive potential of left antisemitism.

I also acknowledge that accumulated hurt of the type many Jews experience when continually confronted with antisemitism, in left-wing spaces both online and physical, can have a profound effect on people's mental well-being, and may well affect the extent to which they feel able to participate in left-wing movements. That is a serious matter, which requires dealing with on its own terms. But hurt and distress are not enough to constitute oppression. Indeed, describing left antisemitism as an oppression could have the effect of blurring our analysis of the very real and immediate structural oppressions – on the basis of colour, gender, sexuality, disability or immigration status – that are deeply imbricated with capitalist class exploitation in a way left antisemitism simply is not.

The left should reject the notion that oppression and relations of power can be *created*, rather than reflected, by the mere expression of ideas. Someone expressing bigoted ideas about someone else does not, in and of itself, create a relationship of structural power between them. Ultimately, insisting on left antisemitism as a form of anti-Jewish oppression will lead us down a blind alley, searching for ways to overthrow the power relation we imagine it reflects, rather than confronting it at the level of *ideas* and seeking to persuade its adherents of different ones.

It bears repeating that analysing a bigotry as not immediately connected to or expressed by a material relation of power and inequality does not make it less bad in a moral sense. In writing this chapter, I acknowledge the risk that some cynical denialist might 'weaponise' it, approximately thus: 'See, even someone writing a whole book opposing left antisemitism says it's not a form of racism and not a form of oppression … even if it *does* exist, it can't be that serious then, can it?'

That would be a profoundly bad-faith reading of my argument, which, I hope I may go some way to warding off by anticipating it. Designating left antisemitism as an ideological bigotry, rather than an oppression that implies primarily political, rather than racialised, hostility to Jews, is an analytical, not moral, argument.

Fundamentally, the significance of the analysis is in the approach it implies to confronting that bigotry.

Racist oppression, and other structural oppressions, must be contested both at the level of ideas and the level of material power. Socialists fight for the labour movement to campaign for reforms to advance and consolidate equality, as part of an over-all anti-capitalist programme that aims to overturn the system in which oppression and inequality are rooted. At the same time, we conduct educational work within the movement against bigoted ideas linked to such oppression and inequality. But left antisemi-tism, unlike racism in general, is a bigotry that must be confronted almost exclusively at the level of ideology. That has implications for what that confrontation must consist of, practically. That will be the focus of this book's next, and final, chapter.

# CHAPTER EIGHT

# HOW TO FIX THE PROBLEM

Left antisemitism cannot be dealt with by bureaucratic procedure, nor by the sanctioning and expulsion of individual antisemites, even in large numbers, from organisations such as the Labour Party. How it *can* be dealt with is perfectly straightforward – a trifling matter of dismantling a political common sense built up in influential sections of the far left over decades, and replacing it with a new common sense based on a reassertion of consistent principles of democracy, internationalism and equal rights that were foundational to the classical Marxist project. Easy.

What this consists of, in a getting-our-hands-dirty, practical sense, is a slightly thornier problem. Whether far-left organisations that have implicitly antisemitic policies about Israel or Zionism can be broken from those policies and maintain anything like their current organisational form is dubious. And left antisemitism is not an abstract problem, but part of a wider malaise stemming essentially from much of the far left's failure to move out from under the shadow of Stalinism and renew socialism's mission – democratic, egalitarian and libertarian, in the sense of seeking to maximise liberty, both collective and individual.

A long-term overcoming of left antisemitism will undoubtedly have to take place in the context of a much wider political transformation and recomposition of the whole socialist movement, and may only be catalysed by a significant upheaval in class struggle, which cannot be brought about at will. Groups on the far left that have a critique of left antisemitism continuing to conduct political-educational campaigning to advance it, and persuade as many activists as they can reach, is a difficult, unglamorous, but necessary task.

But there are additional opportunities today for addressing the problem directly that Steve Cohen, when writing in the 1980s, or even up until his death in 2009, could probably not have predicted. The left surge in the Labour Party from 2015 has meant that, for the first time in a generation or more, people whose ideological formation had been in organisations and milieus where left antisemitism was dominant directly shared a common political space with socialist critics of left antisemitism, in a permanent and ongoing way. This created opportunities for a more direct, head-on confrontation with left antisemitism than had been previously possible. The tools primarily required to conduct that confrontation are not complaints, suspensions and expulsions but debate, polemic and education.

## IDEOLOGICAL CONFRONTATION OR BUREAUCRATIC PROCEDURE?

Much of the writing about the tumult around this issue since 2015 has lamented it as a 'crisis' that should never have happened. I do not see it this way. Undoubtedly, the damage wrought by various scandals could have been limited by speedy and straightforward condemnation from Corbyn's leadership, rather than consistently packaging such condemnation in general opposition to 'all forms of racism', and a mechanical repetition that the scale of the problem was minuscule and, implicitly, therefore not worthy of the attention it was receiving. But definitive avoidance of a confrontation with left antisemitism was a 'what-if?' counterfactual, possible only on the basis of the unpicking and reversal of innumerable historical events stretching back at least to the Stalinist counter-revolution in Russia in the 1920s, and different tendencies winning out in key moments of ideological conflict to determine the hegemonic ideas of the socialist movement. The die was already cast; the problem required running towards, not away from.

I am aware that I risk sounding as though I view the demoralisation experienced by many of those at the centre of the various furores in the Labour Party since 2015 as unfortunate collateral damage in a welcome process of political reckoning. I do not wish to project an air of insensitivity, nor am I by any means entirely personally dispassionate. But I do believe this has been, and continues to be, a necessary, and inevitable, confrontation.

Many attempts to address the issue in the Labour Party have posed the solution in technical, bureaucratic or disciplinary terms. In 2016 the ultra-Blairite Labour Party faction Progress issued an eight-point programme for dealing with antisemitism in Labour, which argued that expressions of antisemitism should lead to a 'lifetime ban' from party membership, foreclosing in advance on the possibility of changing people's minds through argument and debate, and seeming to preclude due process.[1] While quick to identify and call out antisemitism on the left, with a few notable exceptions the Labour right has proved itself inadequate at meaningfully confronting it, including in the opening period of the Corbyn leadership, when much of the Labour Party's administrative machinery remained under the right's control. During the Labour leadership election in early 2020, the right strongly promoted the Board of Deputies' 'Ten Pledges', which adopted the same emphasis on bureaucratic and administrative procedure rather than ideological confrontation.[2]

One pledge was for an 'independent' disciplinary process, calling for an 'independent provider' to process 'all complaints'. While there are good reasons for a party's disciplinary procedures to maintain some structural distance from its leading political committees, making such processes wholly 'independent' from politics is wrong, especially on an issue like antisemitism. The Labour leadership's response to antisemitism needed to be *more* 'political' – more informed by a thorough political understanding of the roots and functioning of antisemitism on the left; more geared towards equipping members with the ideological tools to identify and confront it – not less. There was also more than a hint of irony at the right, which had used its control of the Labour machine to wield the party's rulebook in a nakedly factional way against the far left (including to expel me – twice – for my association with a revolutionary socialist group), supporting pledges that condemned 'partisanship' and 'factionalism'.[3]

The publication, in October 2020, of the Equality and Human Rights Commission (EHRC) investigation into the Labour Party's handling of antisemitism complaints further entrenched the debate on the terrain of the administration of disciplinary processes. That was to some extent inevitable – a body like the EHRC is by its nature legalistic and concerned with procedure. And the Labour Party's complaints procedures were, and are, indeed opaque, slipshod, and inimical to due process in ways that harm both complainants and the accused. But the fusing of the debate on antisemitism in Labour into a debate about the efficiency of complaints procedures has had the ultimate effect of cutting against attempts to refocus discussion on the political fundamentals.

As Michael Richmond put it: 'This is anti-racism as procedure – a search for legal and bureaucratic fixes to a localised outbreak, so that a never-clean institution can be given a clean bill of health again. It shows no interest in what racism is or where it comes from. Antisemitism is barely defined beyond how it interacts with equalities law and party management.'[4] Notwithstanding the nuances, discussed in the previous chapter, around whether antisemitism on the left is best considered as a form of 'racism' at all, Richmond's summary neatly encapsulates the majority responses to antisemitism in Labour: 'legal and bureaucratic fixes' rather than political analysis and ideological confrontation.

All political groups have the right to collectively determine the boundaries of their membership, and deem some beliefs and behaviour incompatible with it. Aspiring to a Labour Party, and wider left, in which antisemitic ideas are clearly understood as such, and clearly understood as incompatible with involvement, is worthy. Imagining we can get to that point entirely, or even primarily, by disciplinary action, expulsions and bans is, at best, naïve. At worst, it is positively counterproductive.

Left antisemitism is not primarily a matter of behaviour that can legislated against at the level of interpersonal conduct. Ideas cannot be expelled or banned. As David Feldman put it: 'The demand for zero tolerance is impossible to meet. Expulsion, though sometimes necessary, will never get to the heart of Labour's problem. You can expel antisemites, but you cannot expel antisemitism.'[5] The necessary response must emphasise political education, discussion and debate far more than complaints procedures and disciplinary sanctions.

Keith Kahn-Harris offered a neat description of one of the common ways antisemitism is transmitted on the left:

> All too often I have seen decent people casually drawing on some of the most ingrained antisemitic tropes without any thought. For example, a feminist academic of my acquaintance – someone whose work I have learned from, someone whose politics I largely share – once liked a fake news story on Facebook that 'the Rothschilds' had been kicked out of Russia by Putin. When I pointed out the long history of the antisemitic Rothschild obsession, she seemed utterly bewildered that what had been the work of a second to express hostility to the banking industry could possibly have mired her in this swamp.[6]

Characterising left antisemitism as largely a matter of unthinking, casual Facebook likes of half-read headlines would be trivialising. But treating the person guilty of such casual unthinking as if they are a dyed-in-the-wool racist who needs to be made the subject of a complaint, rather than someone who needs political education, will not help.

The focus of much of the discussion on relative statistical claims about the scale of the issue, with those seeking to minimise it often pointing to the statistic that, as of mid-2019, only 0.06 per cent of Labour's membership had been 'found guilty' of an antisemitism-related complaint, has also misidentified the problem.[7]

If there was a dispute over whether the Labour Party had a widespread problem with, say, people throwing glasses at each other in meetings, one might reasonably respond to that by attempting to assess its scale, by looking at the number of confirmed reports of such incidents. As a literal matter of interpersonal conduct, one might also reasonably attempt to address it by putting in place more robust disciplinary procedures. Antisemitism cannot be approached that way. While it can obviously impel action, it is not itself an act, instances of which can be statistically measured and perpetrators sanctioned. It is an ideology. The ultimate remedy cannot be for some independent adjudicatory body, standing outside political structures, to assess whether antisemitism has been committed by an individual and then decide on an appropriate sanction. The ultimate remedy can only be to win hegemony for alternative ideas, and establish a political and intellectual culture capable of identifying and rejecting antisemitism.

It should be emphasised that procedural sanctions, such as suspensions and expulsions, as Feldman rightly points out, cannot be ruled out entirely. Kahn-Harris's concept of 'minimal civility' can be a helpful yardstick.[8] For left antisemites whose pursuit of a conspiracy-theorist anti-Zionist politics is so disruptive that it precludes the 'minimal civility' that is a requirement for the collective democratic functioning of any organisation, especially a party as politically diverse as Labour, procedural complaints that result in suspension or expulsion may be the only means of addressing the issue. But while such measures may ameliorate the problem at the level of an individual branch or CLP, they cannot possibly address the wider ideological issue of antisemitism on the left.

To the extent political education has been suggested at all in the discussion about antisemitism in Labour, it has usually been in the context of calls for 'training' – a word that, for me at least, conjures up the notion of something sanitised and corporate, aimed at modifying behaviour and conduct, often superficially – an exercise in 'how to avoid saying the wrong thing'. What is needed is not 'training', but critical education, aimed at changing ideas, and giving people the intellectual tools to think for themselves.

The Labour Party did, eventually, produce an educational resource, the 'No Place for Antisemitism' booklet, which it published in 2019.[9] That was useful, as far as it went. Its contents were largely good. But its publication was not accompanied by any drive to encourage local parties and affiliates to organise workshops, meetings or other events to discuss it. The booklet said: 'Labour exists to promote the social liberation of all people. That's why we are launching a programme to educate our members and empower them to confront oppression, wherever it arises.' Laudable and welcome sentiments indeed. But such a programme was never, in fact, launched. As such, the impact of producing the booklet and publishing it online, while difficult to measure, was probably negligible.

Organising meetings around that resource would have inevitably meant them being attended by denialists and left antisemites. As noted elsewhere, the idea that the confrontation of any bigotry should be a matter of debate, which implies the opportunity for the carriers of the bigotry to express their views, feels instinctively unseemly. Surely we want to limit the airtime those ideas have, rather than increasing it? But it is only via explicit argument against people's existing ideas that their ideas can change. That cannot be done without openly and directly discussing what those ideas are. That does not always have to be done via direct debates – although, as I argue later in this chapter, I believe these have a place – as people may often be less likely to change their minds in the context of a set-piece ideological competition, which forces them to double down on their existing beliefs. But collective education does require an atmosphere of free speech and discussion.

Fear that allowing the expression of antisemitic ideas via confronting them in direct debate or discussion might imperil the physical safety of Jewish people is, I believe, misplaced. It is not beyond imagining that people who think they are serving broadly left-wing goals by daubing 'free Palestine' on a synagogue might make the leap to thinking they are also serving those goals by attacking the people inside it.[10] But currently, the overwhelming evidence is that the greatest threat of violence to Jews is from white nationalists and some Islamists, not leftists. The problem with the carriers of the ideas analysed in this book is less that they are about to start launching physical attacks against Jews and more that their ideas entrench conspiracy-theorist modes of thought that will render the left ideologically hindered and ineffectual, including when it comes to fighting rising antisemitism from the far right. As such, their ideas have to be fought politically, via open debate, rather than 'physically', by exclusion, bans and no-platforming. Exclusionary sanctions should be held in reserve, for use only in extreme and intractable cases of disruptive or abusive behaviour.

We can look to history for inspiration here. In *That's Funny*, Steve Cohen described the efforts of internationalists and anti-racists, both Jewish and non, in the late-nineteenth and early-twentieth-century labour movement and left who waged a determined ideological struggle against the racist-antisemitic policy of the majority of the movement in support of stricter controls on Jewish immigration.[11] Prior to the introduction of the 1905 Aliens Act, Britain had no immigration controls in the modern sense. The end of the nineteenth century saw a growing clamour to introduce them, often posed in explicitly antisemitic terms and with the aim of keeping out Jewish immigrants from eastern Europe. In 1895 the Trades Union Congress adopted a policy in favour of controls, and lobbied the government accordingly. But the internationalists fought back.

Discussing their efforts, the academic Satnam Virdee writes: 'The interventions of socialist activists like Eleanor Marx during these years offered a glimpse into a different way of advancing collective working-class interests that rejected antisemitism and instead reimagined Jewish workers as an integral component of the English (and global) working class.'[12] The pamphlet *A Voice From the Aliens*, written by Jewish socialist and trade-union activist Joseph Finn and published and circulated by Jewish workers' organisations, confronted the antisemitic arguments head on. Finn, Marx and others did not approach the antisemitism they encountered in the movement around them by making complaints against individuals or demanding they be expelled from the movement, but rather by openly contesting their ideas and seeking to win adherents for better ones.

The internationalists were a minority, who had little choice but to undertake the hard work of ideological confrontation against a widespread nationalist common sense. Small groups of socialists calling for the expulsion of the TUC itself from the movement of which it was the main organisational body would have had no prospect of success. But it was no part of the instinct of these heroic people to approach the issue procedurally; they felt a sense of political responsibility to assert their right to equal participation in the movement, and win it to a better policy. We should learn from their example.

In many ways the contemporary balances of forces is more favourable to such an ideological confrontation. Although it represents a default common sense across influential sections of the far left, hardened over decades, today's left antisemitism is surely less widespread and deeply entrenched throughout the wider labour movement than was the nationalist, antisemitic support for immigration controls in the movement of the late nineteenth century. And, unlike left and labour movement support for immigration controls, contemporary left antisemitism is not, in twenty-first-century Britain, an outrider for the racialised violence of the state, so can in a sense be contested on straightforwardly ideological terrain without the shadow of immediate physical threat.

In the aftermath of the EHRC report's publication, Jeremy Corbyn himself was suspended, and had the whip withdrawn, for a tone-deaf and self-exculpating statement he published responding to the report. The Labour Party leadership subsequently launched a wave of suspensions against CLP officers and activists in local parties where motions opposing the action taken against Corbyn were passed – or sometimes even simply discussed. At a JLM event in November 2020, deputy leader Angela Rayner said the party would 'suspend thousands of members' if it needed to.[13]

The spasm of suspensions, which saw bans meted out to officers of CLPs merely for having permitted discussion of motions about the EHRC fallout at their meetings, was an assertion of authority on the part of Starmer's leadership regime, and a way of disciplining the left. Although such procedural toughness was undoubtedly designed to broadcast the 'zero tolerance' attitude, it represents a form of desperate defeatism from a leadership that either has no idea how to conduct an ideological struggle or no inclination to actually do so, and which sees the mass expulsion and suspension of thousands of members for antisemitism as a convenient way of shedding members from the left of the party, where the problem is most concentrated. The implication is that antisemitism is fixed, immutable, almost a force of nature, to which the only possible response is a form of administrative surgery.

But, to extend the medical metaphor, even if one wishes to see antisemitism as a 'virus', we all know from our experiences in 2020–21 that the best protection against a virus is not only to isolate those infected but also to vaccinate as many people as possible. Mass suspensions and expulsions are the equivalent of quarantining anyone believed to be 'infected' – except with no prospect of ever getting out of quarantine or being 'cured'. Conversely, political-educational campaigning aimed at changing and shaping people's ideas can be a vaccine. Even when armed with usable tools like the 'No Place for Antisemitism' booklet, neither the Corbyn nor Starmer leadership ever showed any real interest in seriously deploying them.

It has been left to activists in the party's grassroots to promote meaningful political education and discussion. In 2020 Sheffield Heeley Constituency Labour Party developed its own educational series on antisemitism, without support or encouragement from the national party.[14] Their programme provides a workable model for political education on antisemitism that should be expanded and generalised. Doing so would involve a confrontation with the party bureaucracy: as of early 2021, the party leadership was obstructing CLPs such as Lewes in East Sussex from organising educational events on antisemitism.[15]

Nevertheless, and despite such obstruction, other CLPs have begun to move on the question. Peniston and Stocksbridge CLP in South Yorkshire endorsed a resolution that stated:

Antisemitism is a genuine problem in the Labour Party; denying or minimising that obstructs our ability to tackle it. But an approach that views antisemitism as something that can be addressed primarily through technical bureaucratic measures shows a fundamental misunderstanding of how to challenge it.

A serious political intervention to tackle antisemitism should begin with a campaign of education that allows members to first recognise and then challenge the reactionary thinking that underpins it. Labour can only now do so effectively if it facilitates debate and organises political education enabling members to recognise antisemitism in its various forms – including those which disguise themselves in the language of the left.[16]

Edd Mustill, one of the organisers of the Sheffield Heeley programme, described it in an article for *LabourList*:

The sessions largely followed a facilitated discussion group format with a small amount of preparatory reading and a short introduction. For the first session, we asked people to read Steve Cohen's indispensable text *That's Funny, You Don't Look Antisemitic* and examined the history of antisemitic ideas being entertained and propagated in left-wing circles, which long predates 2015 or 1948. We asked participants to share their own experiences and reasons for taking part, facilitated as a 'round' so that everyone could have their say. Attendees came from across the political spectrum in the party, but all were strongly committed to challenging the policies and actions of the Israeli government towards the Palestinians.

In the second session, we examined the history of Zionism and anti-Zionism as they related to the socialist movement and antisemitism. We took Zionism on its own terms as a form of modern nationalism, which – like other nationalisms – has expressed the national aspirations of an oppressed group while often taking an exclusionary or oppressive stance towards others. We looked briefly at the contribution of Jewish socialists to our movement, including those of the labour-Zionist tradition. We discussed how and why 'Zionism' and Israel can become stand-ins in modern political discourse for the old ideas of the Jewish conspiracy, and whether Zionism is a meaningful political label in contemporary politics in Britain.

In the final session, we considered some contemporary examples of behaviour, language and tropes that have been criticised as antisemitic, including from high-profile figures in the labour movement. We did this not as an exercise in casting judgement about whether person X or Y 'is antisemitic' but to sharpen our own ability to recognise and call out problematic behaviour when we see it. The programme shows that it is possible – and, we believe, necessary – to create the space to discuss the history of antisemitism within and without our party and labour movement in a respectful manner.[17]

Some readers may baulk at the idea this discussion should be 'respectful', and certainly those of us seeking to confront and change them should not respect the content of antisemitic ideas. But, like it or not, a degree of personal respectfulness, Kahn-Harris's 'minimal civility' again, is usually a prerequisite for any discursive or pedagogical exercise aimed at changing someone's mind.

Who exactly is reachable by such an exercise is a matter for judgement. I have no inclination to be 'respectful', beyond a baseline commitment to certain norms of civil conduct, to hardened ideologues of left antisemitism who have been preaching its doctrine for decades. But that layer is a relative minority. The group of people influenced by some left antisemitic ideas, but in an inchoate way that means their thinking is not entirely conditioned by them, and who remain open to discussion, is much wider. There, a 'respectful' approach *is* required. 'Minimal

civility' does not preclude political sharpness, but it is a necessity if the aim is ideological change rather than mere abstract
denunciation.

Some readers may also be uncomfortable with Mustill's statement that the organisers of the educational programme 'were
strongly committed to challenging the policies and actions of the
Israeli government towards the Palestinians', and feel that this
excludes people, and perhaps many Jews, who are more supportive of Israel than this statement leaves room for, from involvement
in delivering political education against antisemitism.

Some nuance is required here. A consistent commitment
to free speech in the labour movement does mean upholding
the right of Labour Party members who defend 'the policies
and actions of the Israeli government' to have their say, just
as it requires critics of Israel to have theirs. Israel is hardly the
only oppressive state with a right-wing nationalist government
to have supporters in the Labour Party – the Starmer leadership performed an unprincipled U-turn over Kashmir following
pressure from Labour Friends of India,[18] but no left group has
advocated the mass expulsion from the Labour Party of Labour
Friends of India supporters, as some on the left have advocated
the expulsion of Labour Friends of Israel and other Zionists. Such
expulsions would be far likelier to reinforce nationalist affinities
than challenge them, while also licensing campaigns of hostility
and suspicion that target minority communities.

Complete agreement with a full set of policies on every international issue is not a viable standard for a mass social-democratic
party of Labour's type. A particular position on Israel/Palestine, or
any other international issue, cannot, therefore, be a precondition
of *involvement* in discussions and education about antisemitism.
As this book has consistently argued, attempts to apply 'no-
platform' approaches to Zionists and Zionism are themselves
logically antisemitic and must be firmly rejected, as must the idea

that any identification with Israel or Zionism, however diffuse or critical, necessarily implies support for Israeli state policy. Indeed, recent evidence, such as the previously discussed protests by the Zionist youth movements Noam and LJY-Netzer against Israeli ambassador Tzipi Hotovely and Israel's bombing of Gaza in April and May 2021 have categorically shown such notions to be false.

But there is no escaping the reality that support for the policies of the Israeli state towards the Palestinians is not compatible with any consistently left-wing worldview. When we oppose the absolute anti-Zionist programme of left antisemitism, we are also advancing an alternative, consistently democratic politics of support for Palestinian rights. That politics should be as integral to the perspectives of the left as opposition to antisemitism. Political-educational campaigning organised from a specifically left-wing point of view should indeed communicate that 'respectfully', but it cannot be flinched from.

Equality and solidarity are not utopian horizons, something to be wished for in the remote future, but must be the guiding principles of struggle today. The confrontation with left antisemitism must be a confrontation *from the left*, which asserts a more consistent application of left-wing principles as the antidote.

Strategic assessments will need to be made about how to practically conduct the confrontation in a given moment. The need to meet left antisemitism with open confrontation and contestation has to be weighed against the need to create an accessible and hospitable movement in which Jewish and non-Jewish critics of left antisemitism are not required to wage continual war against it, to the exclusion of all other political activity. But the desire to 'stamp out' antisemitism with a 'no-tolerance' policy that expels it, one antisemite at a time, cannot, ultimately, be realised. However understandable or well-intentioned it may be, it is a method which, at best, displaces rather than solves the problem. There is no path to a better, politically healthier left that does not involve explicitly naming and challenging what is unhealthy in the current one.

## AN ACTIVE CONFRONTATION WITH ANTISEMITISM, ON AND OF THE LEFT

I conclude, then, with four suggestions for areas of practical activity that socialist activists interested in pursuing active confrontation with left antisemitism within our movement, in the Labour Party and beyond, might consider.

### *Reading groups and collective education*
There is a growing literature that seeks to analyse left antisemitism. Read it, encourage comrades to read it, and then talk about. Organising, via your local Labour Party, campaign group, union branch, or other body, a reading group discussing *That's Funny*, or another similarly accessible text on left antisemitism, provides an immediate framework for discussion of key ideas. While insisting on basic comradely conduct towards each other, such discussions must be conducted in an atmosphere of free speech, with the right to disagree and dissent protected.

Other free and accessible texts include April Rosenblum's pamphlet *The Past Didn't Go Anywhere*, and 'Confronting Antisemitism in the 21st Century', a collection published under the rubric of the *Journal of Social Justice* and edited by the anti-fascist activist Shane Burley, which includes a number of essays referenced in this book. Much of Rosenblum's focus, and of several of the essays in the Burley collection, is on the American left, but these texts are still hugely valuable reading for socialist activists in Britain. And if you have found this book useful, organise meetings to discuss it.

All literature on left antisemitism (including this book!), like all political literature, expresses the perspectives and biases of its author. The purpose of a labour movement reading group on left antisemitism, beyond the basic facilitation of discussion and exposure to new ideas, should be to establish consensus around some fundamentals – opposition to conspiracy theories, opposition to the demonisation of Israel and rejection of 'transcendental', absolute anti-Zionism, while affirming support for Palestinian rights and equality – rather than to demand adherence to a particular perspective in its entirety. For Labour Party activists specifically, the Sheffield Heeley programme and the 'No Place for Antisemitism' booklet are ready-made resources that should be taken up and used.

### Direct debates

The questions of policy, perspective and analysis that underpin left antisemitism – What is Zionism? What is the real extent of Israel's power in the world? Should the Israeli-Jewish national group be entitled to self-determination? – should be openly debated. As noted, head-to-head debates between counterposed positions have their limits as a form of pedagogy, but so do all pedagogical and discursive forms.

Debating with a dyed-in-the-wool partisan of the 'anti-imperialism of fools' the question of whether Zionism exerts a controlling influence on US foreign policy, or whether the state of Israel should be destroyed, may not make much of an immediate dent in that individual's own perspectives. But it can bring the issues out into the open for the much wider layers of activists whose thinking is less worked out and consciously developed, and, as such, more reachable. Left antisemitism persists, at least in part, because of the reflexive adoption of soft versions of its ideas by people who simply have not thought through the implications of, for example, generally supporting national self-determination as a democratic right but believing the Israeli Jews should not be entitled to it. Direct debates can help with that thinking through.

I am sure that many activists, including many sympathetic to the overall arguments of this book, will recoil at the idea that people with such views should be platformed in debates. I understand that instinct. But these ideas exist in our movement, whether we like it or not; better that they are expressed in ways that bring them into direct confrontation with their opposites.

Debates that are not necessarily set-piece confrontations between counterposed, irreconcilable positions, but which allow speakers, and attendees, to explore areas of commonality as well as difference, are also hugely valuable.

### Practical solidarity on Israel/Palestine

I share Steve Cohen's assessment that confrontation with left antisemitism must be consciously fused with class-struggle and internationalist solidarity with struggles for liberation and equality in Israel/Palestine.

In practical terms, this can begin with offering direct solidarity and material support for socialists, internationalists, anti-racists, feminists and labour movement forces in Israel/Palestine, resisting occupation and racism on the basis of a joint Arab–Jewish struggle for equality.

Some focuses for this solidarity might be:

Omdim be'Yachad – a left-wing Arab/Jewish social movement that organises against the occupation and anti-Arab racism, and for equality, based on class struggle around shared interests (www.standing-together.org/english)

Workers Advice Centre-Ma'an – an independent union organising both Israeli-Jewish and Palestinian workers, including Palestinian workers employed in settlements (eng. wac-maan.org.il)

Koah LaOvdim – a trade-union centre based in Israel, also organising both Jewish and Palestinian workers, including those often ignored by Israel's mainstream union federation, the Histadrut (https://workers.org.il)

Democracy and Workers' Rights Centre – a labour-movement NGO based in Ramallah, supporting Palestinian workers' organisation and struggle (dwrc.org)

Combatants for Peace – a joint Palestinian–Israeli initiative campaigning against the occupation on the basis of partnership and reconciliation (https://cfpeace.org)

Refuser Solidarity Network – a network supporting Israelis who refuse mandatory conscription into the military (www.refuser.org)

### *Back to basics*

Confronting left antisemitism cannot be treated as a single-issue campaign. Steve Cohen called his book an 'anti-racist analysis' of left antisemitism. He wanted it to contribute to the construction of a left-wing politics more consistently committed to equality and liberation, and better able to pursue those goals. Although I have queried whether understanding left antisemitism as a form of racism is the most useful explanatory frame, I absolutely share the approach of situating the critique of left antisemitism within a wider effort to transform the left.

Part of this effort involves a back-to-basics reconnection with foundational ideas and approaches that have been distorted or abandoned. A historical materialist analysis of class society is, in and of itself, an answer to the belief that the world is run by a cabal of financiers. A Marxist understanding of capitalism shows that it is not a matter of 'the 1%', who are 'rigging the system'. The responses to situations of national oppression developed by the early revolutionary socialist left, which emphasise democracy and equal rights, provide an alternative to left antisemitic ideas about Israel/Palestine and Zionism. Peeling away the Stalinist-campist historiographies of Israel/Palestine can also strengthen solidarity with the Palestinians by educating about the real history, free from the influence of the 'anti-imperialism of fools'.

A historical understanding of Stalinism as the counter-revolutionary extirpation of the ideals of the Russian Revolution, rather than the legitimate continuation or inevitable end-point of them, reconnects us to the democratic, libertarian core of the original Marxist project. Basic political education about this history and ideas, and how Stalinism has distorted them, is a necessary ideological foundation for a socialism that eschews left antisemitism.

A confrontation with left antisemitism must also be part of a confrontation with other bigotries on the left. Antisemitism is not the only, or even the most intense, bigotry that has a distinct form in left-wing thought and movements. The age of Brexit has intensified a statist left-nationalism that supports tighter immigration controls and the border violence their enforcement requires as allegedly necessary mechanisms for protecting the wages and conditions of local workers, perceived to be under threat of undercutting by migrants. We can also identify an increasingly virulent 'left transphobia', a hostility to the rights of trans people framed in terms of a would-be-radical critique of sexism and defence of women's rights.

Perhaps not coincidentally, these bigotries also find some of their roots in Stalinism, which has been heavily statist and in Britain has tended to be semi-nationalist, and which, as a system of social organisation, was characterised by a profound social conservatism that fed reactionary attitudes to gender and sexuality. Remaking the left means asserting a politics of radical equality against all these reactionary traps.

The long shadow cast over the whole left by the legacy of Stalinism, and the demoralisation flowing from decades of defeat and capitalist triumphalism, have left our movement in a state of disarray. The poison of left antisemitism is one malady amongst several, and in many ways a symptom more than a cause. The road to revival, recomposition and renewal is not an easy one.

But to travel it is necessary. The task we set ourselves – the total revolutionary transformation of a world characterised by exploitation, oppression and inequality, and the construction in its place of a world based on liberty, equality and solidarity – is not achievable with faulty equipment. The historically developed left and labour movement is the only one we have; it is too late to start again from scratch. There is no alternative except to remake and transform our movement on the basis of different, better, ideas.

# APPENDIX I
## SEVEN REASONS WHY

Throughout this book I have attempted to explain the ways in which I think left antisemitism inhibits socialist politics, and why I think a confrontation with left antisemitism is imperative. But, in an age of ephemeral communication, many of us, including myself, sometimes find it easier to digest arguments in relatively bite-sized form. I also acknowledge that, because this book has been presented as a series of essays essentially confronting what left antisemitism *is*, arguments about the practical consequences of a failure to confront it may have been lost in the mix.

If you came to this book as a sceptic, I hope its chapters have convinced you that left antisemitism exists. If you came to it as someone who already accepted the existence of the phenomenon, I hope the book has given you a clearer sense of its substance and origins. I offer in this appendix, then, seven reasons *why* I think the socialist left must confront antisemitism within our movement, with contingent explanation of the consequences of not doing so:

1. Left antisemitism is a form of bigotry, which necessarily implies hostility to most Jews alive. Opposition to bigotry, and support for equality, should be foundational principles for the left.

2. Failure to recognise and confront antisemitism in our own movement inhibits efforts to confront it elsewhere, including in its most potentially deadly forms.

3. Left antisemitism, in both its primitive and contemporary forms, is a type of conspiracy theory. Conspiracy-theorist

thinking runs counter to class-struggle socialist politics, which must be based on rational, materialist analysis of capitalism. Capitalism is not a conspiracy, it is a clear system of class exploitation, the workings of which are conducted primarily in the open. To overthrow capitalism, we need an accurate understanding of what it is. The anti-capitalism of a movement that does not reject conspiracy-theorist thinking will be at best ineffective and at worst reactionary.

4. Although antisemitism on the left is not always, or necessarily, racialised, it sometimes can be. Accepting, as a legitimate part of our movement, a politics rooted in the idea of Jews as a racialised other not only harms Jews but also inevitably blunts our opposition to racism as such, by accommodating with the idea of racialised othering of certain peoples.

5. Demonising – that is, ascribing the status of a unique, essential evil – Israel and Zionism, and over-inflating the extent of their power, fundamentally miseducates and misleads the people our movement aims to persuade about how imperialism really functions. It also invariably has the effect of diminishing our focus on other instances of national and colonial oppression.

6. Left antisemitism does not help the Palestinians. By making demands for the destruction of Israel, and an insistence on the illegitimacy of Israeli-Jewish self-determination, a precondition of progress, policies that could actually lead to material redress for the Palestinians in the here-and-now are sidelined. It also creates artificial and unnecessary barriers to building Jewish, and especially Israeli-Jewish, solidarity with the cause of Palestinian freedom. The Palestinians do not need the permission of, or approval from, Israeli Jews to struggle for liberation, but the balance of forces in Israel/Palestine means that a progressive outcome for that struggle will require social upheaval in Israel itself. A politics of Palestinian solidarity

that requires a denial of Israeli-Jewish national rights essentially forecloses on the possibility of such upheaval.

7. The existence of left antisemitism, like all forms of antisemitism, inhibits attempts to persuade Jews of revolutionary-universalist ideas, by reinforcing the apparent need for a particularist, even separatist, politics. Any attempt to develop Jewish consciousness beyond Zionism must involve an unflinching confrontation with all forms of antisemitism, including left antisemitism.

# APPENDIX II
## AN EXCHANGE ON THE 2019 GENERAL ELECTION

Shortly before the December 2019 general election I met with Rabbil Sikdar to discuss our disagreements, and our common ground, on how to respond to antisemitism in the Labour Party in the context of the election. What follows is an edited transcript of our exchange. It was published by *The Clarion* magazine in March 2020.[1]

Rabbil is a left-wing activist involved in anti-racist politics, who was at the time a member of both the Labour and Cooperative parties. He has since left Labour, although he remains a member of the Cooperative Party. He is the author of the article 'As a Left-Wing Muslim, I Cannot Vote for Corbyn's Labour', published by *UnHerd* on 8 November 2019.[2]

**DR:** Could you summarise the arguments you made in your article?

**RS:** In that article, I articulated why I, as a British Muslim with left-wing political leanings, could not support Jeremy Corbyn's leadership of the Labour Party, and why I won't be voting for Labour in this election, despite being a member of the Labour and Cooperative Parties. My feeling is that the party is too institutionally racist to support, and voting for it in these conditions would be to greenlight that. I won't be voting in this election; I'm still a Labour Party member, and it would be wrong for me to vote for another party.

**DR:** I'd question the description of Labour as 'institutionally' racist or antisemitic, but I definitely agree there's a serious problem with antisemitism within Labour and on the wider left, and maybe with some other forms of bigotry as well. But how would you respond to the argument that a Labour vote has always involved a degree moral compromise? For example, voting for Labour through the mid-2000s was to vote for the party of detention centres and hostile policies towards asylum seekers; voting for Labour at any point throughout its history has always involved having to come to terms with reactionary aspects of its policy or culture. It's never had a clean slate in terms of political morality, so what is it about this election in particular that has tipped the balance for you?

**RS:** I've always objected to the idea that Labour is, straightforwardly, an 'anti-racist party'.

Historically, that's never been true. It's been a progressive party, yes, but the idea that it's been 'anti-racist' erases a lot of the history of the party, for example in terms of its stances towards refugees, immigrants and asylum seekers. But the difference for me now is that there is an ethnic minority group in this country, and within the party itself, actively saying they feel unsafe. I'd compare it to Brexit. Brexit didn't create bigotry and racism, but it did inflame those things.

Clearly, there were problems during the New Labour years – Margaret Hodge, for example, made some comments that were praised by the BNP. That needed to be called out, and maybe wasn't called out enough. But the situation now feels qualitatively worse in terms of the British Jewish community feeling that the Labour Party is hostile to them.

**DR:** I agree with you about the inadequacy of describing Labour as an 'anti-racist party'. Some of the responses to the antisemitism issue have taken the form of people essentially retconning Labour's history, claiming that the Labour Party has somehow always been a beacon of consistently anti-racist politics. It's usually accompanied by hagiographical defences of Jeremy Corbyn himself, typically using the phrase 'lifelong anti-racist', as if anyone comes out of their mother's womb with a fully formed anti-racist consciousness, as if anyone is beyond criticism.

Clearly there have been plenty of times throughout history when the Labour Party, either in government or in opposition, has been complicit in, or even a driver of, state-level racism, and I'd argue there have been times when Labour policies, or the rhetoric and culture coming from figures within the party, has made particular ethnic minority communities feel unsafe, for example Roma and Traveller communities being targeted by Labour councils.

**RS:** To go back to the comparison with Brexit, my view at the time was that if you voted Leave, you were voting for a UKIP platform. Whether you consciously thought that way or not, whether you actively wanted to or not, you were voting for a campaign that was unavoidably shaped by right-wing nationalist forces, and the rhetoric of which was explicitly about 'there are too many migrants in the country'.

I feel the same here. Even though Labour's policies aren't antisemitic, if you vote for Labour you're voting for a party led by, shaped by, people who are either responsible for or who have failed to confront antisemitic rhetoric. Corbyn himself, and too many of his close allies, are steeped in this kind of rhetoric, including conspiracy-theorist rhetoric about Israel.

In 2016, I voted Remain because I saw how threatened and upset my Romanian and other immigrant-background friends were. I couldn't vote for Leave, for the thing that was causing them to feel threatened. Similarly, I couldn't look Jewish friends in the face having voted for the thing that's making them feel threatened now.

I understand the argument that the impulse to change this has to come from within to some extent, and going forward I hope there are enough people inside the party prepared to confront these problems. But for me personally, as someone who also faces racism and bigotry, I see Labour in the same way I see Brexit. Brexit was the green light for people to come out and say all sorts of awful things about, and to, ethnic minorities and immigrants. Similarly, the Corbyn leadership of Labour has been a green light for people – online, in Momentum groups, in other Labour left spaces – to say bigoted things about, and to, Jewish people. Corbyn didn't create these problems. He's a product of this tendency I'm talking about, this strand of antisemitic leftism, he didn't create it. But in my view he has accelerated it.

**DR:** It might be interesting to return to the question of Corbyn's personal role; I think that's a complicated question. But just to pick up on your Brexit analogy; while I don't think the political terrain of a general election is the same as the political terrain of a binary plebiscitary referendum, wasn't Remain a flawed and morally compromised option as well? I very strongly agree with you about the referendum, I'm strongly pro-Remain and think Brexit is a fundamentally reactionary project that will lead to an emboldening of nationalism and racism. I hold no brief for the European Union as a set of institutions, and in fact am an opponent of those institutions, but I believed a Leave victory would create conditions in which it was harder to conduct class struggle, and to struggle for progressive politics, than if Remain won.

Similarly, despite a vote for Labour being a flawed option in many ways, I think a Labour victory and a Labour government will create conditions in which it's easier to address social problems in a progressive way – including, perhaps counter-intuitively, problems within the Labour Party itself – than the conditions which will be entrenched if the Tories win.

**RS:** This is something I'm grappling with, as I obviously know that if Labour don't win, the Tories will, and that's something I don't want either. And I know that a Labour victory would bring some positive things and social advances with it.

But we've got polls showing that 87% of British Jews say they'd feel less safe if Jeremy Corbyn became prime minister. On Brexit, you had at least some pro-Remain politicians understanding that the EU needed reform; I haven't seen anything from Corbyn that convinces me he'd really be capable of confronting this problem and regaining the trust of the Jewish community if Labour were to win. I see that from moderates within the party, people like Wes Streeting, Jess Phillips and Stella Creasy, but not from the Corbyn-supporting left. If Labour win, their response will be 'What incentive is there to change anything? People like us; we won.' I don't want British Jews to feel less safe.

**DR:** The question of feelings and perceptions of being threatened is complicated, and I think it needs some unpacking. It's important to discuss these things in a way that isn't insensitive to or dismissive of people's concerns and fears, but I think feelings and perceptions aren't a sufficient basis for drawing political conclusions.

Jews in Britain are not systemically oppressed. I'm not going be denied a tenancy, or a job, or a place at an educational institution because I'm Jewish. I'm not going to face brutality from the police because of my ethnicity. Just in an objective sense, we don't suffer the same systemic oppression and marginalisation that other ethnic minority communities do.

Clearly, antisemitic hate crimes do take place, and Jews do suffer physical and verbal attacks, and there is a view from some on the left that antisemitism is essentially now a historical relic in Britain that doesn't really require any special attention. That's obviously deeply wrong and dangerous.

It is important, though, to understand how antisemitism actually functions, and particularly, for the focus of our exchange, how it functions and manifests on the left. Primarily, antisemitism in Britain doesn't manifest either via systemic marginalisation and exclusion, or, on the whole, via physical attacks, but rather functions as an ideological nexus.

That's not to minimise it; something that functions on the level of ideology can have a hugely toxifying effect on all sorts of areas of political life, and if allowed to fester can in fact descend into the material quite easily. But it is important to acknowledge the specificities of different forms of bigotry and not flatten them out.

For me, the immediate threat of left antisemitism is not that I think Jeremy Corbyn supporters are likely to start beating me or my parents up in the street if Labour win the election, it's that the conspiracy-theorist ideas which comprise antisemitism – about finance, about Israel and Zionism, and so on – will poison any attempt to build a socialist political project if they're not confronted and uprooted. As someone who wants to see left-wing politics advance in this country, I believe that will always be held back and distorted if this source of toxicity is allowed to fester.

The conversation I want to have, and have had, with Jews who have these concerns is about saying yes, left antisemitism is real, but the only way it's going to be fixed is from within. What it requires is for people on the grassroots of the Labour Party to develop an analysis and a critique of what this is, where it comes from, and to uproot it.

You mentioned Wes Streeting, Stella Creasy and Jess Phillips. I don't want to imply they have no right to a view or an intervention on this issue because they're Blairites, and I don't think there's much to be gained by attempting to police who within the Labour Party does and doesn't have the right to comment. But even if one thinks they've made a broadly positive intervention, I don't think they've got the answers. Some of what's limited about what I've seen from that wing of the party is precisely that there is a flattening out of the specificities.

The idea that the best thing someone can do if they think there's a problem with antisemitism in the Labour Party is to join the Labour Party is not necessarily an easy argument to make. But I genuinely believe there's no shortcut around convincing people of that.

**RS:** That's a totally legitimate argument. For Labour to fix this problem, there have to be strong voices within the party challenging the entrenched left-wing narratives that promote antisemitic conspiracy theories.

I just don't think a Labour Party that's just won a general election will be sufficiently introspective to allow for that challenge to take place. We've seen it in the past; in times of victory, there's pressure to close ranks. It creates the impression that there are no problems that need fixing. You saw some of that after the 2017 election, and I think that effect would be amplified were Labour to win on 12 December. Where is the pressure or incentive to have those difficult conversations, to undertake that soul-searching, to reform the political culture going to come from if Labour is in government?

A jolt and a shake-up is required to really open up those introspective conversations. Ultimately, I don't think it can happen while Corbyn is leader. He can't be separated from his baggage. We need a leader that's pro-Palestine without the baggage of Corbyn's past associations and his complicity in promoting conspiracy-theory narratives.

For me, there's also an issue here around the left's analyses of structural and systemic racism. The simplistic argument on the left is that because British Jews are not systemically or economically oppressed, they don't need our solidarity. But the structural demonisation of a group doesn't need to be rooted in the economic. For example, Arab Americans were not a particularly economically downtrodden group, there was a comfortably consolidated Arab-American middle class, many in fact were Republican voters. But they still faced substantial demonisation and racism in the aftermath of 9/11.

The left needs to confront this and understand that, yes, the structural and the systemic are features of racism – you can face discrimination in housing, you can face police brutality – but even when a community doesn't experience that, they can still face racism. So even though the Jewish community may not face discrimination in the job market, or the housing market, or from the police, they can still face discrimination from racist tropes and stereotyping. We can see that in incidents like the one on the Tube recently; that man didn't need to be working-class or poor to experience that racism.* I do, of course, acknowledge that if the Tories win, racists and right-wingers will be emboldened, who are also likely to be antisemitic. It's really a lose–lose situation for the Jewish community.

**DR:** You've talked about Corbyn's personal role, about this problem being unsolvable while he's leader because of his background. I actually feel the extent to which the debate has become bogged down in questions about Corbyn himself, as an individual, has been very unhelpful.

I think there is a quite unhealthy, almost personality-cultist, attitude towards Corbyn throughout a lot of the party, which is really dangerous on its own terms. What that's led to is a whole series of uncritical, hagiographical defences of him, people

---

* See Jane Dalton, 'Tube Passengers Unite to Challenge Man Hurling Antisemitic Abuse at Jewish Family', *Independent*, 23 November 2019. Available at: www.independent.co.uk/news/uk/home-news/train-abuse-jewish-family-antisemitism-london-tube-racist-a9214316.html

talking about him as if he's absolutely unimpeachable and beyond any reproach whatsoever, on any issue, and what that produces in its turn is people talking about him as if he's an evil mastermind and that he's the problem on a personal, individual level, which I think is equally nonsensical. These positions have become mutually reinforcing.

For what it's worth, I'm not sure Corbyn is necessarily as politically sophisticated on a lot of these issues as either his supporters or his detractors claim. I think he has assimilated, to a large degree, a simplistic view of world politics where political forces, up to and including at the level of states, can be divided into 'good' and 'bad', with Israel on the 'bad' side and anyone who opposes Israel therefore on the 'good' – hence his association with and apologism for people like [Palestinian Islamist] Raed Saleh.

That worldview has its origins in something much more deeply rooted; a lot of it comes from Stalinism. While I don't at all think Corbyn is a Stalinist in the sense that people close to him, like [Seumas] Milne and [Andrew] Murray, are, his political formation has taken place in milieus where those ideas were dominant, or at least very prominent. But he's not the originator of it. That's not to let him off the hook for where he's said or done problematic things; clearly, he's not just an empty vessel that other people have poured ideas into. But say Corbyn goes – so what? That worldview, and ideological offshoots of it, will still be present and influential throughout the left.

Corbyn's personal role, for me, is fundamentally secondary to whether or not there are enough people at the grassroots prepared to meaningfully confront and grapple with these issues. Whether or not Corbyn himself is ever going to really confront what's problematic about his past associations and views, I can't say; probably not. But I think a sufficient groundswell at the grassroots of the party could have a transformative effect on the culture of the party as a whole, whoever the leader was.

To return to the question of the election, I think that unless one intends to stand in every election oneself, ensuring that you'll always have a candidate to vote for whose views accord exactly with your own, any vote for anyone will be on some level ostensibly contradictory and a compromise. In 2005, the first election I voted in, a vote for Labour was a vote for the party of the Iraq war and Private Finance Initiatives. In 2017, a vote for Labour was a vote for a party making a manifesto commitment to end free movement. So I've voted for Labour on a number of occasions when they had many policies I disagreed with and believed would make society worse. But I did so because I saw that vote as part of a wider project which was about advancing working-class interests in politics, voting for a party fundamentally based on the labour movement, and acknowledging that you can vote for that party at the same time as disagreeing with some things about the party and fighting to change them. I think the same is true in this election.

**RS:** I agree that Corbyn going won't, by itself, fix the problem. The problem predates Corbyn. The need to transform the political culture within the Labour Party, to educate people about the antisemitic tropes around Israel and Zionism, will still be there. That will take years, it will probably need to happen over a generation. I just don't see that reform happening if Labour win. I think the party is so entirely controlled by Corbyn and his supporters, and therefore influenced by their culture, that there's no prospect for those reforms to take place if Labour win and that control is entrenched.

We've talked a lot about voting for a party even when you disagree with certain policies, but this isn't fundamentally a matter of formal policy. Take the Tories, for example: they don't have specific policies that are about directly, specifically targeting British Muslims in a racist way. There's no proposal to ban the burqa from public spaces, for example. Nevertheless, British Muslims still feel very threatened by the prospect of ongoing Boris Johnson government, because of the comments he's made and the rhetoric he and others have used. Similarly, there are no Labour policies that directly target British Jews, but a Labour government will be one led by someone who has used antisemitic rhetoric and has proved incapable of addressing the problem or approaching it with empathy. Why will he be more likely to do so if he's just become the prime minister? Once Corbyn goes, I think more space will open up to be more critical and push for changes.

**DR:** I do find it profoundly unhelpful when people on the left essentially tell Jews concerned about antisemitism in Labour to just get over it and vote Labour anyway, basically saying 'take one for the team'. But there's a bit of an irreconcilable problem there, because if you're saying 'Labour has to lose for this problem to get solved', you're implicitly saying 'the Tories have to win', so you're telling all the people who'll be victims of their government, including many Jews, to 'take one for the team' as well.

We do have to weigh up, in aggregate, which outcome will create conditions more conducive to prosecuting the class struggle, or even to advancing progressive politics on a basic level if one prefers to look at it that way. For me there's no question that a Labour victory is the better outcome. There is an unseemly element to that assessment, which could be taken as saying that the negatives and risks are less important than the potential positives, but perhaps where we differ is that I don't agree that the potential space to confront left antisemitism within Labour will be decisively closed down in the event of a Labour victory, and in fact could, in some ways, open up.

You're right that a thumping defeat for Labour would lead to a shake-up, Corbyn would probably resign, and maybe there'd be some soul-searching. But that would also mean the unleashing of an absolute tidal wave of reaction and bigotry, we'd probably see Johnson lurch further towards Trumpian rhetoric, and those are certainly not conditions in which advancing progressive politics will be any easier. Quite the reverse. Given the extent to which Johnson wants to align with Trump and Orban, they're also not conditions in which I think antisemitism is likely to recede, either.

The 'Corbyn phenomenon' in the Labour Party, by which I don't mean him as an individual but rather the surge around his leadership that's seen the Labour Party become a mass force and via which political life inside the party has become reanimated, is itself contradictory. It's got a lot of unhealthy elements – the incipient personality-cultism, the uncritical attitude to the leadership, and obviously there are conspiracy-theory narratives present – but it isn't limited to, or wholly, or even largely, defined by those elements. It's also a phenomenon based on enthusiastic, often quite open-minded young people, who've become radicalised by their experiences and found an expression for that within the Labour Party.

Those people are the potential agency for the transformation of political culture that's necessary. But if the movement those people feel themselves to be aligned with and part of is essentially ended by being electorally smashed by a rampantly reactionary Tory Party, and dissolves into demoralisation, a lot of people who might've become active participants in this transformational effort are likely to drift out of politics altogether.

**RS:** I accept that my analysis is based on a form of accelerationism, which is something I'm usually opposed to. It's also a largely personal position, and I understand that there are people who'll vote Labour for what I think are entirely legitimate reasons. Some of my position is shaped by the fact that I live in a safe Labour seat; would I feel the same way if I lived in a marginal? I can't say for sure.

Ultimately, I feel more comfortable on the level of my own personal morality in preparing to face down the reactionary consequences of a Boris Johnson victory, and fight against them, than telling British Jews they need to take a hit for me. I would be deeply uncomfortable about saying that, in the same way I was uncomfortable with the idea of voting for Leave in 2016.

I am dreading a Tory victory and the right-wing nationalism that will unleash. I am dreading what will happen to my family; my mother wears the hijab, I know she's likely to face increased racism. It's not a position I've arrived at lightly, of course I'm sick of the Tories being in government. But the type of Labour government we need, one that doesn't just have a good policy platform for the life of one parliament but which can fundamentally change the ways in which we talk about and relate to ethnic minorities in this country, isn't going to be provided by the Labour Party under its current leadership. I would have no confidence in the ability of a Labour government under this leadership to identify and confront institutional racism when they've failed to identify and confront it within their own ranks. I would have no confidence that they'd be able to adequately support victims of bigotry when I've seen how they've gaslit so many of their own Jewish members.

I understand and empathise with many of the reasons many people will vote for Labour. But on a personal level, given all of this, I don't feel comfortable giving them the confidence of my vote.

**DR:** I did want to ask your view on something which is related to all this, but which is somewhat separate, which I've been thinking about following the Chief Rabbi's statement today.* There's a whole long tradition on the left, including on the Jewish left specifically,

---

* See Ephraim Mirvis, 'What Will Become of Jews in Britain if Labour Forms the Next Government?' *The Times*, 25 November 2019. Available at: www.thetimes.co.uk/article/ephraim-mirvis-what-will-become-of-jews-in-britain-if-labour-forms-the-next-government-ghpsdbljk

of critiquing the role of official communal leaderships, and not viewing ethnocultural or religious communities as homogeneous but understanding them as spaces riven by conflicts of class interest and other power relations, for example gender and sexuality, which the left should see as potential bases for organisation.

I acknowledge that, when a community faces bigotry or oppression, it's possible and often easy for such a critique to be misheard as an attack on the community as a whole, but I think it's important this critique is rediscovered and reasserted, and for the left to develop an approach to ethnic minority communities that doesn't entrench the existing power relations within them, which doesn't confer a special status on their official leaderships, and which in fact is about developing radical critiques of the power relations and dominant ideologies within the community. This is a big topic to touch on at the end of our conversation, but I wondered what your thoughts on this were.

**RS:** I come from a liberal strand within the Muslim community, and have been frustrated over the years with self-appointed community spokespeople trying to speak on behalf of very diverse communities, and I always felt there were attempts to portray the British Muslim community as a homogenous bloc. There is a problem with accepting the views of official leaders as representative of the entire community. Within the Muslim community today, imams often reflect the viewpoints of their own generation rather than today's Muslim youth; there's a massive disconnect there which the left doesn't necessarily understand.

But there are instances in which it's possible and necessary to engage with these groups. That doesn't mean having to agree with them on everything, but it does mean engaging with them when they're expressing something that is widely felt within their community. Take the Muslim Council of Britain. I'd be wary of any political party that set too much store by what they say, or took it to be representative of all British Muslims. But where the MCB are intervening around an issue like Islamophobia and the demonisation of Muslims in the media, they're articulating something that's not just felt by people from the same generation and same class as the people who lead MCB, but is widely felt across the British Muslim community, irrespective of sect, class, cultural group, gender, and so on. Similarly, when the Chief Rabbi comes out and tells people not to vote for the Labour Party, and 87% of British Jews say they'd feel less safe under a Labour government, you have to say we do have a real problem here.

Generally speaking, I agree that we should be wary of community spokespeople and critical of power relations within ethnic minority groups. Today amongst British Muslims, particularly in online spaces, there's a burgeoning Muslim feminist movement, which is producing discourses around issues like hijab; slut-shaming; modesty; and family violence and honour. Muslim women are leading these discussions, often in the face of very defensive responses from Muslim men, and a grassroots conversation is taking place. The left should be supporting that internal dissent within communities, but at the same time, when official leaderships are articulating views that are widely held within the community, we have to listen to it – not because it's the MCB or the Chief Rabbi saying it, but because it's something many people across these communities feel, which the left has to engage with and respond to.

# APPENDIX III
## SELECTED ADDITIONAL WORKS

Throughout this book, I have adapted, and in some cases directly reproduced, elements of my existing work on the issue of left antisemitism. This appendix collates a number of the original sources from which these elements were drawn. If you google a phrase from this book and find it is also included in some other piece I've written not listed here, or based on something I've said on Twitter, rest assured that I have only plagiarised myself.

'The Left and Antisemitism', *Solidarity* 403, 4 May 2016; www.workersliberty.org/story/2017-07-26/left-and-anti-semitism

'How the Labour Left Can Combat Antisemitism', *The Clarion*, 3 March 2018; https://theclarionmag.org/2018/03/03/how-the-labour-left-can-combat-anti-semitism/

'Corbyn, Anti-Zionism, and Antisemitism', *Solidarity* 477, 29 August 2018; www.workersliberty.org/story/2018-08-27/corbyn-anti-zionism-and-antisemitism

'What Momentum's Video Does and Doesn't Say About Antisemitism on the Left', *The Clarion*, 14 November 2018; https://theclarionmag.org/2018/11/14/what-momentums-video-does-and-doesnt-say-about-antisemitism-on-the-left/

Video: 'Left Antisemitism: What It is and How to Fight It', 29 November 2018; www.workersliberty.org/story/2018-11-29/video-left-antisemitism-what-it-and-how-fight-it

'The Rabbi and the Real Issue', *Solidarity* 526, 7 November 2019; www.workersliberty.org/story/2019-11-27/rabbi-and-real-issue

Video: 'What is Left Antisemitism, and How Can It be Confronted?', with Daniel Randall, 29 October 2020; www. workersliberty.org/story/2020-10-29/video-what-left-antisemitism-and-how-can-it-be-confronted-daniel-randall

# AUTHOR'S NOTE

I want to become the kind of Jew the antisemites warned against: the cosmopolitan of no fixed identity. And I hope you are willing to surrender your own tribal, ethnic, nationalist, and religious identities and allegiances. Join me as a traitor to your own traditions. Become cosmopolitans!

*Steve Cohen, 'Writing as a Jewish Traitor: An Imagined Disputation with My Comrades on Antisemitism'*[1]

During the final stages of editing this book, Israel's May 2021 bombing of Gaza and a wave of international protest in response to it thrust many of the issues discussed here further into the spotlight, and posed anew the question of how the left can build a movement of internationalist solidarity with the Palestinians that is also a movement against antisemitism. Steve Cohen believed those exigencies were fused. I agree with him. I was only able to insert some passing references to the events of May 2021 into the book; with more time, and perhaps in a future edition, I am keen to reflect on them further.

Given the subject matter, writing this book has not exactly been what one might call 'enjoyable'. Nevertheless, writing it has been invaluable in reassessing, clarifying and refining my own ideas. As I say in the introduction, I hope I've been able to communicate them in a way that is persuasive and, at the very least, thought provoking.

Although this book is not a sequel to *That's Funny, You Don't Look Antisemitic*, it exists in a space Steve Cohen's work helped to open. I have referred extensively to Cohen's work, and I hope comrades who value it feel I have honoured its legacy, even where I have differed from his ideas.

Throughout this book I have deliberately not generally referred to Jews as 'we' and 'us'. Where I have used 'we' and 'us', it has been in reference to the socialist movement. I did this because I wanted to convey that I do not lean on or appeal to my own Jewishness to claim authority or validity for my argument. I appeal only to political ideas, and assessments and conclusions informed by those ideas, which I believe to be correct.

Notwithstanding this, in the course of writing this book, I have inevitably reflected on my own identity as a Jewish social-ist and socialist Jew – a militant atheist and secularist; opposed to communalism, nationalism, and particularism; committed to universalism, but still profoundly Jewish. I am reminded of Isaac Deutscher's concept of 'the non-Jewish Jew', radical and revolu-tionary Jews who went through and beyond their Jewish identity and experience to advance a 'message of universal human eman-cipation'.[2] The idea of the 'non-Jewish Jew' is in some ways echoed in Cohen's concept of the 'anti-Zionist Zionist', two categories that seek new, higher syntheses through the dynamism of contra-diction. I am well aware that I am scrabbling around in the dirt compared to the 'non-Jewish Jews' Deutscher surveyed – Spinoza, Marx, Luxemburg, Trotsky and others – but I find the concept of the 'non-Jewish Jew' an inspiring one nonetheless.

I think, too, of Cohen's words on his Jewishness from 2006:

I want to become un-Jewish – a person of the world. However to become un-Jewish means first working through a Jewish identity in order to un-identify. It is all I know. It is my bedrock. The positive image I have is bounc-ing on a trampoline called 'Jewish'. I bounce higher and higher until one day I bounce beyond the power of gravity

and become a free-floating human. We should all try it –
Jews, Muslims, whoever. It sure would make the world a far
more energetic place.[3]

I am greatly drawn to this image. While I feel in many ways
*more* rooted in my Jewishness now than I did when I began,
writing this book has very much been part of bouncing on that
trampoline. The achievement of a collective human identity that
leaves all conflicts of ethnic, national, and cultural difference
behind, or rather fuses what is best in all cultures into a universal
synthesis, which will render all bigotries and chauvinisms distant
memories from humanity's brutal past, will be the work of many
generations. I fully expect to be bouncing on the trampoline of
my Jewishness for the rest of my life. But the endeavour of revolutionary socialism is, in part, the process of charting a course
towards that future universal horizon.

I never met Steve Cohen personally, and 'know' him only
through his writing and the recollections of comrades he worked
with. He died with capitalism still very much intact, with the
working-class movement and the left greatly weaker than it was
when he began his political life, and with left antisemitism still
entirely too widespread. But he left behind work that people
like me have been able to put to continued use in the attempt to
remake our movement, and, through it, the world.

*That's Funny* was first published in 1984, this book in 2021.
I hope this book is less needed in thirty-seven years' time than
*That's Funny* is today. If not, then if anyone finds it even half as
useful as I found *That's Funny*, it will have achieved something.

Throughout this book, I have sought to emphasise that I see
left antisemitism as a symptom of wider maladies that distort
left-wing politics. I therefore see confrontation with it as part of
a necessary work of ideological transformation of the left, such
that our movement will be able to achieve its aim of the revolu-

tionary transformation of society. Whether we will succeed in that transformation and ultimately achieve that aim is a matter of what might be called fighting hope, rather than absolute faith. Socialism is not a millenarian attractor history is drawing us inevitably towards. It is a future that must be consciously fought for, in battles we are not guaranteed to win, and which mostly end in defeat.

I end, then, and at the risk of attempting too grandiose a conclusion for what is ultimately a polemical intervention into intra-left debates, with some words on that matter from Hal Draper – an American Jewish socialist and one of the foremost theoreticians and organisers of the 'Third Camp' tradition of dissident, heterodox Trotskyism:

> The socialist revolution, once observed Rosa Luxemburg, is a war in which there is necessarily a continuous series of 'defeats', followed by only one victory. Nothing can be guaranteed, of course, except the honour and dignity of fighting for a new and better world, rather than the vileness of adapting one's mind and heart to a vile one.[4]

# NOTES

## CHAPTER 1: INTRODUCTION

1 Eric K. Ward, 'Skin in the Game: How Antisemitism Animates White Nationalism', *The Public Eye*, Summer 2017. Available at: www.politicalresearch.org/2017/06/29/skin-in-the-game-how-antisemitism-animates-white-nationalism

2 'Another Local Labour Party Demands Investigation into Israeli #steerorsmear', Skwawkbox, 3 February 2017. Available at: https://skwawkbox.org/2017/02/03/another-local-labour-party-demands-investigation-into-israeli-steerorsmear/

3 'Siobhain McDonagh Links Anti-Capitalism to Antisemitism in Labour', *LabourList*, 4 March 2019. Available at: https://labourlist.org/2019/03/siobhain-mcdonagh-links-anti-capitalism-to-antisemitism-in-labour

4 Aaron Amaral, 'An Insidious Dialectic: Antisemitism, Corbyn, and the Fight for the Labour Party', interview with David Renton, *Tempest*, 13 November 2020. Available at: www.tempestmag.org/2020/11/an-insidious-dialectic/

5 For more on the origins and early usage of the 'socialism of fools' label, see Chapter Four.

6 See Brendan McGeever and Satnam Virdee, 'Antisemitism and Socialist Strategy in Europe, 1880–1917: An Introduction', *Patterns of Prejudice* 51, 3–4, 5 September 2017, pp. 221–34. Available at: www.tandfonline.com/doi/full/10.1080/0031322X.2017.1349606

7 See Max Shachtman, 'Palestine: Pogrom or Revolution?', *The Militant* 2, 15, 1 October 1929, p. 5. Available at www.marxists.org/archive/shachtma/1929/10/palestine.htm

8 Quoted in Mark Osborn, *Solidarność: The Workers' Movement and the Rebirth of Poland in 1980–81* (London: Workers' Liberty, 2020), p. 23.

9 See Tony Kushner, 'Jewish Communists in Twentieth-Century Britain: The Zaidman Collection', *Labour History Review* 55, 2, October 1990.

10 See Sean Matgamna, 'Free Speech for Zionists!', *Workers' Action* 77, 29 October 1977; Jane Ashworth, 'Banned for Being Jewish', *Socialist Organiser* 216, 13 February 1985; John O'Mahony, 'Don't Ban Zionists!', *Socialist Organiser* 221, 28 March 1985. All included in *Arabs, Jews, and Socialism*, 2019. Available at: www.workersliberty.org/files/3rd-ajs.pdf

11 Jewish Labour Movement, Twitter post, 28 December 2019. Available at: https://twitter.com/jewishlabour/status/1210991963937345536

12 Momentum, Twitter post, 24 January 2019. Available at: https://twitter.com/peoplesmomentum/status/1088423914550820865

13   Steve Cohen, *That's Funny, You Don't Look Antisemitic* (London: No Pasaran Media, 2019), p. 1.

## CHAPTER 2: WHAT IS LEFT ANTISEMITISM?

1   David Feldman, 'Labour Can Expel Antisemites – But That Won't "Root Out" Antisemitism in Our Culture', *Guardian*, 8 April 2020. Available at: www.theguardian.com/commentisfree/2020/apr/08/education-labour-antisemitism-party-keir-starmer

2   Moishe Postone, *Antisemitism and National Socialism* (London: Chronos Publications, 2000), p. 7. Available at: www.thesparrowsnest.org.uk/collections/public_archive/12410.pdf

3   See Tom Buchanan, *East Wind: China and the British Left, 1925–1976* (Oxford: Oxford University Press, 2012), p. 18, and Emmet Larkin, *James Larkin, 1876–1947: Irish Labour Leader* (London: Pluto Press, 1989), p. 15.

4   Nancy L. Green, 'Socialist Antisemitism, Defence of a Bourgeois Jew and Discovery of the Jewish Proletariat: Changing Attitudes of French Socialists Before 1914', *International Review of Social History* 30, 3, December 1985, pp. 374–99, p. 374.

5   Quoted in Francis Wheen, *Karl Marx* (London: Fourth Estate, 1999), p. 340.

6   Pierre-Joseph Proudhon, 'On the Jews' (1847). Available at: www.marxists.org/reference/subject/economics/proudhon/1847/jews.htm

7   *La Guerre Sociale*, 3 January 1912, p. 2, quoted in Edmund Silberner, 'Anti-Jewish Trends in French Revolutionary Syndicalism', *Jewish Social Studies* 15, 3–4, July–October 1953, pp. 195–202, p. 196.

8   *La Guerre Sociale*, 3 January 1912, p. 2, quoted ibid., p. 196.

9   *Libre Parole*, 4 April 1911, p. 3, quoted ibid., p. 197.

10  Green, 'Socialist Antisemitism', pp. 381–2.

11  See Hal Draper, 'Marx and the Economic-Jew Stereotype', from *Karl Marx's Theory of Revolution*, vol. 1: *State and Bureaucracy* (New York: Monthly Review Press, 1977), pp. 591–608, and Robert Fine, 'Rereading Marx on the "Jewish Question": Marx as a Critic of Antisemitism?', in Marcel Stoetzler (ed.), *Antisemitism and the Constitution of Sociology* (Lincoln: University of Nebraska Press, 2014), pp. 137–59.

12  Steve Cohen, *That's Funny, You Don't Look Antisemitic* (London: No Pasaran Media, 2019), p. 3.

13  'Zionism, Antisemitism, and the Left', interview with Moishe Postone, *Solidarity* 166, 4 February 2010. Available at: www.workersliberty.org/story/2010-02-05/zionism-anti-semitism-and-left

14  Moishe Postone, 'History and Helplessness: Mass Mobilization and Contemporary Forms of Anticapitalism', *Public Culture* 18, 1, 2006, pp. 93–110, p. 99.

15  April Rosenblum, *The Past Didn't Go Anywhere: Making Resistance to Antisemitism Part of All of Our Movements* (2007), p. 1. Available at: www.aprilrosenblum.com/thepast

16  Chapter Three, 'The Re-emergence of Primitive Antisemitism on the Left', aims to explore this phenomenon in greater detail, and asks what might have shaped it.

17  See Leon Trotsky, 'Thermidor and Antisemitism', *New International* 7, 4, May 1941. Available at: www.marxists.org/archive/trotsky/1937/02/therm.htm

18  See Max Shachtman, 'Palestine – Pogrom or Revolution?' *The Militant* 2, 15, 1 October 1929, p. 5. Available at: www.marxists.org/archive/shachtma/1929/10/palestine.htm

19  See Brendan McGeever, *Antisemitism and the Russian Revolution* (Cambridge: Cambridge University Press, 2019).

20  'Tragi-comedy in Prague', *New York Times*, 22 November 1952.

21  See Stan Crooke, 'The Stalinist Roots of "Left" Antisemitism', *Workers' Liberty* 10, May 1988. Available at: www.workersliberty.org/node/16575

22  Cohen, *That's Funny*, p. 18.

23  Gilbert Achcar, 'The Arabs and the Holocaust: A Response', *The New Republic*, 9 November 2010. Available at: https://newrepublic.com/article/78998/arabs

24  Jordan Kutzik, 'This "Antifa" Group Was Also Zionist, Pro-Palestinian and Yiddish-Speaking – and It's Trending', *Forward*, 3 June 2020. Available at: https://forward.com/news/448022/antifa-yiddish-zionist/

25  See Dan Tamir, 'When Jews Praised Mussolini and Supported Nazis: Meet Israel's First Fascists', *Haaretz*, 20 July 2019. Available at: www.haaretz.com/israel-news/.premium.MAGAZINE-when-jews-praised-mussolini-and-supported-nazis-meet-israel-s-first-fascists-1.7538589

26  Isaac Deutscher, 'Israel's Spiritual Climate', *The Reporter*, 27 April and 11 May 1954. Available at: www.marxists.org/archive/deutscher/1954/israel.htm

27  Maxime Rodinson, *Israel: A Colonial-Settler State?* (London: Pathfinder, 1973), pp. 91–3.

28  See Sean Matgamna, 'The Development of Workers' Liberty's Idea on Israel and Palestine', *Solidarity* 505, 8 May 2019. Available at: www.workersliberty.org/story/2019-05-08/development-workers-libertys-ideas-israel-and-palestine

29  See, for example, Dr Yvonne Ridley, Twitter post, 23 September 2016. Available at: https://twitter.com/yvonneridley/status/779319419646406656

30  Keith Kahn-Harris, *Strange Hate: Antisemitism, Racism, and the Limits of Diversity* (London: Repeater Books, 2019), p. 82.

31  Friedrich Engels, letter to J. Bloch in Königsberg (1890). Available at: www.marxists.org/archive/marx/works/1890/letters/90_09_21.htm

32  Stephen Miller et al., 'The Attitudes of British Jews Towards Israel', Department of Sociology, School of Arts and Sciences, City University London, 2015. Available at: http://yachad.org.uk/wp-content/uploads/2015/11/British-Jewish-Attitudes-Towards-Israel-Yachad-Ipsos-Mori-Nov-2015.pdf

33  See Sue Hamilton, 'The Left-Wing Student Movement in the 1980s', *Workers' Liberty* 40, May–June 1997. Available at: www.workersliberty.org/story/2019-03-17/left-wing-student-movement-1980s

34  David Feldman, 'The David Miller Case: A Textbook Example of Anti-Zionism Becoming Vicious Antisemitism', *Haaretz*, 4 March 2021. Available at: www.haaretz.com/israel-news/david-miller-textbook-case-of-anti-zionism-becoming-vicious-antisemitism-1.9585115

35  Lee Harpin, 'Bristol Professor Attacks Starmer Over "Zionist" Money', *Jewish Chronicle*, 27 April 2020. Available at: www.thejc.com/news/uk/bristol-professor-attacks-starmer-over-zionist-money-1.499258

36  Labour Left Alliance, Facebook post. Available at: www.facebook.com/watch/live/?v=2735672193376538&ref=watch_permalink

37  See email from David Miller to *The Tab* in Twitter post by Ben Bloch, 18 February 2021. Available at: https://pbs.twimg.com/media/EuhUtp6XAAE2qJt?format=jpg&name=large. See also quotes at Union of Jewish Students, 'Pattern of Behaviour'. Available at: www.ujs.org.uk/pattern_of_behaviour

38  Feldman, 'The David Miller Case'.

39  See Working Group on Syria, Propaganda, and Media, 'Members'. Available at: http://syriapropagandamedia.org/about/members

40  Vanessa Beeley, Twitter post, 12 January 2017. Available at: https://twitter.com/VanessaBeeley/status/819512858329366528

41  See Tom Wainwright, Twitter post, 21 February 2021. Available at: https://twitter.com/TomNwainwright/status/1363601306519281667

42  See undated open letter to Professor Hugh Brady, President and Vice-Chancellor, University of Bristol, from supporters of David Miller. Available at: https://supportmiller.org/open-letter

43  Tom Mills, Twitter post, 19 February 2021. Available at: https://twitter.com/ta_mills/status/1362799008016715779

44  Kerry-Anne Mendoza, Twitter post, 19 February 2021. Available at: https://twitter.com/TheMendozaWoman/status/1362688565377961985

45  John O'Mahony, 'Don't Ban Zionists', *Socialist Organiser* 221, 28 March 1985. Available at: www.workersliberty.org/story/2019-06-20/arabs-jews-and-socialism-1-anti-zionism-and-antisemitism

46  Kahn-Harris, *Strange Hate*, p. 164.

47  For more on the origins, and early usage, of the 'socialism of fools' label, see Chapter Three.

48  'Zionism, Antisemitism, and the Left'.

49  See, for example, Rohini Hensman, *Indefensible: Democracy, Counter-Revolution, and the Rhetoric of Anti-Imperialism* (Chicago: Haymarket Books, 2018); Bryant William Sculos, '"Campism" and the "New" (Anti-) Imperialisms', *New Politics* 18, 1, Summer 2020, Whole Number 69; Daphne Lawless, 'Against Campism: What Makes Some Leftists Support Putin?', *Fightback*, 5 November 2015. Available at: https://fightback.org.nz/2015/11/05/against-campism-what-makes-some-leftists-support-putin/

50 Steve Cohen, 'For the Third Camp – Yes to Palestinian Liberation! No to Antisemitism!', 19 June 2007. Available at: https://workersliberty.org/story/2017-07-26/third-camp-yes-palestinian-liberation-no-anti-semitism-0

51 Image available at: https://images-na.ssl-images-amazon.com/images/I/519 kW-dHrhL._SX321_BO1,204,203,200_.jpg

52 Cohen, *That's Funny*, p. 18.

53 'Why and How the Left Has Shifted on Israel', interview with Susie Linfield, *Solidarity* 513, 17 July 2019. Available at www.workersliberty.org/story/2019-07-17/why-and-how-left-has-shifted-israel

54 Edward Said, 'Barenboim and the Wagner Taboo', *Al-Ahram Weekly On-line* 547, 16–22 August 2001. Available at: www.mafhoum.com/press2/58C31.htm

55 Martin Thomas, 'How to be Pro-Palestinian Without Being "Anti-Zionist"', *Solidarity* 484, 31 October 2018. Available at: www.workersliberty.org/story/2018-11-16/how-be-pro-palestinian-without-being-anti-zionist

56 *Socialist Worker* 1224, quoted in Dale Street, 'Three Decades of *Socialist Worker* on Antisemitism', *Solidarity* 534, 12 February 2020. Available at: www.workersliberty.org/story/2020-01-27/three-decades-socialist-worker-antisemitism

57 Sina Arnold and Blair Taylor, 'Antisemitism and the Left: Confronting an Invisible Racism', *Journal of Social Justice*, 9, 2019, p. 18. Available at: http://transformativestudies.org/wp-content/uploads/Blair-Taylor-and-Sina_Arnold.pdf

58 The *Socialist Worker* referred to here is the newspaper of the now-defunct International Socialist Organisation (ISO), a US Trotskyist tendency. The ISO was at one time linked to the UK Socialist Workers Party (SWP), whose newspaper is also called *Socialist Worker*. Unless otherwise stated, references to '*Socialist Worker*' throughout this book are to the newspaper of the UK SWP.

59 Daniel Fischer, 'In Support of Joint Struggle', *New Politics* (Online Features), 15 March 2021. Available at: https://newpol.org/in-support-of-joint-struggle/

60 Marcel Stoetzler, 'Capitalism, the Nation, and Societal Corrosion: Notes on "Left-Wing Antisemitism"', *Journal of Social Justice* 9, 2019, p. 2. Available at: http://transformativestudies.org/wp-content/uploads/Marcel-Stoetzler.pdf

61 See David Feldman, Ben Gidley and Brendan McGeever, 'Labour and Antisemitism: A Crisis Misunderstood', *Political Quarterly* 91, 2, April–June 2020. Available at: https://politicalquarterly.blog/2020/05/29/the-labour-party-and-antisemitism-a-crisis-misunderstood/

62 Arnold and Taylor, 'Antisemitism and the Left', p. 25.

## CHAPTER 3: THE RE-EMERGENCE OF PRIMITIVE ANTISEMITISM ON THE LEFT

1 Michael Segalov, 'If You Can't See Antisemitism, It's Time to Open Your Eyes', *Guardian*, 28 March 2018. Available at: www.theguardian.com/commentisfree/2018/mar/28/antisemitism-open-your-eyes-jeremy-corbyn-labour

2   Quoted ibid.

3   See 'Labour Suspends Activist Over Alleged Antisemitic Comments',
    BBC News, 5 May 2016. Available at: www.bbc.co.uk/news/uk-england-
    kent-36203911

4   See Harold Brackman, 'Jews Had a Negligible Role in the Slave Trade', *New
    York Times*, 14 February 1994. Available at: www.nytimes.com/1994/02/14/
    opinion/l-jews-had-negligible-role-in-slave-trade-183202.html. Winthrop
    D. Jordan, 'Slavery and the Jews', *The Atlantic*, September 1995. Available
    at: www.theatlantic.com/magazine/archive/1995/09/slavery-and-the-jews/
    376462/

5   See 'What's Wrong with Chris Williamson?', Bob from Brockley, 29 June
    2019. Available at: http://brockley.blogspot.com/2019/06/whats-wrong-
    with-chris-williamson.html

6   'The Work of the Labour Party's Governance and Legal Unit in Relation to
    Antisemitism, 2014–2019', The Labour Party, March 2020, p. 13. Available
    at: https://cryptome.org/2020/04/Labour-Antisemitism-Report.pdf

7   Ibid., p. 274.

8   Ibid., p. 235.

9   Ibid., p. 287.

10  Ibid., p. 235.

11  Ibid., p. 269.

12  See Tom Cotterill, 'Labour Activist Resigns as Portsmouth Momentum
    Organiser Amid Antisemitism Probe', iNews, 18 April 2018. Available at:
    https://inews.co.uk/news/politics/labour-activist-resigns-portsmouth-
    momentum-organiser-anti-semitism-probe

13  See Benjamin Kentish, 'Momentum Activists Accused of "Anti-Zionist
    Ranting" in Labour Antisemitism Row', *Independent*, 6 August 2018.
    Available at: www.independent.co.uk/news/uk/politics/labour-party-
    antisemitism-momentum-barnet-jews-jeremy-corbyn-israel-a8473501.html

14  'New World Order', a motif of conspiracy theories which claim that some
    force is working to impose an authoritarian world government.

15  'The Work of the Labour Party's Governance and Legal Unit in Relation to
    Antisemitism, 2014–2019', p. 779.

16  Ibid., p. 287.

17  See 'What's wrong with Chris Williamson?', Bob from Brockley blog.

18  See Alison Flood, 'Penguin Stops Printing Pedro Baños Book After
    Antisemitism Claims', *Guardian*, 27 June 2019. Available at: www.
    theguardian.com/books/2019/jun/27/pedro-banos-how-they-rule-the-
    world-penguin-antisemitism-julia-neuberger

19  Quoted in Alan Johnson, 'Institutionally Antisemitic: Contemporary Left
    Antisemitism and Crisis in the British Labour Party', *Fathom*, 2019, p. 34.
    Available at: https://fathomjournal.org/wp-content/uploads/2019/03/
    Institutionally-Antisemitic-Report-FINAL-6.pdf

20  Dan O'Donoghue, 'North Tyneside Councillors Slammed for Sharing
    "Antisemitic" Post on Social Media', *Chronicle Live*, 26 August 2016.

Available at: www.chroniclelive.co.uk/news/north-east-news/north-tyneside-councillor-slammed-sharing-11803945

21  Justin Cohen, 'Labour Drops Council Candidate Who Posted About "Rich Families of the Zionist Lobby"', *Jewish News*, 15 November 2017. Available at: https://jewishnews.timesofisrael.com/labour-drop-council-candidate-who-posted-about-rich-families-of-the-zionist-lobby/

22  Kate McCann, Harry Yorke and Gordon Rayner, 'Labour Quietly Reinstated Six Councillors Who Posted Antisemitic Messages', *Daily Telegraph*, 29 March 2018. Available at: www.telegraph.co.uk/politics/2018/03/29/labour-quietly-reinstated-six-councillors-posted-anti-semitic/

23  See Caroline Mortimer, 'Former Labour Candidate Accused of Antisemitism After Retweeting Far-Right Meme', *Independent*, 8 February 2017. Available at: www.independent.co.uk/news/uk/politics/labour-anti-semitism-claims-candidate-fair-right-twitter-meme-a7570181.html

24  Marcel Stoetzler, 'Capitalism, the Nation, and Societal Corrosion: Notes on "Left-Wing Antisemitism"', *Journal of Social Justice*, 9, 2019, p. 2. Available at: http://transformativestudies.org/wp-content/uploads/Marcel-Stoetzler.pdf

25  'Zionism, Antisemitism, and the Left', interview with Moishe Postone, *Solidarity* 166, 4 February 2010. Available at: www.workersliberty.org/story/2010-02-05/zionism-anti-semitism-and-left

26  Michael Richmond, 'On "Black Antisemitism" and Anti-Racist Solidarity", 30 July 2020. Available at: https://newsocialist.org.uk/black-antisemitism-and-antiracist-solidarity

27  Werner Bonefeld, 'Anti-Globalisation and the Dangers of Nationalism and Antisemitism', undated, pp. 12–13. Available at: http://biblioteca.clacso.edu.ar/ar/libros/cuba/if/marx/documentos/22/Anti%20globalisation%20and%20the%20danger....pdf

28  Luke Hardy, 'Learning Lessons in Dark Times', *Solidarity* 546, 4 May 2020. Available at: www.workersliberty.org/story/2020-05-04/learning-lessons-dark-times

29  Matt Bolton and Frederick Harry Pitts, *Corbynism: A Critical Approach* (Bingley: Emerald Publishing, 2018), p. 214.

30  Edd Mustill, 'Capitalism is Not a Conspiracy', *The Clarion*, 21 May 2018. Available at: https://theclarionmag.org/2018/05/21/capitalism-is-not-a-conspiracy

31  See David Feldman, Ben Gidley and Brendan McGeever, 'Labour and Antisemitism: A Crisis Misunderstood', *Political Quarterly* 91, 2, April–June 2020. Available at: https://politicalquarterly.blog/2020/05/29/the-labour-party-and-antisemitism-a-crisis-misunderstood

32  For an example, see image at: www.thejewishstar.com/uploads/original/20200916-095854-George%20Soros%20puppetmaster.jpg

33  Werner Bonefeld, 'Antisemitism and the Power of Abstraction: From Political Economy to Critical Theory', in Marcel Stoetzler (ed.), *Antisemitism*

and the Constitution of Sociology (Lincoln: University of Nebraska Press, 2014), pp. 314–32, p. 314.

34  Gilad Atzmon, 'Holocaust Day – the Time is Ripe for a Jewish Apology', Gilad Online, 28 January 2014. Available at: https://gilad.online/writings/holocaust-day-the-time-is-ripe-for-a-jewish-apology.html

35  See Michael Moynihan, 'Busted', Tablet, 6 December 2011. Available at: www.tabletmag.com/sections/news/articles/busted

36  Spencer Sunshine, 'The Right Hand of Occupy Wall Street', The Public Eye, Winter 2014. Available at: www.politicalresearch.org/2014/02/23/the-right-hand-of-occupy-wall-street-from-libertarians-to-nazis-the-fact-and-fiction-of-right-wing-involvement#8

37  Daniel Taylor, 'David Graeber's Anarchism and the Occupy Movement', Red Flag, 5 September 2020. Available at: https://redflag.org.au/node/7356

38  Sunshine, 'The Right Hand of Occupy Wall Street'.

39  'The Trump Way', interview with Leo Panitch, Jacobin, 22 December 2016. Available at: www.jacobinmag.com/2016/12/donald-trump-workers-infrastructure-immigrants-jobs/

40  'Donald Trump's Argument for America', campaign advertisement, 4 November 2016. Available at: www.youtube.com/watch?v=vST61W4bGm8

41  Bolton and Pitts, Corbynism, p. 213.

42  Ellen Meiksins Wood, The Retreat From Class: A New 'True' Socialism (London: Verso, 1986).

43  'Jewish Leaders' Letter and Jeremy Corbyn's Reply', BBC News, 26 March 2018. Available at: www.bbc.co.uk/news/uk-politics-43540795

44  Dale Street, 'The "Idiot of Vienna"', Solidarity 566, 7 October 2020. Available at: https://workersliberty.org/story/2020-09-30/idiot-vienna

45  Quoted ibid.

46  Quoted ibid.

47  Quoted ibid.

48  Quoted ibid.

49  Ibid.

50  Will, Chino, Saudade and Mamos, How to Overthrow the Illuminati, 2013, p. 6. Available at: https://overthrowingilluminati.wordpress.com/

51  Ibid., p. 26.

52  Grayzone website, https://thegrayzone.com/tag/george-soros/

53  Alex Rubinstein, Twitter post, 19 January 2020. Available at: https://twitter.com/RealAlexRubi/status/1351599030460153862

54  See quotes and links in Alexander Reid Ross, 'These "Dirtbag Left" Stars are Flirting with the Far Right', Daily Beast, 9 March 2021. Available at: www.thedailybeast.com/these-dirtbag-left-stars-are-flirting-with-the-far-right

55  See 'The Canary in the Coalmine', Everybody Hates a Tourist, 30 June 2019. Available at: https://everybodyhatesatourist.wordpress.com/2019/06/30/the-canary-in-the-coalmine/

56  George Galloway, Twitter post, 28 February 2021. Available at: https://twitter.com/georgegalloway/status/1366063132402147329

57  Emily Prince, 'George Galloway Backs Nigel Farage's New Brexit Party', *New European*, 18 April 2019. Available at: www.theneweuropean.co.uk/brexit-news/george-galloway-endorses-nigel-farage-45536

58  Tom Embury-Dennis, 'Steve Bannon and George Galloway "Hug" in Kazakhstan After Learning Theresa May Has Resigned', *Independent*, 24 May 2019. Available at: www.independent.co.uk/news/world/asia/theresa-may-resigns-steve-bannon-george-galloway-hug-brexit-a8928816.html

## CHAPTER 4: THE ANTI-IMPERIALISM OF FOOLS: THE STALINIST ROOTS OF LEFT ANTISEMITISM REVISITED

1   Quoted in Stan Crooke, 'The Slánský Trial', *Workers' Liberty* 3, 36, 2012. Available at: www.marxists.org/history/etol/newspape/wl/wl3-36.pdf

2   Martin Thomas, 'Like It or Not, Stalinism is Still a Live Force', *Solidarity* 533, 5 February 2020. Available at: www.workersliberty.org/story/2020-02-05/it-or-not-stalinism-still-live-force

3   Karl Marx, *The German Ideology* (1845). Available at: www.marxists.org/archive/marx/works/1845/german-ideology/ch01b.htm

4   Leon Trotsky, 'Stalinism and Bolshevism' (August 1937), reproduced in *Socialist Appeal* 1, 7, 25 September 1937, pp. 4–5, and 1, 8, 2 October 1937, pp. 4–5. Available at: www.marxists.org/archive/trotsky/1937/08/stalinism.htm

5   See, for example, Rohini Hensman, *Indefensible: Democracy, Counter-Revolution, and the Rhetoric of Anti-Imperialism* (Chicago: Haymarket Books, 2018); Bryant William Sculos, '"Campism" and the "New" (Anti-) Imperialisms', *New Politics* 18, 1, Summer 2020, Whole Number 69; Daphne Lawless, 'Against Campism: What Makes Some Leftists Support Putin?', *Fightback*, 5 November 2015. Available at: https://fightback.org.nz/2015/11/05/against-campism-what-makes-some-leftists-support-putin/

6   Gilbert Achcar, 'How to Avoid the Anti-Imperialism of Fools', *The Nation*, 8 April 2021. Available at: www.thenation.com/article/politics/anti-imperialism-syria-progressive/

7   Sean Matgamna, *The Left in Disarray* (London: Phoenix Press, 2015), p. 56.

8   Leon Trotsky, 'Thermidor and Antisemitism' (February 1937), reproduced in *New International* 7, 4, May 1941. Available at: www.marxists.org/archive/trotsky/1937/02/therm.htm

9   Ibid.

10  Max Shachtman, 'Palestine: Pogrom or Revolution?', *The Militant* 2, 15, 1 October 1929, p. 5. Available at: www.marxists.org/archive/shachtma/1929/10/palestine.htm

11  'Zionism, Antisemitism, and the Left', interview with Moishe Postone, *Solidarity* 166, 4 February 2010. Available at: www.workersliberty.org/story/2010-02-05/zionism-anti-semitism-and-left

12  Quoted in Crooke, 'The Slánský Trial'.

13  Ibid.

14  Ben Cohen, 'Surviving Stalin's Purges', *Tablet*, 26 February 2013. Available at: www.tabletmag.com/sections/news/articles/surviving-stalins-purges

15  Ibid.

16  Izabella Tabarovsky, 'Soviet Anti-Zionism and Contemporary Left Anti-semitism', *Fathom*, May 2019. Available at: https://fathomjournal.org/soviet-anti-zionism-and-contemporary-left-antisemitism/

17  Mark Osborn, *Solidarność: The Workers' Movement and the Rebirth of Poland in 1980–81* (London: Phoenix Press, 2020), p. 24.

18  William Korey, *Russian Antisemitism, Pamyat and the Demonology of Zionism* (Oxford: Routledge, 2013), p. 19.

19  Ibid., p. 66.

20  V. Skurlatov, *Zionism and Apartheid* (1975), p. 39, quoted in Stan Crooke, 'The Stalinist Roots of "Left" Antisemitism', *Workers' Liberty* 10, May 1988. Available at: www.workersliberty.org/node/16575

21  V. Kiselev et al., *International Zionism: History and Politics* (1977), p. 12, quoted in Crooke, 'Stalinist Roots'.

22  D. Soifer, *The Collapse of Zionist Theories* (1980), p. 5, quoted in Crooke, 'Stalinist Roots'.

23  Soifer, *The Collapse of Zionist Theories*, p. 95, quoted in Crooke, 'Stalinist Roots'.

24  V. Bolshakov, *Zionism in the Service of Anti-Communism* (1972), p. 96, quoted in Crooke, 'Stalinist Roots'.

25  I. Mints et al., *Zionism: Theory and Practice* (1973), p. 169, quoted in Crooke, 'Stalinist Roots'.

26  Mints et al., *Zionism: Theory and Practice*, p. 21, quoted in Crooke, 'Stalinist Roots'.

27  M. Mitin et al., *The Ideology and Practice of International Zionism* (1978), p. 62, quoted in Crooke, 'Stalinist Roots'.

28  Mitin et al., *The Ideology and Practice of International Zionism*, p. 49, quoted in Crooke, 'Stalinist Roots'.

29  M. Davydov et al., *We Pass Judgement on Zionism* (1973), p. 7, quoted in Crooke, 'Stalinist Roots'.

30  Bolshakov, *Zionism in the Service of Anti-Communism*, p. 27, quoted in Crooke, 'Stalinist Roots'.

31  Soifer, *The Collapse of Zionist Theories*, p. 22, quoted in Crooke, 'Stalinist Roots'.

32  Skurlatov, *Zionism and Apartheid*, p. 118, quoted in Crooke, 'Stalinist Roots'.

33  Bolshakov, *Zionism in the Service of Anti-Communism*, p. 67, quoted in Crooke, 'Stalinist Roots'.

34  Kiselev et al., *International Zionism: History and Politics*, p. 113, quoted in Crooke, 'Stalinist Roots'.

35  Ibid.

36  Crooke, 'Stalinist Roots'.

37   Quoted in John Strawson, 'Communists for the Jewish State: British
     Communists and the *Daily Worker* in 1948', *Fathom,* September 2020.
     Available at: https://fathomjournal.org/communists-for-the-jewish-state-
     british-communists-and-the-daily-worker-in-1948/#_edn1
38   Ibid.
39   *World News and Views* 50, 1953, p. 591, quoted in June Edmunds, *The Left
     and Israel* (London: Palgrave Macmillan, 2000), p. 113.
40   Tony Kushner, 'Jewish Communists in Twentieth-Century Britain: The
     Zaidman Collection', *Labour History Review* 55, 2, 1990, pp. 66–75, p. 36.
41   Ibid., p. 71.
42   Ibid.
43   Ibid.
44   Edmunds, *The Left and Israel*, p. 114.
45   Ibid, pp. 116–17.
46   Kushner, 'Jewish Communists in Twentieth-Century Britain', pp. 71–2.
47   Ibid., p. 72.
48   Bert Ramelson, 'The Middle East: Crisis, Causes, Solutions', CPGB pamphlet
     (1967), pp. 36–7.
49   Ibid., p. 41.
50   Ivor Montagu, 'A Peace Policy for Israel', *Labour Monthly*, September 1969,
     pp. 410–14, pp. 410–11).
51   Ibid., p. 412.
52   *Morning Star*, 8 June 1982, p. 3, quoted in Edmunds, *The Left and Israel*,
     p. 118.
53   *Morning Star*, 9 October 1982, p. 3, quoted in Edmunds, *The Left and Israel*,
     p. 118.
54   Ibid.
55   CPGB pamphlet, 'A Land With People', May 1982, quoted in Edmunds, *The
     Left and Israel*, p. 118.
56   'Israel's Iron Fist Leaves Death Trail', *Socialist Worker* 928, 23 March 1985.
57   See Rowena Mason, 'Ken Livingstone Repeats Claim About Nazi–Zionist
     Collaboration', *Guardian*, 30 March 2017. Available at: www.theguardian.
     com/politics/2017/mar/30/ken-livingstone-repeats-claim-nazi-zionist-
     collaboration
58   Leon Trotsky, 'On the Jewish Problem', *Fourth International* 6, 12, December
     1945, pp. 377–9. Available at: www.marxists.org/archive/trotsky/1940/xx/
     jewish.htm
59   Ibid.
60   See 'The Trotskyists and the Creation of Israel', *Workers' Liberty* 3, 13, July
     2007. Available at: www.workersliberty.org/story/2017-07-26/trotskyists-
     and-creation-israel-introduction
61   Robert Fine, 'How Trotskyists Debated Palestine Before the Holocaust',
     *Workers' Liberty* 14, July 1990. Available at: www.workersliberty.org/
     story/2010/01/07/how-trotskyists-debated-palestine-holocaust

62  See 'The Jewish Question and Israel: Resolution Adopted by the Independent Socialist League', *New International* 17, 4, July–August 1951, pp. 222–31. Available at: www.marxists.org/history/etol/newspape/ni/vol17/no04/isl.html

63  Hal Draper, 'How to Defend Israel', *New International* 14, 5, July 1948, pp. 133–7. Available at: www.marxists.org/archive/draper/1948/07/israel.htm

64  Tony Cliff, *The Struggle in the Middle East* (1967 pamphlet), edited and republished in *International Struggle and the Marxist Tradition, Selected Works*, vol. 1 (London: Bookmarks, 2001), pp. 43–51. Available at: www.marxists.org/archive/cliff/works/1990/10/struggleme.htm

65  'Talkin' 'Bout a Revolutionary', interview with Ian Birchall, *International Socialist Journal* 131, Summer 2011. Available at: http://isj.org.uk/talkin-bout-a-revolutionary/

66  Paul Hampton, 'Birchall's Cliff: "If You Seek His Memorial, Look Around You"', *Solidarity* 215, 7 September 2011. Available at: www.workersliberty.org/story/2011/09/07/birchalls-cliff-if-you-seek-his-memorial-look-around-you

67  *Socialist Worker*, 20 October 1973, quoted in Steve Cohen, *That's Funny, You Don't Look Antisemitic* (London: No Pasaran Media, 2019), p. 65.

68  Cohen, *That's Funny*, pp. 66–7.

69  'No Expulsion', *Socialist Worker* 928, 23 March 1985.

70  Dave Glanz, 'The Brutal Logic of Zionism', *Socialist Worker* 929, 30 March 1985.

71  John Rose, *Israel: The Hijack State* (London: Bookmarks, 1986). Available at: www.marxists.org/history/etol/document/mideast/hijack/index.htm

72  Quoted in Sami Moubayed, '69 Years on, al-Nakba is History and Iran is the Arabs' Enemy', *Arab Weekly*, 14 May 2017. Available at: https://thearabweekly.com/69-years-al-nakba-history-and-iran-arabs-enemy/

73  Ibid.

74  See David Kaiser, 'What Hitler and the Grand Mufti Really Said', *Time*, 22 October 2015. Available at: https://time.com/4084301/hitler-grand-mufi-1941/

75  Tony Cliff, 'A New British Provocation in Palestine', *Fourth International* 7, 9, September 1946, pp. 282–4. Available at: www.marxists.org/archive/cliff/works/1946/07/provocation.htm

76  Ernest Mandel, 'Introduction', in *50 Years of World Revolution: An International Symposium*, 3rd edn (New York: Pathfinder Press, 1971), pp. 11–34, p. 26.

77  Werner Cohn, 'From Victim to Shylock and Oppressor: The New Image of the Jew in the Trotskyist Movement', *Journal of Communist Studies* (London) 7, 1, March 1991, pp. 46–68.

78  See Ernest Mandel, 'World Revolution Today – Trotskyism or Stalinism?', *International Socialist Review* 31, 4, June 1970, pp. 34–8. Available at: www.marxists.org/archive/mandel/1970/xx/worldrev.htm

79  Dale Street, '"Anti-Zionism", Antisemitism, and the German New Left', *Workers' Liberty* 3, 63, July 2018. Available at: https://workersliberty.org/files/wl63.pdf

80  'Dedication', *50 Years of World Revolution: An International Symposium*, p. 7.

81  Clare Cowen, *My Search for Revolution: & How We Brought Down An Abusive Leader* (Kibworth: Troubador Publishing, 2019).

82  See John O'Mahony, 'The 1980s Left and Antisemitism', *Solidarity* 471, 30 May 2018. Available at: www.workersliberty.org/story/2018-06-01/1980s-and-left-antisemitism

83  *Socialist Worker*, 28 November 1987, quoted in 'The Socialist Workers Party on the Iran–Iraq War, 1987', LibCom, 12 September 2008. Available at: https://libcom.org/library/the-socialist-workers-party-iran-iraq-war-1987

84  See Camila Bassi, '"The Anti-Imperialism of Fools": A Cautionary Story on the Revolutionary Socialist Vanguard of England's Post-9/11 Anti-War Movement' *ACME: An International Journal for Critical Geographies* 9, 2, 2010, pp. 113–37. Available at https://acme-journal.org/index.php/acme/article/view/863

85  Raya Jalabi, 'Critics Question Catholic Nun's "Alternative Story" on Syria Civil War', *Guardian*, 5 December 2013. Available at: www.theguardian.com/world/2013/dec/05/catholic-nun-mother-agnes-syria-civil-war

86  Cliff, 'A New British Provocation in Palestine'.

87  Phil Marfleet, 'Revolution Continues Beyond the Poll in Egypt', *Socialist Worker*, 29 May 2012. Available at https://socialistworker.co.uk/images1412/txt/issue2305.txt

88  Richard Seymour, 'Israel Kills More in Lebanon: Media Blackout Protests', *Leninology*, 22 July 2006. Available at: www.leninology.co.uk/2006/07/israel-kills-more-in-lebanon-media.html. It should be noted that Richard Seymour is no longer a member of the SWP, and has in recent years written articles acknowledging the existence of left antisemitism. Whether he has explicitly revised his previous campist worldview, I do not know.

89  Nick Clark, 'No "Peace or Prosperity" in Palestine', *Socialist Worker*, 1 February 2020. Available at: https://socialistworker.co.uk/art/49540/No+peace+or+prosperity+in+Palestine

90  Isabelle Ringrose, 'Cruel Britannia: The Bloody Truth About the British Empire', *Socialist Worker*, 29 August 2020. Available at: https://socialistworker.co.uk/art/50554/Cruel+Britannia+the+bloody+truth+about+the+British+Empire

91  Paul Whiteley et al., 'Oh Jeremy Corbyn! Why Did Labour Party Membership Soar After the 2015 General Election?', *British Journal of Politics and International Relations* 21, 1, 2019, pp. 80–98, p. 87.

92  'Corbyn and the Labour Left Opposed the East European Regimes', Ukraine Solidarity Campaign, 27 February 2018. Available at: https://ukrainesolidaritycampaign.org/2018/02/27/tory-liars-corbyn-and-the-labour-left-opposed-the-east-european-regimes/

93  'Workers' Democracy in Eastern Europe', Early Day Motion 210, 14
    December 1989. Available at: https://edm.parliament.uk/early-day-
    motion/1846

94  'MPs, Peers, Trade Unionists, Labour and Human Rights Activists in
    Support of Lee Cheuk Yan', Labour Movement Solidarity with Hong Kong,
    14 February 2021. Available at: https://uklaboursolidaritywithhk.wordpress.
    com/2021/02/14/lcksupporters/

95  Press TV, 12 August 2012. See clip at: www.youtube.com/watch?v=
    KW2r3ZmVcRM

96  See Rajeev Syal, 'Jeremy Corbyn Says He Regrets Calling Hamas
    and Hezbollah "Friends"', *Guardian*, 4 July 2016. Available at: www.
    theguardian.com/politics/2016/jul/04/jeremy-corbyn-says-he-regrets-
    calling-hamas-and-hezbollah-friends. Footage at www.youtube.com/
    watch?v=isPnvofGWjA

97  Quoted in Yonah Jeremy Bob, 'Islamic Movement Leader Salah Convicted
    to Racist Incitement on Appeal', *Jerusalem Post*, 10 November 2014.
    Available at: www.jpost.com/Arab-Israeli-Conflict/Islamic-Movement-
    leader-Salah-convicted-of-racist-incitement-on-appeal-381337

98  Jeremy Corbyn, column in the *Morning Star*, 1 July 2011, quoted in
    Mathilde Frot, 'Corbyn Wrote "We must stand up to Zionist lobby" Over
    Blood-Libel Cleric's Ban', *Jewish News*, 2 April 2019. Available at: https://
    jewishnews.timesofisrael.com/corbyn-wrote-we-must-stand-up-to-zionist-
    lobby-over-blood-libel-clerics-ban/. Corbyn article reproduced at: https://
    static.timesofisrael.com/jewishndev/uploads/2019/04/D3ITjW1X4AAwtv9.
    jpg

99  Aaron Amaral, 'An Insidious Dialectic: Antisemitism, Corbyn, and the Fight
    for the Labour Party', interview with David Renton, *Tempest*, 13 November
    2020. Available at: www.tempestmag.org/2020/11/an-insidious-dialectic/

100 See Communist Party of Britain International Bulletin, Summer 2020.
    Available at: www.communistparty.org.uk/wp-content/uploads/2020/06/
    International-Bulletin-No-2-2020.pdf

101 See Hadash website: http://hadash.org.il/english/

102 See, for example, the work of Ran Greenstein and Musa Budeiri on the
    Communist Party tradition in Israel and Palestine.

103 See Mary Davis, 'Contestation Between Anti-Zionism and Antisemitism',
    Open Democracy, 27 July 2016. Available at: www.opendemocracy.net/en/
    opendemocracyuk/contestation-between-anti-zionism-and-antisemitism;
    Phil Katz and Mary Davis, 'The Socialism of Fools: Antisemitism
    in the Labour Party?', *Morning Star*, undated. Available at: https://
    morningstaronline.co.uk/article/f/socialism-fools-anti-semitism-labour-
    party

104 Karl Marx and Friedrich Engels, 'Chapter III. Socialist and Communist
    Literature', *Manifesto of the Communist Party* (1847). Available at: www.
    marxists.org/archive/marx/works/1848/communist-manifesto/ch03.htm

105 Sean Matgamna, *The Left in Disarray* (London: Phoenix Press, 2017), p. 220.

106 Marcel Stoetzler, 'Capitalism, the Nation, and Societal Corrosion: Notes on "Left-Wing Antisemitism"', *Journal of Social Justice* 9, 2019, p. 13 (emphasis in original). Available at: http://transformativestudies.org/wp-content/uploads/Marcel-Stoetzler.pdf

107 Mostafa Omar, 'What Do Socialists Say About Hamas?', *Socialist Worker*, 31 July 2014. Available at: https://socialistworker.org/blog/critical-reading/2014/07/31/what-do-socialists-say-about-h

108 'Hamas's History of Resistance', *Socialist Worker*, 6 January 2009. Available at: https://socialistworker.co.uk/art/16497/Hamass+history+of+resistance

109 'Whoever Wins the Israeli Elections Will Oppress Palestinians', *Socialist Worker*, 10 February 2009. Available at: https://socialistworker.co.uk/art/16783/Whoever%20wins%20the%20Israeli%20elections%20will%20oppress%20Palestinians

110 See 'The Jewish Question and Israel: Resolution Adopted by the Independent Socialist League', *New International* 17, 4, July–August 1951, pp. 222–31. Available at: www.marxists.org/history/etol/newspape/ni/vol17/no04/isl.html

## CHAPTER 5: TOWARDS AN 'ANTI-ZIONIST ZIONISM'

1 James Wright, 'Almost All the Sources in That Panorama Hatchet Job Have Leading Roles in an Anti-Corbyn Organisation', The Canary, 11 August 2019 www.thecanary.co/feature/2019/08/11/almost-all-the-sources-in-that-panorama-hatchet-job-have-leading-roles-in-an-anti-corbyn-organisation/

2 Mahmoud Darwish in *Notre Musique* (dir. Jean-Luc Goddard, 2004), quoted in Joey Ayoub, 'The Jewish and Arab Questions, and European Fascism', 22 May 2021. Available at: https://joeyayoub.com/2021/05/22/the-jewish-and-arab-questions-and-european-fascism/

3 Ayoub, 'The Jewish and Arab Questions'.

4 Leon Trotsky, *Stalin: An Appraisal of the Man and His Influence* (1938–40), chapter 5. Available at: www.marxists.org/archive/trotsky/1940/xx/stalin/ch05.htm

5 Edward Said, 'What Israel Has Done', *The Nation*, 6 May 2002. Available at: www.thenation.com/article/archive/what-israel-has-done

6 *Socialist Worker* 1224, quoted in Dale Street, 'Three Decades of *Socialist Worker* on Antisemitism', *Solidarity* 534, 12 February 2020. Available at: www.workersliberty.org/story/2020-01-27/three-decades-socialist-worker-antisemitism

7 Nahuel Moreno, *On Palestine* (Buenos Aires: Ediciones El Socialista, 2015), p. 5. Available at: www.marxists.org/archive/moreno/1982/on-palestine.pdf

8 Scott Cooper, 'Every Jew Should be Unequivocally Anti-Zionist', Left Voice, 13 May 2021. Available at: www.leftvoice.org/every-jew-should-be-unequivocally-anti-zionist/

9 Nick Clark, 'New Government in Israel Poses a Fresh Threat to the

Palestinians', *Socialist Worker* 2702, 22 April 2020. Available at: https://socialistworker.co.uk/art/49942/New+government+in+Israel+poses+a+fresh+threat+to+Palestinians

10   See D. Soifer, *The Collapse of Zionist Theories* (1980), quoted in Stan Crooke, 'The Stalinist Roots of "Left" Antisemitism', *Workers' Liberty* 10, May 1988. Available at: www.workersliberty.org/node/16575

11   John Strawson, 'Communists for the Jewish State: British Communists and the *Daily Worker* in 1948', *Fathom*, September 2020. Available at: https://fathomjournal.org/communists-for-the-jewish-state-british-communists-and-the-daily-worker-in-1948/

12   Isaac Deutscher, *The Non-Jewish Jew and Other Essays* (Oxford: Oxford University Press, 1968), quoted in Michael Mirer, 'Isaac Deutscher Redux', *Jewish Currents*, 4 July 2017. Available at: https://archive.jewishcurrents.org/isaac-deutscher-redux/

13   Sean Matgamna, 'How to Wipe Out Left Antisemitism', *Solidarity* 404, 11 May 2016. Available at: www.workersliberty.org/story/2017-07-26/how-wipe-out-left-anti-semitism

14   Quoted in Lee Harpin, '"Jews are Christ killers" Banner at Anti-Israel Protest', *Jewish News*, 22 May 2021. Available at: https://jewishnews.timesofisrael.com/jews-are-christ-killers-banner-at-anti-israel-protest/

15   Iyad el-Baghdadi, Twitter post, 6 June 2020. Available at: https://twitter.com/iyad_elbaghdadi/status/1269191173282975745

16   After Donald Trump's now-infamous statement, referring to a far-right march and an anti-fascist counter-protest, that there were 'very fine people on both sides', 'to both sides [something]' has entered leftist discourse as a verb, describing the drawing of a patently false equivalence between two sides that are clearly highly imbalanced, in either a material or moral sense.

17   See Daniel Fischer, 'In Support of Joint Struggle', *New Politics* (Online Features), 15 March 2021. Available at: https://newpol.org/in-support-of-joint-struggle/

18   Keith Kahn-Harris, *Strange Hate: Antisemitism, Racism, and the Limits of Diversity* (London: Repeater Books, 2019), p. 194.

19   Spencer Sunshine, 'Looking Left at Antisemitism', *Journal of Social Justice* 9, 2019, p. 34. Available at: http://transformativestudies.org/wp-content/uploads/Spencer-Sunshine.pdf

20   In polling conducted by the Palestine Centre for Policy and Survey Research in December 2020, 45 per cent of respondents said ending the occupation and establishing a Palestinian state should be the main goal of Palestinian struggle, with just 29 per cent stating that securing the right of return to all pre-1948 territory should be the main goal. See: www.pcpsr.org/en/node/829

21   Ayman Odeh, 'My People Know Our Past', *Haaretz*, 23 April 2021. Available at: www.haaretz.com/opinion/.premium-my-people-know-our-past-1.9738536

22  Frequently Asked Questions, 'Two States, One Homeland: An Open Land for All'. Available at: www.alandforall.org/english/?d=ltr

23  Sina Arnold and Blair Taylor, 'Antisemitism and the Left: Confronting an Invisible Racism', *Journal of Social Justice*, 9, 2019, p. 18. Available at: http://transformativestudies.org/wp-content/uploads/Blair-Taylor-and-Sina_Arnold.pdf

24  International Holocaust Remembrance Alliance, 'Working Definition of Antisemitism'. Available at: www.holocaustremembrance.com/resources/working-definitions-charters/working-definition-antisemitism

25  Tony Greenstein, 'The Abuse of Antisemitism to Silence Free Speech on Israel', Brighton BDS YouTube channel, 3 May 2017 (emphasis added). Available at: www.youtube.com/watch?v=M5PKI__M14k?t=177

26  'This is Apartheid', B'Tselem, 12 January 2021. Available at: www.btselem.org/publications/fulltext/202101_this_is_apartheid

27  See, for example, Fabio Damen, 'The Palestinian Tragedy', Communist Workers' Organisation, undated. Available at: www.leftcom.org/en/articles/2002-12-01/the-palestinian-tragedy

28  'Neither Israel Nor Palestine: No War But the Class War', International Communist Tendency statement, 20 May 2021. Available at: www.leftcom.org/en/articles/2021-05-20/neither-israel-nor-palestine-no-war-but-the-class-war

29  Edward Said, 'Barenboim and the Wagner Taboo', *Al-Ahram Weekly* (Online) 547, 16–22 August 2001. Available at: www.mafhoum.com/press2/58C31.htm

30  'Against Israel's New Coalition', interview with Maisam Jaljuli and Asaf Yakir, *Solidarity* 545, 28 April 2020. Available at www.workersliberty.org/story/2020-04-27/against-israels-new-coalition

31  'West-Eastern Divan Orchestra Violates Boycott', statement by the Palestinian Campaign for the Academic and Cultural Boycott of Israel, Electronic Intifada, 24 March 2010. Available at: https://electronicintifada.net/content/pacbi-west-eastern-divan-orchestra-violates-boycott/1040

32  Jewish Voice for Labour, Twitter post, 28 November 2020. Available at: https://twitter.com/JVoiceLabour/status/1332717740281507841

33  Steve Cohen, 'I Would Hate Myself in the Morning', *Solidarity* 94, 4 June 2006. Available at: www.workersliberty.org/story/2017-07-26/i-would-hate-myself-morning

34  Statement by M&S technical food director David Gregory, quoted in Corporate Occupation, 'Apartheid in the Fields: From Occupied Palestine to UK Supermarkets (2020 Update), Part 7.6: M&S', 14 February 2020. Available at: https://corporateoccupation.org/2020/02/14/apartheid-in-the-fields-from-occupied-palestine-to-uk-supermarkets-2020-update-part-7-6-ms/

35  'Marks and Spencer: Ally of Israel', *Fight Racism! Fight Imperialism!* 160, April–May 2001. Available at: www.revolutionarycommunist.org/campaigns/palestine-campaign/1353-marks-and-spencer-ally-of-israel

36 Corporate Occupation, 'Apartheid in the Fields'.

37 Martin Thomas, 'How to be Pro-Palestinian Without Being "Anti-Zionist"', *Solidarity* 484, 31 October 2018. Available at: www.workersliberty.org/ story/2018-11-16/how-be-pro-palestinian-without-being-anti-zionist

38 Jordan Kutzik, 'This "Antifa" Group Was Also Zionist, Pro-Palestinian and Yiddish-Speaking – and It's Trending', *Forward*, 3 June 2020. Available at: https://forward.com/news/448022/antifa-yiddish-zionist/

39 Isaac Deutscher, 'Israel's Spiritual Climate', *The Reporter*, 27 April and 11 May 1954. Available at: www.marxists.org/archive/deutscher/1954/israel. htm

40 Barry Finger, 'Zionism and the Left, from Arendt to Chomsky: A Review of Susie Linfield's *The Lion's Den*', *Solidarity* 511, 20 June 2019. Available at: www.workersliberty.org/story/2019-06-20/zionism-and-left-arendt-chomsky

41 See 'Trotskyists and the Creation of Israel', *Workers' Liberty* 3, 13, July 2007. Available at: www.workersliberty.org/trotskyists-and-creation-israel-workers-liberty-313

42 Musa Budeiri, *The Palestine Communist Party 1919–1948* (Chicago: Haymarket Books, 2010), p. 168.

43 W. E. B. Du Bois, 'Not Separatism', *The Crisis* 17, 4, Whole No. 100, February 1919, p. 166.

44 Eldridge Cleaver, *Post-Prison Writings and Speeches* (New York: Ramparts/ Vintage, 1969), pp. 67–9.

45 Brian Klug, 'Israel, Antisemitism, and the Left', *Red Pepper* (special issue on Israel/Palestine), November 2005. Available at: https://jfjfp.com/israel-antisemitism-and-the-left/

46 Sunshine, 'Looking Left at Antisemitism'.

47 Deutscher, *The Non-Jewish Jew and Other Essays*, pp. 136–7.

48 Said, 'Barenboim and the Wagner Taboo'.

49 Steve Cohen, *That's Funny, You Don't Look Antisemitic* (London: No Pasaran Media, 2019), p. 62.

50 Steve Cohen, 'For the Third Camp – Yes to Palestinian Liberation! No To Antisemitism!', 19 June 2007. Available at: www.workersliberty.org/ node/8708

51 Steve Cohen, 'There Must Be Some Way Out Of Here', in *That's Funny*, p. xii.

52 Martin Thomas, 'Socialists and the National Question', *Socialist Organiser* 567 and 568, 24 June and 8 July 1993. Available at: www.workersliberty.org/ index.php/story/2011/07/14/socialists-and-national-question

53 Steve Cohen, 'Writing as a Jewish Traitor: An Imagined Disputation with My Comrades on Antisemitism', 31 October 2006. Available at: www. workersliberty.org/node/7203

54 Iyad el-Baghdadi, Twitter posts, 25 June 2019. Available at: https://twitter. com/iyad_elbaghdadi/status/1143489082842079234 and https://twitter. com/iyad_elbaghdadi/status/1143489084490420226

55  Cohen, 'For the Third Camp'.

## CHAPTER 6: THE LEFT AND JEWISH COMMUNITIES: SOME RECENT TRENDS

1   Ephraim Mirvis, 'What Will Become of Jews in Britain if Labour Forms the Next Government?' *The Times*, 25 November 2019. Available at: www. thetimes.co.uk/article/ephraim-mirvis-what-will-become-of-jews-in-britain-if-labour-forms-the-next-government-ghpsdbljk

2   Rushaa Louise Hamid, 'New Polling Shows Tensions Remain Strong Between Labour and the British Jewish Community', Survation, 25 March 2019. Available at: www.survation.com/new-polling-of-british-jews-shows-tensions-remain-strong-between-labour-and-the-british-jewish-community/

3   See screenshot at https://149363154.v2.pressablecdn.com/wp-content/uploads/2019/11/Holly-Rigby-00.png

4   See Michael Barker, 'Why Chief Rabbi Ephraim Mirvis is Wrong About Labor [sic] Antisemitism', CounterPunch, 29 November 2019. Available at: www.counterpunch.org/2019/11/29/why-chief-rabbi-ephraim-mirvis-is-wrong-about-labor-anti-semitism; Emily Apple, 'There's One Crucial Sentence Missing from the Mainstream Media's Coverage of the Chief Rabbi's Comments', The Canary, 26 November 2019. Available at: www. thecanary.co/opinion/2019/11/26/theres-one-crucial-sentence-missing-from-the-mainstream-medias-coverage-of-the-chief-rabbis-comments; 'Here's the Real Reason Chief Rabbi Mirvis Attacked Jeremy Corbyn and Labour: He's a TORY (and a Racist It Seems)', Vox Political, 26 November 2019. Available at: https://voxpoliticalonline.com/2019/11/26/heres-the-real-reason-chief-rabbi-mirvis-attacked-jeremy-corbyn-and-labour-hes-a-tory-and-a-racist-it-seems

5   'Pan-European Jewish Organisation Sends Letter of Support to Corbyn', Skwawkbox, 27 November 2019. Available at: https://skwawkbox.org/2019/11/27/pan-european-jewish-organisation-sends-letter-of-support-to-corbyn/

6   See Rumy Hasan, 'How the Left Should Work with Muslims', *What Next?*, October 2003. Available at: www.whatnextjournal.org.uk/Pages/Politics/Rumy.html; 'Fighting for Secularism Amongst London's Bengalis', interview with Ansar Ahmed Ullah, *Solidarity* 308, 8 January 2014. Available at: www. workersliberty.org/story/2014/01/08/fighting-secularism-among-londons-bengalis

7   Steve Cohen, *That's Funny, You Don't Look Antisemitic* (London: No Pasaran Media, 2019), p. xxxv.

8   See Lee Harpin, 'Revealed: Charedi Anti-LGBT Education Activist Jeremy Corbyn Met is Biggest Donor to Anti-LGBT Birmingham Protesters', *Jewish Chronicle*, 24 July 2019. Available at: www.thejc.com/news/uk/chared-anti-lgbt-education-activist-jeremy-corbyn-met-is-biggest-donor-to-anti-lgbt-birmingham-1.486747

9   Cohen, *That's Funny*, p. 91.

10  See, for example, 'The Wrong Kind of News/Jews', Jewish Voice for Labour, 18 March 2019. Available at: www.jewishvoiceforlabour.org.uk/article/the-wrong-kind-of-news-jews/

11  'Orthodox activists' unpublished statement to *Jewish Chronicle*: "Jeremy is a Long Friend of Our Community"', Skwawkbox, 17 September 2019. Available at: https://skwawkbox.org/2018/09/17/orthodox-activists-unpublished-statement-to-jewish-chronicle-questions-representative-groups-credentials/

12  Keith Kahn-Harris, *Strange Hate: Antisemitism, Racism, and the Limits of Diversity* (London: Repeater Books, 2019), p. 82.

13  See images at https://bit.ly/3wLqklE and www.saasuk.org/wp-content/uploads/2020/11/image-1-489x1024.png

14  Eldad Levy, 'Anti-Zionist Neturei Karta are No Friend to the Palestinian National Struggle', *+972 Magazine*, 28 November 2012. Available at: www.972mag.com/anti-zionist-jews-are-no-friend-of-the-palestinian-national-struggle/61002/

15  Assaf Uni, 'Neturei Karta Delegate to Iranian Holocaust Conference: I Pray for Israel's Destruction "In Peaceful Ways"', *Haaretz*, 6 January 2007. Available at: www.haaretz.com/1.4947225

16  Tom Harris, 'Neturei Karta: Enemies Not Allies', Left Foot Forward, 31 January 2014. Available at: https://leftfootforward.org/2014/01/neturei-karta-enemies-not-allies/

17  'On Neturei Karta', Socialists Against Antisemitism, 24 January 2019. Available at: www.saasuk.org/2019/01/24/on-neturei-karta/

18  Interview between Rabbi Beck of Neturei Karta and Patrick Harrington of Third Way Publications, Neturei Karta USA, 1 July 1991. Available at: www.nkusa.org/activities/interviews/rabbibeck.cfm

19  Spencer Sunshine, 'Looking Left at Antisemitism', *Journal of Social Justice* 9, 2019, p. 8. Available at: http://transformativestudies.org/wp-content/uploads/Spencer-Sunshine.pdf

20  Ibid., pp. 8–9.

21  John Elder, 'Rising Antisemitism Cannot be Tackled Without Addressing Israel's Crimes', *Morning Star*, 18 June 2018.

22  'Statement on the Result of Board of Deputies' Israel Debate', Board of Deputies of British Jews, 23 August 2020. Available at: www.bod.org.uk/statement-on-the-results-of-board-of-deputies-israel-debate/

23  Mathilde Frot, '38 Deputies Urge Board to Condemn Israel's Annexation Plans', *Jewish News*, 13 May 2020. Available at: https://jewishnews.timesofisrael.com/33-board-deputies-urge-representative-body-to-condemn-israels-annexation-plans/

24  See Yachad UK, Twitter post, 21 May 2021. Available at: https://twitter.com/YachadUK/status/1395736950057967617

25  See video in Keith Kahn-Harris, Twitter post, 22 May 2021. Available at: https://twitter.com/KeithKahnHarris/status/1396177800806162433

26  Keith Kahn-Harris, Twitter posts, 22 May 2021. Available at: https://twitter.com/KeithKahnHarris/status/1396177800806162433 and https://twitter.com/KeithKahnHarris/status/1396178700161400838

27  Robert Cohen, 'The Jewish Establishment's "War Against Corbyn" Risks Bringing Real Antisemitism to Britain', Mondoweiss, 29 July 2018. Available at: https://mondoweiss.net/2018/07/establishments-bringing-semitism/

28  David Miller, quoted in Lee Harpin, 'Bristol University Professor Calls for "End" of Zionism as "Functioning Ideology of the World"', Jewish Chronicle, 15 February 2021. Available at: www.thejc.com/news/uk/bristol-university-professor-calls-for-end-of-zionism-as-functioning-ideology-of-the-world-1.511837

29  See image at https://i0.wp.com/www.jewthink.org/wp-content/uploads/2021/02/cst-lecture-image.jpg?w=813&ssl=1

30  Keith Kahn-Harris, 'Into the Flatlands with Professor David Miller', JewThink, 22 February 2021. Available at: www.jewthink.org/2021/02/22/into-the-flatlands-with-professor-david-miller/

31  Cathy Nugent, 'Uphold Free Speech, Fight Antisemitism', Solidarity 584, 3 March 2021. Available at: www.workersliberty.org/story/2021-03-02/uphold-free-speech-fight-antisemitism

32  Rose Schneiderdamn, 'When Freedom of Speech is Under Attack, What Do We Do? Sit Down, Write a Blog Post', Jewdas, 21 February 2021. Available at: www.jewdas.org/david-miller/

33  William J. Fishman, East End Jewish Radicals, 1875–1914 (Nottingham: Five Leaves Publications, 2004), pp. 157–8.

34  Ibid., p. 156.

35  Ibid., p. 159.

36  Jewish Labour Movement, Twitter post, 9 May 2021. Available at: https://twitter.com/JewishLabour/status/1391332656898510848

37  Noam Masorti Youth, Facebook post, 19 April 2021. Available at: www.facebook.com/NoamUK/posts/10158008390762187

38  LJY-Netzer, Twitter post, 16 May 2021. Available at: https://twitter.com/LJYNetzer/status/1393910125228871680

39  'Against Israel's New Coalition', interview with Maisam Jaljuli and Asaf Yakir, Solidarity 545, 27 April 2020. Available at www.workersliberty.org/story/2020-04-27/against-israels-new-coalition

40  Keith Kahn-Harris, Strange Hate, p. 203.

41  Ibid., p. 214.

42  See Alexander Meleagrou-Hitchens, 'Spinwatch Must Offer Right of Reply', Guardian, 13 July 2010. Available at: www.theguardian.com/commentisfree/libertycentral/2010/jul/13/spinwatch-right-reply-david-miller

## CHAPTER 7: LEFT ANTISEMITISM, RACISM, AND OPPRESSION

1   For a thought-provoking examination of the relationship between anti-Black racism and antisemitism, see Michael Richmond, 'On 'Black Antisemitism' and Anti-Racist Solidarity', New Socialist, 30 July 2020. Available at: https://newsocialist.org.uk/black-antisemitism-and-antiracist-solidarity/

2   Keith Kahn-Harris, *Strange Hate: Antisemitism, Racism, and the Limits of Diversity* (London: Repeater Books, 2019), p. 141.

3   Emily Ward, 'Black and Jewish: A Conversation with Nadine Batchelor-Hunt', Jewish Women's Archive, 22 September 2020. Available at: https://jwa.org/blog/black-and-jewish-conversation-nadine-batchelor-hunt

4   Eric K. Ward, 'Skin in the Game: How Antisemitism Animates White Nationalism', *The Public Eye*, Summer 2017. Available at: www.politicalresearch.org/2017/06/29/skin-in-the-game-how-antisemitism-animates-white-nationalism

5   'Zionism, Antisemitism, and the Left', interview with Moishe Postone, *Solidarity* 166, 4 February 2010. Available at: www.workersliberty.org/story/2010-02-05/zionism-anti-semitism-and-left

6   Martin Thomas, 'Distinctions on Left Antisemitism', *Solidarity* 455, 24 November 2017. Available at: www.workersliberty.org/story/2017-11-24/distinctions-left-antisemitism

7   See Satnam Virdee, 'Socialist Antisemitism and its Discontents in England, 1884–98', *Patterns of Prejudice* 51, 3–4, pp. 356–73. Available at: www.tandfonline.com/doi/full/10.1080/0031322X.2017.1335029

8   See Daniel Randall, '1905 and All That: How the Labour Movement Debated Britain's First Immigration Control', Labour Campaign for Free Movement, 13 August 2017. Available at: www.labourfreemovement.org/1905-and-all-that-how-the-labour-movement-debated-britains-first-immigration-control/

9   David Feldman, Ben Gidley and Brendan McGeever, 'Labour and Antisemitism: A Crisis Misunderstood', *Political Quarterly* 91, 2, April–June 2020. Available at: https://politicalquarterly.blog/2020/05/29/the-labour-party-and-antisemitism-a-crisis-misunderstood/

10  Camila Bassi, 'Racism, Antisemitism, and the Left', *Solidarity* 454, 15 November 2017. Available at: www.workersliberty.org/story/2017-11-15/racism-anti-semitism-and-left

11  Brian Klug, 'Israel, Antisemitism, and the Left', *Red Pepper* (special issue on Israel/Palestine), November 2005. Available at: https://jfjfp.com/israel-antisemitism-and-the-left/

12  Frantz Fanon, *The Wretched of the Earth* (Paris: François Maspero, 1961), quoted in Thomas, 'Distinctions on Left Antisemitism'.

13  Nahuel Moreno, *On Palestine* (Buenos Aires: Ediciones El Socialista, 2015), p. 5. Available at: www.marxists.org/archive/moreno/1982/on-palestine.pdf

14  Thomas, 'Distinctions on Left Antisemitism'.

15  Bassi, 'Racism, Antisemitism, and the Left'.

16  Sean Matgamna, 'Antisemitism and the Left: An Open Letter to Tony Cliff',
    *Workers' Liberty* 14, July 1990. Available at: www.workersliberty.org/files/
    wl14cliffletter.pdf

17  Thomas, 'Distinctions on Left Antisemitism'.

18  Tony Greenstein, 'Debate Between Tony Greenstein and Daniel Randall
    of the Alliance for Workers' Liberty', Tony Greenstein's Blog, 7 November
    2016. Available at: https://azvsas.blogspot.com/2016/11/debate-between-
    tony-greenstein-daniel.html?m=0

19  April Rosenblum, *The Past Didn't Go Anywhere: Making Resistance to
    Antisemitism Part of All of Our Movements* (2007), p. 8. Available at: www.
    aprilrosenblum.com/thepast

20  For a study of the antisemitic origins of the 'Cultural Marxism' conspiracy
    theory, see Joan Braune, 'Who's Afraid of the Frankfurt School? "Cultural
    Marxism" as an Antisemitic Conspiracy Theory', *Journal of Social Justice*, 9,
    2019. Available at: http://transformativestudies.org/wp-content/uploads/
    Joan-Braune.pdf

21  Community Security Trust, 'Antisemitic Incidents Report', 2020, p. 22.
    Available at: https://cst.org.uk/public/data/file/7/2/Incidents%20Report%20
    2020.pdf

22  Karl Marx and Friedrich Engels, *The German Ideology* (1845–6). Available
    at: www.marxists.org/archive/marx/works/1845/german-ideology/

23  Ward, 'Black and Jewish'.

## CHAPTER 8: HOW TO FIX THE PROBLEM

1   Richard Angell, 'We Need This Action Plan to Tackle Antisemitism
    Within Labour', *LabourList*, 6 April 2016. Available at: https://labourlist.
    org/2016/04/we-need-this-action-plan-to-tackle-anti-semitism-within-
    labour

2   Board of Deputies of British Jews, '"Rebuilding will take more than mild
    expressions of regret" – the Board of Deputies Launches Its Ten Pledges for
    Labour Leadership and Deputy Leadership Candidates', 13 January 2020.
    Available at: www.bod.org.uk/bod-news/rebuilding-will-take-more-than-
    mild-expressions-of-regret-the-board-of-deputies-launches-its-ten-pledges-
    for-labour-leadership-and-deputy-leadership-candidates/

3   See Daniel Randall, 'Expelled for Being a Socialist', *Solidarity* 414, 31 August
    2016. Available at: www.workersliberty.org/story/2017-07-26/expelled-
    being-socialist

4   Michael Richmond, 'Anti-Racism as Procedure', *Protocols* 8, December 2020.
    Available at: https://prtcls.com/article/richmond_labour-antisemitism

5   David Feldman, 'Labour Can Expel Antisemites, But That Won't "Root
    Out" Antisemitism in Our Culture', *Guardian*, 8 April 2020. Available at:
    www.theguardian.com/commentisfree/2020/apr/08/education-labour-
    antisemitism-party-keir-starmer

6    Keith Kahn-Harris, *Strange Hate: Antisemitism, Racism, and the Limits of Diversity* (London: Repeater Books, 2019), p. 82.

7    Sienna Rodgers, 'Jennie Formby and Tom Watson Exchange Letters in Antisemitism Row', *LabourList*, 12 July 2019. Available at: https://labourlist. org/2019/07/jennie-formby-and-tom-watson-exchange-letters-in-antisemitism-row/

8    Kahn-Harris, *Strange Hate*, p. 200.

9    Sienna Rodgers, 'Labour Launches New Antisemitism Education Material', *LabourList*, 21 July 2019. Available at: https://labourlist.org/2019/07/labour-launches-new-antisemitism-education-material

10   In 2020, synagogues in Graz, Austria (www.timesofisrael.com/free-palestine-graffiti-sprayed-on-austrian-synagogue/), Los Angeles, California (https://jewishjournal.com/los_angeles/316561/los-angeles-synagogue-vandalized-with-free-palestine-f-israel-graffiti/) and Kenosha, Wisconsin (https://forward.com/fast-forward/453400/kenosha-synagogue-vandalized-with-free-palestine-graffiti-jacob-blake/) had 'Free Palestine' graffiti sprayed on them.

11   Steve Cohen, *That's Funny, You Don't Look Antisemitic* (London: No Pasaran Media, 2019), pp. 28–33.

12   Satnam Virdee, 'Socialist Antisemitism and Its Discontents in England, 1884–98', *Patterns of Prejudice* 51, 3–4, 20 June 2017, pp. 356–73. Available at: www.tandfonline.com/doi/full/10.1080/0031322X.2017.1335029

13   Lizzy Buchan, 'Angela Rayner Says Labour Will Suspend "Thousands" of Members Over Antisemitism if Necessary', *Daily Mirror*, 29 November 2020. Available at: www.mirror.co.uk/news/politics/angela-rayner-says-labour-suspend-23088719

14   Edd Mustill, 'How Our Local Party Developed an Educational Programme on Antisemitism', *LabourList*, 7 August 2020. Available at: https://labourlist. org/2020/08/how-our-local-party-developed-an-educational-programme-on-antisemitism/

15   'Educational Event About Antisemitism Stopped', Momentum Inter-nationalists, 22 January 2021. Available at: https://momentuminternationalists.org/2021/01/22/educational-event-about-antisemitism-stopped/

16   'Penistone & Stocksbridge CLP Call for Antisemitism Education', Momentum Internationalists, 3 February 2021. Available at: https://momentum internationalists.org/2021/02/03/penistone-stocksbridge-clp-call-for-antisemitism-education/

17   Ibid.

18   Sienna Rogers, 'Keir Starmer Repositions Labour on Kashmiri Conflict', *LabourList*, 30 April 2020. Available at: https://labourlist.org/2020/04/keir-starmer-repositions-labour-on-kashmiri-conflict/

## APPENDIX II: AN EXCHANGE ON THE 2019 GENERAL ELECTION

1   'Labour, Antisemitism, Antiracist Politics and the General Election', *The Clarion*, 10 March 2020. Available at: https://theclarionmag.org/2020/03/10/labour-antisemitism-and-the-general-election/
2   Rabbil Sikdar, 'As a Left-Wing Muslim, I Cannot Vote for Corbyn's Labour', *UnHerd*, 8 November 2019. Available at: https://unherd.com/thepost/as-a-left-wing-muslim-i-cannot-vote-for-jeremy-corbyns-labour/

## AUTHOR'S NOTE

1   Steve Cohen, 'Writing as a Jewish Traitor: An Imagined Disputation with My Comrades on Antisemitism', *Solidarity* 107, 22 February 2007. Available at: www.workersliberty.org/story/2017-07-26/writing-jewish-traitor-imagined-disputation-my-comrades-anti-semitism
2   Isaac Deutscher, 'Message of the Non-Jewish Jew' (1968). Available at: www.marxists.org/history/etol/newspape/amersocialist/deutscher01.htm
3   Cohen, 'Writing as a Jewish Traitor'.
4   Hal Draper, 'Why Socialists Look to the the Working Class as the Force for Social Progress', *Labor Action* May Day special, 1955. Available at: www.workersliberty.org/story/2013/10/08/why-socialists-look-working-class-force-social-progress

# INDEX